Foucault and Religi

MW00998983

Jeremy Carrette's book opens new vistas in the dialogue between cultural criticism and religious thinking. His recovery of this forgotten religious strand in Foucault's writing enables us to better understand why some of Foucault's ideas have suffered such misinterpretation. While a major contribution to Foucault studies, Carrette's real achievement is to have performed a reading of Foucault in the spirit of Foucault and not from the limited perspective of an academic discipline. In rescuing Foucault's exercises in reconciling the bodily and the spiritual, Carrette's study advances the contemporary transformation in the field of religious understanding. He shows us Foucault's religious questions but his greatest success is that, in doing so, he gives new excitement and urgency to our own.

James Bernauer, Professor of Philosophy, Boston College

Foucault and Religion is the first major study to discuss the role of religion in the work of Michel Foucault. Carrette offers us a challenging new look at Foucault's work and addresses a religious dimension that has previously been neglected. We see that there is a complex religious sub-text which anticipates Foucault's infamous unpublished volume on the theme of Christianity.

Carrette argues that Foucault offers a twofold critique of Christianity by bringing the body and sexuality into religious practice and exploring a political spirituality of the self. He shows us that Foucault's creation of a body theology through the death of God reveals how religious beliefs reflect the sexual body. Carrette also questions the notion of a mystical archaeology and exposes the political technology of confession.

Anyone interested in understanding Foucault's thought in a new light will find this book a truly fascinating read.

Jeremy R. Carrette is Lecturer in Religious Studies at the University of Stirling. He is the editor of *Religion and Culture by Michel Foucault*.

Foucault and Religion

Spiritual corporality and political spirituality

Jeremy R. Carrette

London and New York

First published 2000
by Routledge
11 New Fetter Lane, London EC4P 4EE

Simultaneously published in the USA and Canada
by Routledge
29 West 35th Street, New York, NY 10001

Routledge is an imprint of the Taylor & Francis Group

Typeset in Times by Taylor & Francis Books Ltd
Printed and bound in Great Britain by MPG Books Ltd, Bodmin

British Library Cataloguing in Publication Data
A catalogue record for this book is available from the British Library

Library of Congress Cataloging in Publication data
Carrette, Jeremy R.
Foucault and religion: spiritual corporality and political
spirituality/Jeremy Carrette.
p. cm.
Includes bibliographical references and index.
1. Foucault, Michel–Contributions in philosophy of religion. 2.
Religion–Philosophy. I. Title.
B2430.F724C365 1999   99–31682
210′.92–dc21   CIP

ISBN 0-415-20259-0 (hbk)
ISBN 0-415-20260-4 (pbk)

To the memory of my father and mother

David Alan Carrette

1938–1989

Susan Carrette

1940–1998

Contents

Preface   ix
Acknowledgements   xiii
Abbreviations of main texts by Foucault   xvi

Introduction: Approaching Foucault's work on religion   1

1 Outline of Foucault's work and the question of religion   7

2 Silence and confession   25

3 Surrealism and the religious imagination   44

4 Male theology in the bedroom   63

5 Mystical archaeology   85

6 Body and belief   109

7 Towards a political spirituality   129

Conclusion: Religion after Foucault   142

Notes   153
Bibliography   183
Index   209

Preface

> I am not where you are lying in wait for me, but over here, laughing at you?
> ... Do not ask me who I am and do not ask me to remain the same: leave it
> to our bureaucrats and our police to see that our papers are in order. At least
> spare us their morality when we write.
>
> Foucault (1969a) *The Archaeology of Knowledge*, p. 17

Foucault wrote to be free but everywhere he is in chains. The slow process of locating, defining and appropriating him has turned man into icon and complex texts into soundbites. If Foucault was previously 'over there' laughing at those who put his papers in order (those who had tried to define and position him), he would now be in hysterics at the limits imposed on his texts. In the light of such a situation it is perhaps time to ask a whole new set of questions about the politics of reading Foucault. How can we, for example, read his texts outside the disciplinary regimes that have so far appropriated his work? How can we let his writings find a voice, a texture and a complexity outside the packaged and predictable interpretations of previous readings? How can we release him from the chains of commodified knowledges which highlight, reify and stereotype the complex folds of a thinker? How can we take his work out of the reductive introductions, the shortsighted dismissals, the obscure categories, the normalising labels and the rash generalisations? How can we begin to make his work as complex as the life of the man? How can we extend, elaborate and elucidate what has been hidden and marginalised in his work? How can we learn to read the richness of Foucault's texts from the outside?

By raising these questions I am not suggesting that there is 'real' Foucault to be discovered in some original free-floating space, but rather suggesting that it is necessary to find an interdisciplinary and historically located reading which seeks to appreciate the breadth and complexity of his work. The questions I am posing become even more significant in the light of the publication of *Dits et écrits* (and the English translations arising from that work) and the publication of the Collège de France lectures. There is now a possibility to appreciate the intricate developments and subtle nuances of Foucault's writing in a new light. Foucault scholarship, it would seem, is about to enter a second wave of examination from the initial explosion of interest. As Arnold Davidson makes clear, the publication of *Dits et écrits* in 1994 'requires us to rethink the place of Foucault in twentieth-century intellectual life, allows us to rediscover the scope and importance of his work, and, above all, to recognise his continued philosophical force'.[1]

To begin an examination of the religious nature of Foucault's writing may appear to some to be yet another disciplinary appropriation, but this work is not so much about applying Foucault to themes in religion or theology as an attempt to examine the religious tropes of his writing in order to explore how he reflected upon and examined religious and theological ideas. This work seeks to enter the richness of Foucault's texts, to retrieve and fold texts together, in order to discover a 'religious question' at the heart of his work. In this sense I am seeking to appreciate the diversity of his work by opening the space for thinking about a forgotten strand of his writing.

Those with an allegiance to the history or disciplinary parameters of philosophical analysis and those who have no appreciation of the interdisciplinary work of religion and cultural studies, which incorporates French literary ideas, continental philosophy, queer theory and feminism, will find this work grinds against their sanitised worlds. For I am not seeking to locate Foucault in the historical context of philosophy or theology – a task completed in the fragments of other studies.[2] This work does not seek to force Foucault into any disciplinary straitjacket but rather reads him 'across disciplines' by closely following the contours of his varied and dynamic work. My reading of Foucault seeks in this sense to follow his disruptive spirit rather than locate him in any single disciplinary context – something which will be of irritation to those in the Anglo-American tradition which attempts to force Foucault into restrictive disciplinary frames. This tension has been identified by Gayatri Chakravorty Spivak, who states:

> I would like to suggest that the United States approach to Foucault, on either side of the debate, is generally within the same side of a clash of epistemes. Both Gutting on the one hand and Dreyfus and Rabinow on the other like Foucault and want to save him for philosophy. But if an episteme can be taken, loosely, to be one level of social *pouvoir savoir*, then these colleagues seem to inhabit a rather different one from Foucault's. .... One feels the tension of making Foucault fit for the consumption of American students and colleagues; the will to regularize him, normalize him, disciplinarize him.[3]

While I acknowledge the importance of mapping the intellectual trajectories of Foucault's thinking in, for example, philosophy and the history of science, I do not seek to restrict or limit Foucault to any specific disciplinary frame in the exploration of the question of 'religion' – not least because, as Asad and King have illustrated, the concept of 'religion' is itself a Western discursive construct bound up with a series of power relations.[4] My attempt in this work is to read Foucault through the literary/religious/cultural tropes of his writing in order to unfold an understanding of 'religion' inside his work. My style is therefore more sympathetic to experimental ways of thinking found in avant-garde French writings than with the annals of traditional philosophy. In this sense my work at times plays into what Gerald Bruns saw as a 'refusal of philosophy' in the work of Blanchot.[5] My attempt is therefore to read Foucault with the fluidity and disruption of such writers as Bataille and Blanchot in order to recover the forgotten fragments of his early 'religious' work.

My work also reacts against those thinkers who wish to bring Foucault and other post-structuralist writers into the conventions and traditions of Christian theology. While Foucault's work holds many possibilities for developing theological ideas and while there have been some very useful theological engagements with him, I separate these developments from his own project. I maintain that Foucault was an atheist and that his work on religion does not sustain a traditional theological worldview. The creative location of Foucault in the tradition of negative theology, for example, is a secondary theological redaction (interesting and valid in its own right) which does not find internal support in his work – except in the very general sense of his work being located within a European post-Christian intellectual context and the possibility of making analogical comparisons with his own linguistic strategies. What I seek to show is that Foucault's engagement with theological themes radically transforms and destabilises the field of religious understanding. Religion after Foucault can never be the same – there is a distinctive break with the historical location and understanding of religion.

Some may want to argue that my use of the word 'religion' in this work is vague and ambiguous, but it is precisely the unsettling of the certainty of the signifier 'religion' that informs Foucault's work. I wish to show that Foucault's writing questions the politics of religious experience and that he uses the words 'religion' and 'spirituality' in a way which disrupts traditional conceptions. The central force of my reading of Foucault is to show how what I call a 'spiritual corporality' and a 'political spirituality' undermine the traditional space of religion as understood in Western Christian society. After Foucault 'religion' is taken out of its privileged realm and brought into the body politic and into the heart of culture. This reading of religion will always be difficult to anyone hoping to use Foucault to support traditional religious belief and practice.

The bringing together of religious discourse and sexuality in the work of Foucault may also frustrate anyone who wishes to deny the influence of the Marquis de Sade and Georges Bataille on his thinking about religion. One anal(ytical) critic has gone as far as to describe my reflections on bodily fluids in relation to Foucault and body theology as 'tasteless'.[6] Ironically such responses can only be described as anti-Foucauldian, in so far as they show no appreciation of Foucault's interest in the politics of sexual practice.

Foucault was challenging the boundaries of our thinking, he was disrupting the binary categories of our thought. My work seeks to take Foucault seriously, which means acknowledging sexually explicit acts, both heterosexual and homosexual, and linking them to religion, as Bataille, Sade and Foucault all do in their work. The style and structure of my work is often meant to be provocative and suggestive as a strategy to thinking differently about religion as it is developed in Foucault's work. The ideas may be challenging; they may offend a traditional theology and philosophy which wants to ignore the body, sexuality and queer politics. There are too many thinkers who want to neatly package religious knowledge into comfortable academic straitjackets, suppressing emotional uncertainties and interpersonal insecurities in intellectual and institutional structures which deny the political and erotic nature of religious discourse and practice.

I therefore read and write about Foucault not through the tradition of philosophy or Christian belief but as someone taking the fragments of his work on religion seriously. To read Foucault 'unplugged' will never be easy for anyone wanting to read him according to the restrictions of disciplinary knowledge. I seek in effect to follow a close textual and historically specific reading that allows space for a series of forgotten fragments of 'religious' discourse. I regard Foucault as someone challenging the boundaries of thought, someone who is strategically and politically questioning the entire process of the power–knowledge relations of disciplines. Religion after Foucault is never the same and clearly not everyone will be happy about this fact. Foucault was very much aware of the problematic responses to his writing when he stated:

> I know how irritating it can be to treat discourses in terms not of the gentle, silent, intimate consciousness that is expressed in them, but of an obscure set of anonymous rules. How unpleasant it is to reveal the limitations and necessities of a practice where one is used to seeing, in all its pure transparency, the expression of genius and freedom.[7]

We need to read Foucault in the spirit of Foucault rather than in the constraints of disciplinary practice. This book is an attempt to show how Foucault started to think differently about religion.

Acknowledgements

Although this book is in all respects an academic study of the work of Michel Foucault, like Foucault, I see all my work as a reflection of my life. I do not accept the traditional academic dictum that ideas exist outside of the life that forms them, and, contrary to conventional academic practice, I wish to acknowledge the more personal context of my writing and thinking. If Foucault's *The Birth of the Clinic* was to some extent a reflection on his father's medical profession, this book is to some extent a personal response to the life of my father and his ordained ministry. The research for this work began three years after the death of my father and was a creative response to the now empty space of dialogue we had about theology, the politics of the church, and sexuality – it is a reflection of the male love between father and son. My father's pastoral ministry in the Church of England dealt with those on the boundaries of the church – with all those whom the church rejected or would prefer to ignore – his ministry, unlike Christian hypocrisy, was about inclusion and acceptance. This work owes its greatest debt to my father, whose life held the silent tensions of the body and belief; to recall the words of Patricia Dunker's novel on Foucault, he was 'the reader for whom I wrote' (*Hallucinating Foucault*, London: Serpent's Tail, 1996).

As the work began with my father's death, it ended a number of months after the death of my mother. There is no doubt that this work is also testimony to all the unspoken words of love, commitment, dedication and sacrifice that mothers make for their children – those, often unacknowledged, facts that make a life possible. I am indebted to my mother for all she has given to me and all she has made possible for my living and my life, for being there and silently holding.

If the outer contours of this work are shaped by my parents, the more specific details have been influenced by many friends and colleagues who have enriched my thinking over the years. I am above all indebted to my doctoral tutor Professor Grace Jantzen, who has become both colleague and friend. Grace has been a real inspiration through the research, writing and reshaping of this work. She has provided many invaluable critical reflections on various stages of its development. She has also encouraged me to keep believing in my project even as those from more traditional philosophical backgrounds were unable to grasp its political challenge. Like Foucault, Grace has taught me the importance of intellectual courage.

I have also had the privilege to meet and develop many valuable friendships with people working in and around the area of Foucault scholarship. I am particularly indebted to James Bernauer SJ, who has provided enormous support during my research and opened many valuable opportunities to share my work with American audiences. Our friendship continues to be a source of much richness. I am also indebted to David Macey, whose generosity and encouragement from the beginning of my research has been so important. Both David Macey and Margaret Atack have been supportive in many ways not only in the work but during many visits to Leeds. It has also been a special delight to have discovered a friendship with David Halperin during a memorable American Academy of Religion conference in San Francisco. He has provided much needed encouragement, bringing equal measure of care and challenging insight to both my life and my work. The work would never have been possible in its present form without the generous help of my friend Richard Townsend. He opened up aspects of Foucault's texts and ideas beyond my own ability and shared many afternoons discussing French culture.

Working one's way through the Foucault archive is no easy task, and while the archive was kept in the Bibliothèque du Saulchoir I was grateful to Isabelle Seruzier for her help and assistance. Richard Lynch has also provided extremely valuable updates on the archive and indulged me in many discussions about Foucault's work. I am also grateful for comments and suggestions from Lois McNay and Kate Cooper, who provided a challenging context in which to think through the work and gave valuable insights on details of the text. Thanks are also due to Adrian Driscoll at Routledge for encouraging and supporting me in my work, and to Anna Gerber and the production team at Routledge for so efficiently bringing the book to light. In addition, I would like to thank Justin Dyer for his extremely valuable comments on the text and careful copy editing.

The main part of the research for this book took place during my time in West London and many people made the time and space for its emergence possible. I owe a special thank you to Bridget Hinkley for patiently listening to many of the ideas as they developed, for so much support and for the times together at the Serpentine Gallery. I am also grateful to my friends and colleagues at Springhallow Special School for autistic children which grounded my experience during the research. My work at Springhallow taught me much about the limits of the intellectual pursuit in a world of communication disorders, and it particularly enriched my understanding by challenging the normalising powers at work in institutional practices. I am particularly grateful to Lynne Humpheson and Sandra Brown for their insight, support and comments on the work.

Without doubt one of my greatest debts is to my friend and colleague at Stirling University, Richard King. He has followed this work closer than anyone. We have shared many hours engaging in intellectual discussion, visiting book shops and simply laughing. It is a rare and valuable gift to have an intellectual companion who knows you better than you would at times wish to admit. I am also grateful for the support of my friend and acupuncturist Juli Stewart for holding my many fears. My colleagues at the University of Stirling have also been extremely helpful in providing time, space and encouragement to finish this project; I am particularly grateful to Keith Whitelam, Mary Keller and Yvonne McClymont for their support. I am also grateful to many friends and colleagues who have offered me so much in so many different ways, particularly Lucille Cairns, Roy Findlayson, Paul Fletcher, Darrian Gay, Hugh Pyper, Nick Royle, Peter Selby, Sonu Shamdasani, Mark Vernon and, more recently, my most precious 'Jewel' for all that is beyond words. Finally, the love of Tim, Ruth and Simon continues to be invaluable, and without them the last years would have been so much harder. They alone know the real sense of loss behind this work, and it is with them that I dedicate this book to our parents.

A shorter version of chapter 4 appeared in a special issue of the *Bulletin of the John Rylands University Library of Manchester*, vol. 80, no. 3, 1998, pp. 215–33.

Abbreviations of main texts by Foucault

AK	*The Archaeology of Knowledge* [1969] (London: Routledge, 1991)
BC	*The Birth of the Clinic: An Archaeology of Medical Perception* [1963 rev.1972] (London: Routledge, 1991)
DP	*Discipline and Punish: The Birth of the Prison* [1975] (London: Penguin, 1991)
HF	*Historie de la folie à l'âge classique* [1961] (Paris: Gallimard, 1972)
HS1	*The History of Sexuality, Volume 1: An Introduction* [1976] (London: Penguin, 1990)
HS2	*The Use of Pleasure: The History of Sexuality, Volume 2* [1984] (London: Penguin, 1992)
HS3	*The Care of the Self: The History of Sexuality, Volume 3* [1984] (London: Penguin, 1990)
MC	*Madness and Civilization: A History of Insanity in the Age of Reason* [1967] (London: Routledge, 1991)
OT	*The Order of Things: An Archaeology of the Human Sciences* [1966] (London: Routledge, 1991)
RR	*Death and the Labyrinth: The World of Raymond Roussel* [1963] (London: Athlone, 1987)

Introduction

Approaching Foucault's work on religion

> It is hard for me to classify a form of research like my own within philosophy
> or within the human sciences. I could define it as an analysis of the cultural
> facts characterising our culture.
>
> Foucault (1967c) 'Qui êtes-vous, professeur Foucault?', p. 605

The work of Michel Foucault (1926–84) has been explored in a variety of
ways through the intellectual fields of philosophy, sociology, politics and
literary studies, and his major contributions to these disciplines have been
clearly articulated. However, the task of examining Foucault's work from
the perspective of religion is far more complex. This is not only because he
did not specifically work in the field but because religious studies (an area of
study misunderstood and obscured in the secular academy) is an interdisciplinary subject incorporating aspects of philosophy, sociology, politics and
literature. The current study of religion is now being more accurately articulated as part of an interdisciplinary study of cultures which, unlike the
various modes of cultural studies, takes account of the historical and
contemporary beliefs and practices of a given culture – it does not devalue
or ignore the history and significance of religious beliefs and practices. Such
an interdisciplinary approach finds Foucault's work particularly fascinating
because religion is examined as part of his 'analysis of the cultural facts'. It
is not a matter of separating religion from Foucault's philosophical or
historical work; religion rather exists in the very fabric of such studies.
Foucault takes account of religion in the shaping of Western knowledge,
and it is this dimension which needs to be rescued. It is unfortunate that
most readings of him have obliterated or marginalised the religious content
in the narrow confines of their studies.

In examining the religious dimension of Foucault's writing it is important
to identify the specific methodological approach of my own work in uncovering what I will call his 'religious question'. I am not, for example, seeking
to apply Foucault's methodology to religion or theology, a task already
advanced in the field of the sociology of religion.[1] My aim is rather to
examine his work in order to uncover the religious sub-text of his writing
prior to the emergence of his discussion of Christianity after 1976, and to

show how his work changes in emphasis from this time. I am seeking to show that Foucault's late work on Christianity was not a sudden or abrupt turn to religion, but that he continually drew religion into his work – he recognised religion as a major part of the 'history of the present'.[2]

My approach to Foucault's religious question will be similar (though not identical) to Henry Levinson's seminal assessment of the religious implications of William James' work. Levinson described his work in the following way:

> It is a book of philosophical reconstruction which shows James in his own world, not ours. I have made no effort to develop a comprehensive view of James's work as psychologist, philosopher, psychical researcher, literary critic, and public orator, though James made contributions to his study of religion in each of these roles. But I have tried to follow James's religious investigations wherever they led, even as they spilled over all sorts of proper disciplinary divisions that we make but that he did not.[3]

James, like Foucault, explored religion alongside a wider set of studies, and Levinson's attempt to bracket out the wider issues in James' study is a similar strategy to my own. The extraction of a religious sub-text from Foucault's work may appear fetishistic in nature, especially as Foucault was an acknowledged atheist.[4] But this work seeks to uncover the religious fragments in order to highlight the underlying significance of a religious discourse and to show, as I have indicated, that it was a valid part of Foucault's 'analysis of the cultural facts'.[5] While Foucault's 'religious question' only became a central focus in the late work, it always formed part of his wider studies and was consistently included as a significant part of the 'apparatus' (*dispositif*) of knowledge. However, by isolating the religious texts and trying to understand a separate discourse we are always in danger of distorting Foucault, even if he recommended such an approach in relation to Nietzsche.[6] This work is an attempt to take Foucault's marginal reflections on religion seriously in order to show how they radically challenge traditional religious thinking.

This work, as Levinson notes in relation to his own 'adventure' with James, may appear 'untidy', because it follows 'surprising turns', involves 'subplots' and holds 'unanswered questions'.[7] This is particularly true when exploring Foucault's 'religious question' because he offered no systematic examination of religious themes, or for that matter any other such subject.

Working in such a fragmented landscape means that there is much scope for secondary elaboration, and this highlights once again the dangers of developing imaginary religious worlds from Foucault's work. In order to guard against such excesses my methodology will be primarily textual. Foucault's writing could be, and has been, critically examined and developed from the perspective of the history of religions and theology, but I do *not* seek to develop substantially any of these approaches.[8] My aim is to read Foucault with Foucault, to read the religious strands of his texts alongside each other in order to establish the underlying religious questions hidden in his work. It is to juxtapose and interconnect a whole series of statements about religious ideas and to organise, evaluate and describe the themes held in such fragments. My aim is to 'fold' Foucault's texts upon each other, to establish some coherence and order in the religious ideas held at the margins. Such an exercise is comparable to Gilles Deleuze's commentary on Foucault which describes the 'folds' in Foucault's work, where the 'interiority' of thought is seen as a doubling of what is outside of thought.[9] The 'religious question' in this sense is part of the 'unthought' of Foucault's work. My work aims to shape an 'inside' (an interiority) of his work with the 'outside' (the unthought). It is to explore the 'folds' of his texts in order to reconstruct a 'religious question'. I seek to read the multiple strands of his religious sub-text back on each other, to find Foucault's own 'religious question'.

I will of course introduce other critical methodologies into this textual fabric, but these will not form my main apparatus of inquiry. Thus, for example, I will utilise a number of secondary historical and feminist critiques to illuminate Foucault's writing, but my aim is always to create a space to read his 'religious question' through his own texts rather than consistently examine or outline other critiques to their full extent. This work will therefore isolate and bring together the fragments of Foucault's religious sub-text. From the earliest references in the 1950s and 1960s on the role of religious institutions in the history of madness, through the selective comments in his literary period and the discourse on the death of God, to the more substantial discussion of confession from 1976 till his death, I will attempt to carefully construct his 'religious question' in a way previously unexplored.

The principal aim of this inter-textual reading of Foucault's work, as I have already stated, is to rescue the early strands of his religious sub-text as standing alongside the later and more overt concerns he had with Christianity. I will hope to demonstrate that the later fascination with early Christian history arises out of and complements earlier concerns with religion. This weighting towards the early Foucault is based on two determining factors: first, the 'religious question' in his late work has by virtue of its more overt nature received greater attention in Foucault studies; and, second, the focus on his late work has primarily been concerned, alongside the work of Peter Brown, with the value of his work for understanding the church in late antiquity and has in consequence ignored the critical perspectives which align it with the earlier reflections on religion.[10] I am therefore concerned principally not about the validity of Foucault's reading of religion and theology, but about the way he 'problematises' religious thinking in a philosophical critique of religious ontology.

This work therefore sets out to reveal the underlying religious sub-text in

Foucault's early work in terms of a critique of religious thinking which is, I shall argue, carried forward into the later studies of Christianity in a distinctively different form. I am in effect arguing that there is a single critique of religion in Foucault which emerges in the early work but which shifts in the later work due to a change of emphasis in his approach to religion. My work therefore is mapping a single critique of religion with two distinct edges or forms. I describe these two critiques as a 'spiritual corporality' and a 'political spirituality' by grouping together statements from different periods of Foucault's work, the former emerging in the early work of the 1960s and the latter emerging post-1976. My argument is that these two aspects of Foucault's religious sub-text are mutually dependent and reveal not so much different critiques of religion, as a single interdependent critique of religion. It could therefore be argued that 'spiritual corporality' and 'political spirituality' are applicable to all Foucault's work and that the division is merely one of emphasis.[11]

Outline of the book

In this book I will follow a number of stages of argumentation. I will first (chapter 1) provide an outline of Foucault's work, drawing attention to those aspects of his work that explore religious themes. Those familiar with Foucault's writings will obviously be able to move easily through this section, although it does seek to highlight the religious and theological themes that have been overlooked in other studies. In chapter 2 I orientate the entire study by drawing a theoretical division between 'silence' and 'speech' from Foucault's 1976 work *The History of Sexuality: An Introduction*. This division between silence and speech forms the theoretical lynchpin of my reading of Foucault. It reveals the watershed between the two aspects or dimensions of his religious critique: 'spiritual corporality' (a critique of the silencing powers of religion) and 'political spirituality' (a critique of religious authority in the demand for confession). It is in this sense that I will use 1976 as the division between the notion of early and late work in Foucault. I will demonstrate that Foucault's sub-textual concern with religion prior to 1976 is preoccupied with extrapolating the silenced parts of religion, and that after 1976 he is concerned with religious utterances. In this book I will seek to show how these two aspects of his work form a single religious critique in the same way that he sees silence and speech to be indivisible.

After outlining the theoretical basis of my discussion a substantial part of the work will plot the basis of what I have referred to as Foucault's 'spiritual corporality'. The idea of a 'spiritual corporality' is unfolded through an exploration of Foucault's surrealist and avant-garde background, which I argue is the inspirational source of the 'religious question'. I refer to a 'spiritual corp*orality*' rather than a 'corp*oreality*' because the former indicates *only* 'of the body', as opposed to the latter, which implies body in opposition to 'the spiritual or intangible'.[12] The idea of 'spiritual corporality' will be developed by creating a series of textual graftings or 'folds' with Foucault's religious sub-texts. By bringing together a series of textual fragments I will set out how Foucault's early work can be seen as holding a critique of religion in the form of a 'spiritual coprorality'. I will develop this in three separate stages. I will first entertain the question of a 'religious problem' in Foucault's work in relation to his background in surrealism and show to what extent he suspends and questions 'religious' ideas (chapter 3). I will then in a second stage show how his critical suspension of the 'spiritual' is relocated in the 'corporal' through the work of the Marquis de Sade and the notion of the death of God (chapter 4). I will also argue at this point that any discussion of the body must address the question of gender and seek to show how Foucault's work holds a specifically male religious dimension. In a final stage I will examine Foucault's *The Archaeology of Knowledge* in order to reinforce how his work opposes traditional religious ontology (chapter 5). It is my aim in this chapter to show how Foucault's work rejects models of religious transcendence and opens the way for models of religious immanence.

Once I have established Foucault's idea of a 'spiritual corporality' and his opposition to traditional religious thinking, I will then show how in the mid-1970s his 'religious question' faces a number of tensions and show how it gradually changes in its emphasis. I will argue that in *Discipline and Punish* there is a fundamental tension in his 'religious question' caused by the binary opposition between belief and practice (chapter 6). It is at this point that Foucault begins to submerge his 'spiritual corporality' and starts to develop a different emphasis in his discussion of religion in the form of a 'political spirituality'. I will show how he shifts towards a political concern with religion after 1976 (chapter 7). Finally, I will return to my main argument and show how Foucault's work holds a single critique of religion in the two ideas of 'spiritual corporality' and 'political spirituality'. I will reiterate that as Foucault sees 'silence' and 'speech' as inseparable, so the notions of 'spiritual corporality' and 'political spirituality' are inseparable. My aim is to show how Foucault's work holds a single critique of Christianity with two interrelated dimensions. After Foucault, religion is radically transformed, and in the conclusion I will briefly outline what I see as the distinctive challenges he offers to religious and theological thinking.

The idea of a 'religious question'

It will already be apparent that the signifier 'religion' is a problematic feature of this study, and before exploring Foucault's texts in detail it is important to demarcate the boundaries of the 'religious question' I am suggesting surrounds his work. First, we must constantly bear in mind that Foucault does not provide a distinctive and separate discussion of religion or Christianity. His work on religion often occurs through tangents and oblique associations, where 'religion' and 'Christianity' are selectively introduced in more detailed studies of madness, the avant-garde, language, prisons, sexuality and governmentality. Second, there is also a certain amount of slippage between the concepts of 'religion', 'theology', 'Christianity' and 'spirituality'. Sometimes these terms appear to be synonymous. However, Foucault generally uses the term 'religion' as a kind of overall phenomenological term to refer to any institutionalised faith tradition, though this predominantly means institutionalised Christianity. The term 'spirituality' in a similar fashion appears to refer to any religious faith, but is used, as we shall see, to avoid the word 'religion' and strategically disrupt traditional religious meaning.[13] Foucault's use of the term 'theology' remains exclusively in the Christian tradition; and the references to Christianity always imply an exclusively white, male, Western tradition. In order to anchor my own discussion I will follow this very general framework of terminology, where 'religion' refers to the overall category of institutionalised religious phenomena and 'theology' to the Christian tradition. While it is necessary to locate the terminology for discussion, it is important to remember that the traditional meaning behind these terms is often critically suspended.

The aim of presenting a 'question' around Foucault's allusions to 'religion' is to hold the ambiguity and uncertainty of this referent within his own work. This work seeks to present and demarcate a series of 'religious' and 'theological' questions within his writings, which often seem to have little relationship to each other, but, as will become clear, are part of a wider set of 'force relations' (power) which challenge the coherence of the religious and theological 'subject'. I am seeking in this sense to follow Foucault's own response to surrealism in 1963 by suggesting that there '*may be* a religious question' oscillating in his work, but the coordinates of such a discussion will be radically altered from their traditional contours in the philosophy of religion.[14]

The alteration in traditional religious meaning is brought about by repositioning 'religion' in the space of the body and the politics of the subject. Religion, theology and spirituality are in consequence detached and dislocated from a transcendent order and become strategies which shape, control and dictate the patterns of human experience. The 'truth' of religious discourse is in effect taken out of the binary opposition between spirit and matter and rewritten in terms of the dynamic of power–knowledge and embodiment. Each stage of this work seeks to uncover the sub-textual movements in Foucault's writing which bring about this reorganisation and critique of 'religious' meaning. What I am suggesting is that Foucault's 'religious question' is found in part, like Foucault himself, in the act of its 'disappearance'.

1 Outline of Foucault's work and the question of religion

> Religious discourse, juridical and therapeutic as well as, in some ways, political discourse are all barely dissociable from the functioning of a ritual that determines the individual properties and agreed roles of the speakers.
> Foucault (1970a) 'The Discourse on Language', p. 225

The legacy of Foucault continues to take many twists and turns since his death. On the one hand his work has been condemned as lacking historical accuracy and obscuring philosophical 'truth', while on the other it has been extolled as providing one of the sharpest critiques of Western thought. His private life has been sensationalised in biography and his work held up along with Derrida, Barthes, Irigaray and Lacan in the mythology of the post-modern. It is perhaps, as Foucault declared in 1981, disguised under the pseudonym of 'Maurice Florence', 'doubtless too early to assess the break introduced by Michel Foucault'.[1]

The contours of 'the break' are in part already determined by Foucault's cultural context in the French academic elite: educated at the prestigious École Normale Supérieure in Paris, then through a variety of academic posts in Europe and North Africa, and his arrival in 1970 to the Chair in the History of Systems of Thought at the Collège de France. But Foucault was not content to exist in the isolation of the academy. His work sought to engage in the politics of the asylum, the prison and the regimes of power which attempted to normalize and control. Foucault provided a social analysis which engaged in the intellectual and political struggles of his time; from the French educational structures, the treatment of prisoners, the plight of political refugees, to his support for solidarity in Poland, there was a wider engagement in the protests and battles for social justice. Towards the end of his life he was actively involved in the struggle to find new ways of expressing his gay identity and uncovering the dynamics of sexual politics, a register that arguably determines the entire enterprise of his work.[2]

Foucault's 'break' was also in part a response to the changing role of the intellectual in an ever-shifting political world. He was part of an intellectual 'event' and a wave of critical theory which disrupted the dominant discourses of Western rationalism and opened awkward spaces which remain unresolved and displaced. He was a writer who broke the mould of post-war French thought by challenging the landscape of phenomenology, Marxism and existentialism; a thinker who moved between, in and through traditional academic boundaries, causing anxiety to the Anglo-Saxon disciplinary straitjackets of philosophy, history, literary studies and psychology. Foucault's 'break' was to unfold a new geography of thought, an unfamiliar terrain, which was to unsettle the map of contemporary Western thinking. We encounter Foucault in texts which 'dissolve', 'explode' and 'collapse', in texts which encourage revolt.[3] As the opening lines of his inaugural lecture at the Collège de France make clear, Foucault is found in his 'disappearances'; he is not simply found in the certitudes of historical fragments and philosophical calculation but in the 'enigmatic gesture', in the underground passages, in the silences, in the unthought, in the spaces of the Other, and, as Certeau so poignantly reveals, in the space of laughter.[4] Such a style creates what Bove called a 'problematic of reception'.[5] It presents the paradox of reading Foucault according to the categories of knowledge he so radically questioned.[6]

In order to understand the 'break introduced by Michel Foucault' it is necessary to begin this study by providing an initial outline of his major works. This is particularly important in a work which seeks to explore the sub-textual dimensions of his writing. If we are to understand the context of Foucault's religious thinking, we need to establish the relationship of these ideas to his main texts. In this first chapter I will not seek to wrestle with Foucault's works to find a style which will do justice to the individual force of his ideas, but rather present the broad scope of his thinking in order to locate the religious dimension of his work. This outline will enable me to show how the contours of Foucault's 'analysis of the cultural facts' brush up against the question of religion. It will reveal how he continually made excursions into religious and theological themes. The unique contribution of this work is to take these religious fragments seriously and entertain a 'religious question' hidden in Foucault's writing.

Outline of Foucault's work

Reflecting on his work in 1978, Foucault represented himself as an 'experimenter' rather than a 'theorist'.[7] This differentiation is significant in trying to outline Foucault's work because it reveals the way he develops a series of analyses which reshape the historical object or theme of study by adopting critical indexes in their presentation. Foucault does not formulate neat and consistent objects of knowledge; rather he recasts and redefines the framework of perception. In this respect he argued that he provided 'tools' to examine institutions, practices and concepts.[8] His work seeks to show how knowledge (*savoir*) is shaped by a 'will', by a power, by disciplines and regimes. What Foucault exposed was the ways in which knowledge is controlled, limited and excluded. He revealed the politics of all forms of knowldge.[9] This critical work predominantly exists within an historical–philosophical framework. Foucault develops studies of madness, medicine, prisons and sexuality by writing history according to the 'conditions' which 'constitute' the object of study. He develops a kind of phenomenological discourse inside historical frameworks. In this work, as has been well documented, Foucault was bringing together ideas from the French *Annales* school, with an extended periodization within his historical studies, and the work of Bachelard and Canguilhem in the philosophy of science, in developing a history of the concepts.[10]

Although the broad parameters of Foucault's work can be defined in terms of an historical–philosophical critique, his ideas changed and developed over time within this area. The 'experimental' nature of his enterprise meant that different thematic projects were developed, adapted and redefined throughout his career. He 'continuously made shifts' and introduced new 'fields of analyses' which were unavailable to him in his earlier studies. Foucault's work therefore has an evolving nature, and later concepts, such as the notions of 'power', 'the subject' and 'problematics', meant redefining his perception of his earlier work.[11] There is in this sense, as Hoy makes clear, no 'single Foucault'.[12]

In this introductory outline I will explore Foucault's diverse work in three sections. First, 1954–69, the period dominated by his archaeological thinking. It is from this period that I will later recover a sub-textual religious question based on the repressive nature of religion and the emergence of a 'death of God' discourse. Second, 1970–5, the period in which Foucault unfolds his genealogical work and from which I will later develop a number of sub-textual tensions in his religious thinking between belief and practice. The final section of this introductory outline will cover the period 1976–84, the time when Foucault wrote his multi-volume *History of Sexuality*. This period sees the development of an explicit discussion of Christianity, examining confession and the ethics of self. In each of these sections I will outline the arguments within Foucault's primary texts and then indicate where the religious question emerges. I will not seek at this stage to develop any critical evaluation of his work. My aim is rather to map the landscape of his writing in order to locate the religious question in relation to his principal work.

1954–69

In Foucault's earliest work in the 1950s we can find the rudiments of his critical and historical work. Influenced by Heidegger and phenomenology, on the one hand, and the history of psychology and Marxism, on the other, he wrote two embryonic pieces documenting issues in psychiatry and mental illness. The first piece, an introduction to Ludwig's Binswanger's *Dream and Existence*, attempted to suspend the question of anthropology inside the 'real content of an existence'. Foucault at this point follows the phenomenological task of trying to examine the question of 'man' not through the traditions of psychology and philosophy but through 'his [*sic*] forms of existence'.[13] This consideration of 'concrete existence' took seriously, following Binswanger, the development and history of its content. Foucault, even at this early point of 1954, is working with what he called a 'problematic of foundation', attempting to find the 'conditions of possibility' for anthropology in the analytic of existence. This concern with the 'problematic of foundations' is also found in a second early piece from the 1950s, *Maladie mentale et personnalité*, revised in 1962 and published in English as *Mental Illness and Psychology*. Here Foucault raises two central questions: 'Under what *conditions* can one speak of illness in the psychological domain?' and 'What *relations* can one define between the facts of mental pathology and those of organic pathology?'[14] The object of study in both situations is suspended and questioned through a critical perspective. This dimension of Foucault's work is carried through his entire writings, but the forays into the issues of mental illness and subsequently madness gradually move away from a simple phenomenological and even Marxist question to a wider historical and cultural analysis about how madness is constructed.

The gradual revisions and evolutions from Foucault's work in the 1950s to his later doctoral work published in 1961 can be seen, as Dreyfus has shown, in the revised *Mental Illness and Psychology*. In this work the sections on Marxism and organic pathology have been dropped in favour of a new section, 'Madness and Culture', which arose directly from his doctoral study *Histoire de la folie à l'âge classique* (HF).[15] Foucault is here raising a new set of questions about the object of madness by considering it not from the position of psychiatry but through the conjectured position of the treated patient, though the 'Other' or the 'silence' in the history of psychiatry. The emergent critical edge here is Foucault's attempt to read madness as a defined cultural space. The 'problematic of foundations' continues, as we shall see throughout his work, but this time not so much in terms of phenomenology or normative objects of study and methodology but in terms of his idea of an 'archaeology', a term borrowed from Immanuel Kant.[16]

Foucault's archaeological studies attempt to establish a different basis upon which the objects and concerns of history are established. No longer following the strictures of the history of ideas, he critically suspended the assumptions of disciplinary knowledge and sought to explore the object by considering what he referred to as a 'positive unconscious of knowledge'.[17] This unconscious of knowledge was established by examining the 'discursive structures', the way ideas are formed through discourse. This idea of a 'discourse' is central to Foucault's entire enterprise and it demonstrates clearly the temporality and construction of ideas. Although Foucault acknowledged that the idea of discourse had been used in a variety of ways, in his work it can be seen basically as a group of statements which together have a certain 'modality of existence'; they 'belong to a single system of formation'.[18] Foucault, in the phenomenological tradition, attempts to show how ideas, objects and concepts are 'formulated'.

The basic element of Foucault's analysis of discourse is the 'statement', it is the 'ultimate, undecomposable element', the 'atom of discourse'.[19] The idea of a 'statement' is not to be confused with the sentence and linguistic analysis. The signs of language do not form a statement; it is rather a 'function' which 'cuts across' such unities.[20] The statement is therefore not necessarily a written entity but more broadly, as Dreyfus and Rabinow have stated, a 'serious speech act' which can be spoken, recorded on tape, written in a book or on a poster.[21] The statement always exists within an enunciative field, a network of conditions from which the statement appears. There is always a context, place and condition from which a statement emerges; it has a 'material existence'.[22] This means that all statements are conditioned by institutional determinants and their 'field of use'.[23] Foucault's entire work examines these 'statements' in order to suspend the *a priori* assumptions of knowledge and uncover the laws that govern our knowledge. In this sense, archaeology is an attempt to describe the function of discourses or the 'discursive practice', which Foucault defines as 'a body of anonymous, historical rules, always determined in the time and space that have defined a given period'.[24]

Through his methodological practice of archaeology Foucault elaborates his early phenomenological attempts to explore the 'conditions of possibility' for the emergence of an idea. This practice also radically questions the traditional methods of history by undermining the transcendent assumptions of an historical object.[25] The traditional unities of knowledge such as the *oeuvre*, the book and the author are questioned by examining the conditions in which they are produced and created. There is also a suspension of thematic continuities and categories of historical knowledge. As Foucault so poignantly indicates, the 'a priori does not elude historicity'.[26] This allows him to demonstrate the disunities and discontinuities in history and to expose the underlying ideological unities and teleological assumptions. Archaeology, according to Foucault, is taking 'difference seriously'.[27]

> It establishes that we are difference, that our reason is the difference of discourses, our history the difference of times, ourselves the difference of masks. That difference, far from being the forgotten and recovered origin, is this dispersion that we are and make.[28]

This formulation of archaeology occurred in Foucault's 1969 work *The Archaeology of Knowledge* (AK) and represents to some extent a working through of ideas in his previous studies of madness, medicine and the structure of the human sciences. All of these works follow the archaeological framework to a greater or lesser extent by exploring how specific objects of knowledge are constituted in an historical process. Foucault's doctoral dissertation HF (1961), partly translated in English as *Madness and*

Civilization (1967), was an attempt to examine the archaeology of the silence of the mad. Foucault's study of medicine, *The Birth of the Clinic* (1963), was subtitled 'an Archaeology of medical perception' and his major 1966 work *The Order of Things* was likewise subtitled as 'An archaeology of the human sciences'. Each of these works developed critical historical readings by drawing out the underlying patterns and formations of knowledge.

In *Madness and Civilization* (MC) Foucault focuses on the key division between madness and reason. Reason, according to him, 'subjugates non-reason', and with the 'constitution of madness as mental illness' at the end of the eighteenth century the dialogue between reason and unreason is seen to be broken. The reason of psychiatry silences the voice of the mad. Through a series of historical vignettes, criticized by traditional historians for lacking historical accuracy, Foucault unfolds a history of madness and unreason from the end of the Middle Ages to the present.[29] In each of these representations he portrays the sense of madness as a cultural exclusion, initially filling the gap that had been left by the disappearance of leprosy. It is not surprising in this sense that the work was taken up by the British anti-psychiatry movement. The English edition appeared in a series edited by the leading anti-psychiatrist R.D. Laing and the foreword to the English edition was written by another leading exponent of anti-psychiatry, David Cooper.

The remarkable feature of Foucault's study of madness is its use of a series of powerful images and its interweaving of artistic and literary themes. We are presented with the ship of fools (*Narrenschiff*) carrying the mad away along the rivers of the Rhineland and the Flemish canals, and the landmark of 1656 which founded the Hôpital Général and established the Great Confinement. With the establishment of confinement in the Classical age (the period of the seventeenth and eighteenth centuries which predominates in Foucault's writing), madness became a spectacle of observation and Foucault's work unfolds the 'imaginary landscape' that madness inhabited.[30] Madness was associated with animality and grafted into the passions, hallucinations and delusions in a battle Foucault sets up between reason and unreason. This battle is an attempt by him to demonstrate the interconnected nature of these two domains. The emphasis throughout, as in earlier works, is to show how madness is an historical and cultural 'constitution'.[31]

In mapping the cultural contours of madness, Foucault demonstrated the fragmented conceptions of madness in the seventeenth century in their confusion of bodily and mental states. He showed how in the nineteenth century these would gradually be superimposed with models of morality and psychology. Before this time the therapeutics of madness were based on a diverse series of cures rooted in physical techniques. The emergence of psychological conceptions came with what Foucault saw as the 'The Great Fear'; the fear of confinement giving way to the fear of moral reform. In a 'non-Whiggish' stance, Foucault questioned the moral reforms of madness with Pinel and Tuke in the eighteenth century as a 'strange regression' which reactivated the 'imaginary stigma of disease' found in leprosy.[32]

At the end of the eighteenth century, according to Foucault, unreason and madness were divided. Madness assumed a new conceptual order and history in the face of medical thought, while unreason continued in the work of writers and artists like Hölderlin, Nerval, Nietzsche, Van Gogh and Artaud.[33] This new awareness of madness gave birth to the asylum, the place where 'madness was finally recognised and treated accordingly'.[34] Foucault's work on madness rejected the asylum, moral therapy, Freud and psychoanalysis as silencing the voice of madness. In contrast Foucault valorises the work of art as the space where unreason is heard in the struggle with madness.

The main critical trajectory of Foucault's thinking is seen very clearly in his first work on madness. The broad periodisation taking in the Middle Ages, the Renaissance, the Classical age and the Modern period demonstrates how Foucault models history. He utilises these periods to frame different attitudes and representations of madness which are then held together by a specific literary or poetic image. In his later work *The Order of Things* he will argue that these different periods hold certain 'epistemic' structures which condition knowledge. It is this notion of historical conditioning and structuring which is the central precept of his thinking. As I have emphasised before, Foucault's work continually comes back to the idea of an object of knowledge as 'constituted' in the historical process.

The historical–critical examination of how an object is constructed continues in Foucault's study of the history of medicine. *The Birth of the Clinic* (BC) does not, however, follow the broad periodisation of the study of madness; it seeks rather to concentrate on the details of medical practice at the end of the eighteenth century. The continuity in Foucault's methodology is seen when he states once again that his aim is to find the 'conditions of possibility', in this case of medical experience.[35] His study seeks to examine how the individual was 'constituted' as an object of medical science.[36] In his style of utilising creative images to carry his central ideas, Foucault draws together the work by focusing on the idea of the 'gaze', the act of medical perception. This analysis of the medical gaze is written across the themes of space, language and death, the anatomo-clinical method. In this medical regime we find the 'spatialisation' of the body in medical pathology, the establishment of a relationship between 'words' and 'things' in medical discourse, and the illumination of disease in the opening of the corpse. Foucault's argument is that at end of the eighteenth century there was a 'chronological threshold' which created the historical conditions for disease to be opened up to the 'light of language'.[37] The birth of medicine was made possible through a 'correlation of the visible and the expressible' which was in turn made possible through the 'stable' object of death or the corpse.[38] Once the medical gaze could be anchored by integrating death, medicine could assume a positivity where the patient was enclosed in a 'collective, homogeneous space'.[39] This significantly paved the way for the 'sciences of man', which would be the object of Foucault's next work.

This initial outline of Foucault's early historical–critical studies already reveals how it is possible to develop this methodology to analyse a broad range of 'cultural facts'. It is also possible to see how his methodology could be utilised in theology and religious studies to critically examine religious history.[40] The methodology can be used to question and suspend the assumptions of religious knowledge within an historical framework. It is to recognise, according to Foucault, that we 'are doomed historically to history, to the patient construction of discourses about discourses, and to the task of hearing what has already been said'.[41] This task has already been carried out with great success in a number of areas of religious studies and theology, but my aim, as will become clearer, is to step further inside Foucault's texts not to apply his methodology but to unearth his own religious ideas.

Although there is little material for this task in both MC and BC, Foucault does make a number of allusions to religious history. Religion forms part of the cultural residual which shapes and determines how madness and medicine have been shaped in the West. We may note, for example, how religion in the history of madness was seen as one of the 'safe-guards' of reason and how religion in the establishment of moral treatment represented 'what cannot go mad'.[42] In BC we may only find a brief refer-ence to the shift from a worldview organised by God to the development of medical consciousness, but these minor intimations provide markers to an emergent critical sub-text of religion.

It became clear in MC that Foucault was deeply influenced by literary themes, and between 1962 and 1966 this interest was extended with the publication of a number of literary essays. He wrote extensive pieces on the work of Hölderlin, Blanchot, Bataille and Klossowski. In addition Foucault also published a book-length study of the surrealist writer Raymond Roussel.[43] Some of the literary themes Foucault explored were carried forward into his major 1966 work *The Order of Things* (OT). These literary studies are significant from a religious perspective because they bring Foucault into specific engagement with a religious question on the bound-aries of literature and theology. They show how the space of literature opens up religious ideas. At this time Foucault also starts to entertain issues related to the 'death of God' discourse which was in vogue in avant-garde circles. These themes may be seen as incidental but they infiltrate into his OT and establish a key theoretical relation between theology and language. I will explore the themes from this literary period in later chapters of this work. At this stage I merely wish to register the first signs of a religious discourse behind the scenes of Foucault's wider studies. It is this discourse, previously ignored in Foucault studies, which this work seeks to recover.

In OT Foucault returned to the broad historical–critical perspective found in the study of madness by dividing Western history into three discon-tinuous periods, the Renaissance, the Classical age and the Modern period, each determined by different structures of thought or 'epistemes'. These 'epistemic' structures resembled many of the patterns of current structuralist thinking in France, although Foucault denied any association with such a movement. He defined the 'episteme' in 1969 as 'the total set of relations that unite, at a given period, the discursive practices that give rise to episte-mological figures, sciences, and possibly formalized systems'.[44] The episteme was not so much a type of knowledge as a set of relations for a given period. It was a 'hidden network', 'the fundamental codes of culture' or, as Foucault states, in line with his earlier work, the 'conditions of possibility'.[45] Within this framework Foucault assessed the emergence of the human sciences by examining the development of knowledge in philology, biology and economics, or, as they were constellated in the Classical period, general grammar, natural history and the analysis of wealth.

In OT Foucault disrupts models of historical continuity by illustrating how knowledge is reconstituted in different historical periods. He wants to show how the different configurations of ideas shape our knowledge. This will ultimately destabilize the human sciences and the figure of 'man' which dominate the Modern episteme. To unfold this critique of the positivity of knowledge, Foucault, as the French title, *Les Mots et les choses*, suggests, seeks to establish the relationship between words and things, to establish the order of knowledge, to understand why different relations of ideas are estab-lished. These ideas are initially framed by including a lengthy examination of Velàzquez's painting *Las Meninas*. Foucault shows how the painting plays with the tensions of representation and the gaze in the Classical age by portraying a painter and a mirror reflecting the subjects in the space of the viewer. The painting centres the focus of the work on the question of repre-sentation as it extends across huge periods of history and a whole array of subjects.

In the Renaissance period the world is determined by resemblance. Language and the world form a unity ordained by God. The world is inter-woven with similitudes and signatures. There is, as Foucault indicates, 'a non-distinction between what is seen and what is read', resulting in 'the constitution of a single, unbroken surface in which observation and language intersect to infinity'.[46] The theological emphasis in this world of resemblance as ordered by God is significant in so far as it is the first indica-tion of an emerging theological sub-text in OT. Its significance becomes even more apparent in so far as later epistemes are dependent on the death of God. The shift in representation simultaneously becomes a shift in theo-logical understanding.

Once Foucault has depicted the Renaissance world of resemblance he then demonstrates how an epistemic shift occurred in the Classical age. In the seventeenth century, with the emergence of Port Royal grammar, the arrangement of signs established the connection between the sign and signi-fied. This transition to the Classical world was seen in Cervantes' *Don Quixote*, where the discrepancy between the text and life is outplayed. The sign and signified are separated in a world where knowledge is no longer resemblance but representation. This new order of things allowed for

discrimination and distinction. It created the space for 'order and measure-
ment', for tabulation and analysis.[47] God in this Classical episteme had
given knowledge to interpret the world, including sufficient knowledge to
prove God exists.[48]

The configuration of the Classical episteme emerged out of a 'grid of
kinships' between '*mathesis*' (the science of calculable order) '*taxinomia*' (the
science of empirical order or classifications) and '*genesis*' (the analysis of
empirical orders). This general science of order created the possibility for
general grammar, natural history and the analysis of wealth in an 'exhaustive ordering of the world'.[49] There was an ordering of signs in general
grammar, an ordering of nature in natural history and an ordering of wealth
through money and notions of value, each made possible through the mechanisms of representation. Foucault explored each of these areas in detail. He
attempted to show how each held the 'same conditions of possibility'.[50]
What he was establishing was the 'historicity of knowledge' and how the
shifts within knowledge were based on a series of historical ruptures.[51] What
this also revealed, as Shumway has clearly shown, is how Foucault's
emphasis in the Classical period on language rather than on mathematics
undermined the positivism of science and placed reason within historical
categories.[52]

The transition from the Renaissance to the Classical episteme was
depicted by Cervantes' *Don Quixote*; in a similar fashion Foucault illustrates
the transition from the Classical to the Modern episteme in the novels of the
Marquis de Sade. In the extreme actions of the Sadeian libertine representation found its limit. The conflict between representation and the extremities
of desire demonstrated the opening up of a new space of thought. At the
end of the eighteenth century Foucault argued that there was a new discontinuity which detached thought from the orders of the Classical period. This
radical break was brought about by the 'mutation of Order into History',
the recognition that thought had a history.

In a number of gradual phases the subjects of philology, biology and
economics emerged, not in place of general grammar, natural history and
the analysis of wealth, but in a new area of knowledge, in the 'space they left
blank'.[53] They were established through the recognition of 'great hidden
forces', the recognition that things would be ordered according to a hidden
depth and historical source.[54] The field of modern economics was founded
on the hidden notion of 'labour' which had not previously been part of the
ideas of money, trade and exchange. In biology the 'hidden architecture' of
the 'organic structure' of life took the place of visible taxonomy. And finally,
in the area of language analysis an 'interior "mechanism"' was seen to
organise and structure language through the inflectional system.[55] By taking
key figures in each of the areas, Foucault went on to show how the hidden
aspects of labour, life and language assumed a historicity which 'shattered'
the world of representation.

After describing the shift from the Classical to the Modern episteme

Foucault is drawn back to the question of language. This occurs because of the way the Modern episteme establishes a new configuration of language. What is striking in the modern order of things is the 'demotion of language to the mere status of an object'.[56] This, however, is compensated in the scientific endeavour to find a perfect language and logic, in the critical value of language as an historical reality, and in the emergence of literature as holding a new intensity of language. In this discussion Foucault returns to the theological question through his recognition that language and God are closely bound together. In the Modern era it is words that make God, 'men' and knowledge possible. Foucault at this point highlights what has been implicit throughout OT: the Nietzschean link between grammar and God.[57] The Nietzschean theme continues in the final sections of OT in the link between God, language and 'man' which are brought together in Foucault's final critique of the human sciences.

Towards the end of the work Foucault returns to the great play of representations in Velàsquez's painting of *Las Meninas* to show that in the Classical age there is no consideration of the viewing subject. This, according to Foucault, was because 'man' 'was only a recent invention'.[58] 'Man' became part of the Modern episteme through what he calls the 'analytic of finitude', the space opened up when representation and God collapse and turn the positivity of knowledge back on man's finite being. The figure of man emerges from Kant's resolution of the tension between empiricism ('what is given in experience') and transcendence ('what renders experience possible').[59] It is to resolve the problems of knowledge in the question 'What is man?' This formed what Foucault called 'a strange empirico-transcendental doublet'.[60] This figure of 'man' is, according to him, 'paradoxical' and full of tensions.[61] The very empirical conditions of being in the world that make thought possible prevent any possibility of a sovereign knowledge, such as the transparency of the '*cogito*'. This means, as Freud and others saw clearly, that 'man' is surrounded by the 'unthought', the Other outside of knowledge. The figure of 'man' also faces the tensions of the historicity of being as formulated in life, labour and language. This meant that 'man' was directed to an origin which the 'very fabric' of historicity made it impossible to discover.[62] 'Man' was a being caught in time, a being 'constituted' at a point where all the 'differences', 'dispersions' and 'discontinuities' come together in the Same (the known) struggling at the point of the Other (the unknown).[63]

Foucault brings his extensive archaeological study to its climax by linking, with Nietzsche, the death of 'man' to the death of God. The force of Foucault's work is that we must wake from anthropological sleep by recognising 'man' as a 'constitution' of the modern episteme. Here Foucault heralds the disintegration of 'man' and the possibility of a new epistemic shift. While he recognises psychoanalysis and ethnology (social anthropology) as 'calling into question' the concept of 'man' and offering new possibilities, it is not surprising that he returns at the end of the work to the question of language, for it was in the fragmentation of language that 'man' emerged. Foucault sees language as assuming a new importance as 'man' disappears. He recognises a 'new mode of being in literature' and a ' "return" of language'.[64] In this light Foucault asks: 'Since man was at a time when language was doomed to dispersion, will he not be dispersed when language regains its unity?'[65] Given the relation between God and language, we may also ask: What will happen to God? Later in this work I will examine this theological sub-text in detail and draw out its wider implications.

1970–5

In December 1970 Foucault delivered his inaugural lecture at the Collège de France, following his appointment to the Chair in the History of Systems of Thought, a chair reflecting his own self-styled work in the history of ideas. The inaugural lecture brought forward his earlier work on the 'conditions of possibility' for certain ideas into the wider social domain. Foucault explored the way discourses were controlled and organised, through certain rules of exclusion, classification, ordering and distribution. He identified the conditions under which a discourse could be 'employed'.[66] By examining the 'employment' of a discourse within certain social conditions Foucault gradually enhanced his archaeological work with what he called, following Nietzsche, a 'genealogical' methodology. It explored how a discourse was formed, examining its 'appearance, growth and variation'.[67] If archaeology was the type of analysis which differentiated Foucault's work from social history and philosophical hermenuetics, genealogy, according to Foucault in 1983, was the analysis of (archaeological) discourse according to the constitution of the present, the analysis of discourse as an event.[68] The brief remarks about genealogy in Foucault's inaugural lecture were developed in his 1971 essay 'Nietzsche, Genealogy, History', although even this outline offered none of the precision he had given for his notion of archaeology.[69] Genealogy followed archaeology in undermining the metaphysical and anthropological assumptions of history and sought to offer a 'counter-memory'.[70] Its aim was to remove the 'mask' that covers history by focusing upon those aspects which had previously been ignored or suppressed, notably the body and the will to knowledge (power). Genealogy drew in a spectrum of 'tools' into Foucault's exploration of the history of thought and demonstrated through this methodology how contemporary knowledge had been shaped. With the introduction of genealogy Foucault is no longer exploring the 'conditions of possibility' for a discourse in isolation, but seeking to examine the 'deployment' of discourse or an 'apparatus' (*dispositif*) of knowledge. This has often been conveyed in terms of Foucault broadening his examination to include 'non-discursive' as well 'discursive' practices.[71]

The introduction of this new conceptual apparatus was to have far-reaching implications, and in his 1970 inaugural lecture Foucault hints at his future intentions to examine the penal system, sexuality and confession according to such genealogical strategies. What is particularly striking, from the point of view of this work, is the way Foucault's inaugural lecture draws attention to the importance of religious discourse in the shaping and controlling of Western thought. By the end of the 1970s he would be immersed in studies of the Christian confession.

Foucault's first major work to incorporate his genealogical approach was his 1975 study of penal practice, *Discipline and Punish: The Birth of the Prison* (DP). DP examined the transition in the eighteenth and nineteenth centuries from punishment by torture to incarceration and discipline. The work examined the techniques and technologies of power through which punishment shifted from the 'spectacle' of the body in execution to the disciplining of the 'modern soul' in the prison regime. Following Deleuze and Guattari's *Anti-Oedipus*, Foucault unfolded a 'political technology of the body' which established how a certain 'mode of subjection' gave birth to 'man' as an object of knowledge; it correlated the 'power–knowledge' relationship. According to Foucault, power and knowledge 'directly imply one another', they are bound up in a complex 'network of relations'.[72]

In DP Foucault plots how the mechanisms of torture became politically unstable in their capacity to cause riots and unrest. There was scope for ambiguity in the public ritual which had previously established the sovereign's power. This led eventually in the late eighteenth century to a new system of punishment and a new economy of power. The fundamental weaknesses of monarchical power were replaced by redistributing power though a system of legal punishments. In this new system power could be more effectively exercised and the right to punish was established as a new social contract. The function of this punishment was to prevent 'repetition'.[73] It shifted the focus from the body to the 'representation of the penalty'.[74] Such a system of punishment established a whole series of symbolic or 'analogical penalties'.[75] Eventually, however, the dominant form of punishment became detention and through this models of punitive imprisonment were developed. These models of punishment often had a strong religious basis, not only in adopting monastic models of order, but in developing a concern for the soul. This soul was not strictly a metaphysical entity but a political order covering the body; it was a disciplinary imprisonment of the body.[76]

In penal practice, according to Foucault, the body was made 'docile'.[77] This docility was brought about through the specific manipulation, shaping and use of the body in a disciplinary regime, similar to those found in monasteries, army barracks, workshops and schools. In these disciplinary models the body was transformed through a 'whole machinery of power' which ordered it in both space and time to form a 'new political anatomy'.[78] By documenting the religious, military and educational disciplinary regimes Foucault shows how power is not just a negative force but holds the capacity to 'produce' reality and to constitute individuals.[79] The force of this disciplinary regime manifest itself in the birth of prison and the architectural structure of Jeremy Bentham's panopticon, the circular prison structure where every prisoner is subject to the gaze of authority. Once under the scrutiny of the gaze and the force of disciplinary control the individual is soon faced with new forms of knowledge. In the prison the individual is 'constituted' as an 'object of possible knowledge'.[80] The prison produces an environment for a new understanding of the individual in the science of criminology, which in turn gives birth to the delinquent.[81] Foucault concludes this study of the prison by illustrating how the prison is maintained even though it has been shown to fail in its efforts to prevent crime and reform prisoners. According to him, the prison continued despite its failure because it acted as a mechanism for checking and monitoring illegalities. The prison in fact formed part of a wider 'carceral net' spread throughout society through its institutions and disciplinary mechanisms. The carceral society made the human sciences possible by making 'man' knowable through the power–knowledge matrix. It set up a whole apparatus of medicine, psychology, education and social policy to normalize and control.

The religious content of DP may appear subsidiary to the wider arguments, but if this sub-text is explored in detail we can find an intriguing set of tensions emerging in Foucault's work. DP is significant for it holds a number of distinct religious aspects which remain unresolved. I will explore these in chapter 6, but what we can establish at this point is how Foucault takes seriously the cultural deposits of religion and interweaves religious ideas into his broader archaeological and genealogical studies. This book seeks to explore these aspects of Foucault's work and ascertain their religious and theological significance as a prelude to the more overt studies of Christianity in his late work.

1976–84

It is with Foucault's historical study of sexuality from 1976 that the contours of his 'religious question' are significantly altered. Up to this point the religious content of his work, as we have seen, remained sub-textual and at times of little significance; although, as I will show, it still forms an important critical assessment of religious thinking. After 1976 Christianity assumes a more dominant role in Foucault's work, taking centre stage from 1977 to 1982 when he explored the history of Christian confession in the first five centuries of the church. I hope to show that when Foucault's discussion of Christianity takes a more central role in his work the religious emphasis changes. The religious emphasis prior to 1976 is towards what I have loosely called a 'spiritual corporality', while after 1976 this moves to a concern with a 'political spirituality'. These divisions, which will be explored in detail later in the work, form the broad context of Foucault's 'religious question' and they should not be seen as absolute categories. In the conclusion I will show that they are largely inseparable and that it is possible to see aspects of each throughout Foucault's work. By drawing out the religious nature of Foucault's earlier work I am seeking to rescue a certain unconscious dimension of his knowledge – his unashamedly Christian, and more specifically Catholic, cultural inheritance.[82] It above all shows that Foucault's work on religion is by no means restricted to his late project on the history of sexuality.

Foucault's *History of Sexuality* has a complex evolution which has been well documented by his biographers.[83] It began with a small introductory volume, *La Volonté de savoir*, in 1976. This first volume proposed a further five to follow but none of these were to appear. The second to be written was a study of Christianity, *Les Aveux de la chair* ('Confessions of the Flesh'), but this remains unpublished according to an interpretation of Foucault's request not to publish any 'unfinished' work.[84] After many changes of order and content two further volumes in his *History of Sexuality* did appear in the final year of his life, *L'Usage des plaisirs* ('The Use of Pleasure') and *Le Souci de soi* ('The Care of the Self'). These last two volumes related to the Greco-Roman world and were initially prepared to set the scene for Foucault's reading of the Christian understanding of the flesh.

The first volume of Foucault's *History of Sexuality* continued his archaeological and genealogical strategies in an examination of the development of modern sexual discourse in the West. He attempted to show that what he called the 'repressive hypothesis' of sexual discourse was fundamentally mistaken and that sexuality was a deployment of power linked to the body.[85] The central argument of his study showed how sexuality was not a natural given but something which was historically constructed. Sexuality, according to Foucault, was produced through the strategies of power–knowledge.[86]

Foucault rejected the Victorian myth that sex was repressed by showing how since the seventeenth century sex had been put into discourse. Sex was not silenced but positively promoted in discourse, resulting in an 'explosion' of sexual discourse in the eighteenth and nineteenth centuries. In Foucault's analysis this was to a large extent established by the practice of confession in Western Christendom. In the confession sex was linked to the truth of the individual; it provided the register through which the individual subject was known. The techniques and mechanisms of confession were eventually appropriated in a '*scientia sexualis*', whereby the will to knowledge of sex in confession was reconstituted in scientific terms.

In the practices of medicine, psychiatry and pedagogy of the nineteenth century a new sexual discourse emerged by linking the confession to a personal examination and to the establishment of a sexual aetiology. These practices produced 'sexuality' by positioning the discourse of sex inside certain frameworks of interpretation and extrapolating rules of the normal and pathological. To some extent Foucault saw this discussion of the history of sexuality as forming an 'archaeology of psychoanalysis'; it exposed the limitations of psychoanalysis and unveiled its 'normalizing functions'.[87]

In Foucault's analysis 'sexuality' was created through the 'deployment' or 'apparatus' (*dispositif*) of a 'subtle network of discourses, special knowledges, pleasures and powers'.[88] Following on from his earlier work DP, Foucault demonstrates how power positively determines the nature of sex and pleasure. This power was not a judicial model of law but 'the multiplicity of force relations'.[89] In this sense power was everywhere; it was an 'unstable' network of force relations operating throughout society. While sex had previously been connected to a 'deployment of alliance' concerned with permitted and forbidden relations in marriage and kinship, the 'deployment of sexuality' sought to extend control over the body and its pleasures and also to extend control over populations. Sexuality was therefore seen to arise from a 'complex political technology' and to form part of the mechanism through which power was exercised over life.[90]

In the final section of the work Foucault continued this theme of power over life by showing how from the seventeenth century the sovereign's power was replaced by an 'anatomo-politics of the human body' (disciplinary power) and a 'bio-politics of the population' (the demographic regulation of life). The emergence of bio-power had enormous consequences not only in forming an 'indispensable' platform for capitalism by inserting bodies into the 'machinery of production', but also by taking control of life in such a way as to normalize society. The discussion of bio-power illustrates how Foucault's short introduction to his study of sexuality extends over a vast terrain of issues often without satisfactory analysis. He is throwing up a whole series of connections which emerge from the understanding of sexuality as a political deployment of power. The work concludes by suggesting that a 'counterattack' to the deployment of sexuality could perhaps be found in a new 'economy of bodies and pleasures'.[91] This opening up of a broad spectrum of issues behind the subject of 'sexuality' was a prelude to an even greater theoretical adjustment in subsequent volumes of his work.

In volume two of the *History of Sexuality, The Use of Pleasure* (HS2), published some eight years after the introductory work, Foucault acknowledged that there had been a 'theoretical shift' and that the work appeared in a form 'altogether different' from that originally anticipated.[92] The gap between the publication of the first and second volumes is significant not only in terms of how he redefined his work but also in terms of his exploration of religious themes. The interest in Christian confession was clearly visible in the introductory volume, and by continuing this interest under the rubric of 'governmentality' (the government of nation-states and individual self-government), Foucault refocused his work in terms of the constitution of the modern 'subject' and the 'ethics of self'. I will explore this period of his work in greater detail in chapter 7, because, like the intermediary period between HF and OT, it forms a second vital field of studies outside his main works where religious themes are examined. It was also during this period that his final work on Christianity took shape.

In his final studies Foucault reconceptualised his work in terms of how individuals were made into 'subjects'; not only subjects of knowledge and subjects of power, as his previous work had demonstrated, but desiring subjects. The shift in his thinking was coupled with a move from exploring the techniques of domination in human societies (power) to an exploration of the techniques or technologies of self.[93] This meant that his later volumes of his history of sexuality were recast in terms of a 'hermeneutics of self'. According to Foucault, the fundamental axis of sexual ethics could be seen to rest upon the 'self's relation to itself' (*rapport à soi*). The final two published volumes of his work explore this theme in detail in the Greco-Roman world. What Foucault demonstrated was that the concerns of sexual morality did not vary enormously between the Greco-Roman world and Christianity. What did change, according to him, were the techniques of self which shaped sexual practice.

What Foucault was trying to do was explore how concerns with sex were 'problematised', a term which I shall show later also characterised his work on religion. In line with all his previous studies, Foucault was trying to ascertain how an object was 'constituted', in this case 'sexuality'. It meant analysing 'the conditions' under which a culture framed who they were and how they lived, or, more precisely, it meant analysing their 'arts of existence'.[94] In HS2 Foucault explored these issues in Greek culture of the fourth century BC, and in *The Care of the Self* (HS3) he explored the same issues in the Greek and Latin texts of the first two centuries CE. The unpublished fourth volume, *Confession of the Flesh*, was to examine Christian documents in the first five centuries CE. The three volumes formed an account of the 'practices of self' in early and late antiquity and demonstrated that the thematics of sexual austerity were not unique to Christianity.

In HS2 Foucault examined a selection of Greek texts written by philosophers and doctors in their consideration of '*chrēsis aphrodisiōn*' (the use of pleasures). In these texts the central concern was with the right use of pleasure, according to such things as time, manner, conduct, personal regimen and status. There were no set codes which permitted or restricted actions, rather an attitude of self-mastery. It demanded a certain relationship with oneself where the individual was not enslaved to the pleasures. As a result of this regulation or art there developed an economy of austerity in relation to the body (dietetics), marriage (economics) and love of boys (erotics), which Foucault outlined in detail. The food one ate and the relations one established were all part of an art of self, maintaining health, household and honour. In this world love was a relationship to truth, a shared quest on the path to self-mastery and wisdom.

Having already established themes of sexual austerity in Greek literature Foucault's next volume, HS3, showed how these themes were transformed.

He sought to establish that new techniques of self gradually emerged which strengthened the theme of austerity prior to developments within Christianity. This change occurred not through the adoption of a new code but through 'an intensification of the relation to oneself by which one constituted oneself as the subject of one's acts'.[95] According to Foucault, there developed in the first two centuries of the common era 'a kind of golden age in the cultivation of the self' which took up Socrates' earlier principle to 'take care of oneself'.[96] In the texts of such writers as Epicurus, Seneca and Marcus Aurelius, Foucault showed how there developed a whole process of writing and speaking about oneself in order to develop care for the body and satisfaction of one's needs. It resulted in 'a whole art of self-knowledge' where the ills of the body and soul were treated through physical and mental exercises.[97] While this reflected many of the earlier concerns of Greek society, it differed in so far as the bridging of medicine and ethics brought about a 'tighter structuring of life' and a more detailed self-examination.[98] It is, however, important to realize that it did not bring about stricter prohibitions in sexual ethics but rather placed a different emphasis on pleasure through the art of living.

Foucault's work on the Greco-Roman period originated from problems in his initial introduction to his study of Christianity, and in many ways these works can be seen as an extended preparation for the themes of sexual austerity in Christianity. HS2 and HS3 continually stress the movement towards a world where restraint and the art of living in relation to sexual pleasure are modified through an ethical substance based on 'finitude, the Fall and evil'.[99] Christianity modifies the earlier moral system by developing new techniques of self and new modes of ethical subjection. In Foucault's lectures and essays on Christianity we see how confession brought about a new ethics of self through the process of self-renunciation.[100] But the final words of his study of Christianity remain at present unpublished.

The unpublished volume on Christianity is symbolic of the way important religious questions in Foucault's work are left at the margins. As this outline of his work reveals, there is a 'religious question' hidden beneath the more prominent cultural sounds of his *oeuvre*. But the distant echoes of Foucault's 'religious question' remain unexamined; they gently vibrate in the fragments of his primary texts, strike chords in his numerous articles and lectures, and finally become dampened in an unpublished symphony. It is the task of this work to listen to the fragmented sounds of a 'religious question' hidden in Foucault's work – to show the emergence of his religious thinking prior to his final work on Christianity.

2 Silence and confession

> I think that any child who has been educated in a Catholic milieu just before
> or during the Second World War had the experience that there were many
> different ways of speaking as well as many forms of silence.
>
> Foucault (1982g) 'The Minimalist Self', p. 3

In Foucault's work there are a series of fragmented religious ideas which
have been neglected in the examination of his wider arguments. In order to
bring some coherence to these ideas I wish to hold these fragments together
by framing them within Foucault's discussion of 'the said as much as the
unsaid'.[1] I want to show how silence operates alongside confession in the
formation of two central dynamics in Foucault's unveiling of religious
discourse. Throughout his work there is a sub-textual questioning of 'religion' as he examines discourses, institutions, architectural forms, regulatory
decisions and propositions, which inescapably involves an examination of
the silences.[2] What we find in bringing together the religious strands of
Foucault's work in this way is a critique of religion based on the politics of
what can be said and what cannot be said in the religious domain. His work
can therefore be seen as an attempt to identify the underlying forces which
control and shape the religious 'subject' and as an exercise to uncover the
silenced and subjugated discourses of religion. While Foucault never formulated such a clear position about his overall work on religion, my sub-textual
reworking takes its inspiration from the centrality of silence within his own
writings.

The idea of silence can be confusing because of the different ways it operates in Foucault's work. Silence assumes a key hermeneutical significance
alongside the Christian confession in his 1976 publication *La Volonté de
savoir*, the first volume of his *History of Sexuality* (HS1). The importance of
silence is reiterated in a 1982 interview with Stephen Riggins where
Foucault, forgetting his earlier ambiguities about silence in AK, expresses
his regret that silence had been 'dropped' from our culture. Foucault recalls
in this respect the Japanese culture of silence and the 'specific form of expe-
riencing' found in the silence of early Greek and Roman societies. He also
returns to the idea of silence in his 1982 Vermont lectures, exploring the

pedagogical relationships in Stoicism, where the master/teacher speaks and the disciple keeps silent, and he also notes the Pythagorean rule of the five-year silence of disciples.[3] This art of listening was developed in opposition to the dialogic form found in Plato and displays a positive dimension of silence. Foucault further explains in the 1982 interview that he is 'in favour of developing silence as a cultural ethos'.[4] These comments reflect the way he transforms the nature of silence in his late works into an ethical and aesthetic form which contrasts sharply with some of his earlier oppressive models of silence.

Foucault's reappraisal of silence in his later work is part of a broader utilization of the concept which often assumes a pivotal position. There is the silence of the mad, the enigmatic silences at the limits of language, the silence of prisons, the mythic silence of sexuality and the later interest in different forms of cultural silence. The theme constantly resurfaces and acts as a strange undercurrent to Foucault's many varied historical and philosophical discussions. This dimension of his work becomes even more poignant when we consider how silence forms part of the political and social effects of discourse and how a discussion of the Christian confession, the act of utterance, rests awkwardly on a theory of non-binary opposition between speech and silence. Despite Foucault's continual introduction of the concept of silence, it assumes a varied and confused position, moving precariously between other ideas. What is particularly striking in terms of Foucault's 'religious question' is his failure to fully appreciate the implications of the interconnected nature of silence to his work on confession.

In order to locate Foucault's 'religious question' I want to start by exploring this dynamic of silence and confession in the later work and return to his earlier work to show how his exploration of religious discourse carries through these ideas. It is methodologically easier to start an examination of Foucault's work on religion with his later studies because of the more overt engagement with issues of religion during this period. The importance of this approach becomes even more apparent when we consider that Foucault provides no coherent statement about religion and we can therefore anchor the more fragmented earlier references from this base. By framing the 'religious question' within the later discussions between 1976 and 1982 I am also prioritising the period when Foucault formulated his unpublished work on Christianity, *Confessions of the Flesh*. If this period reflects his most concentrated reflections on religion, and Christianity in particular, then it arguably provides the most useful starting point for a consideration of his entire 'religious question'. I propose therefore to gather a series of statements on Christianity from HS1 in 1976 to Foucault's 1982 American lectures on confession and then position these statements within the 'apparatus' (*dispositif*) of the said and unsaid which forms a key theoretical practice in his work. Silence and confession, as we shall see, are the constructs around which Foucault not only develops his wider critique of religion but also builds a new political ordering of the religious 'subject'.

This chapter therefore forms the conceptual axis around which I will develop the ideas of a 'spiritual corporality' and a 'political spirituality' existing at the heart of Foucault's work on religion.

Silence and confession

Foucault consistently interprets Christianity in his work from 1976 as a 'confessional religion', a religion that requires the subject to 'speak truth-fully'.[5] As he writes in 1982:

> Christianity is not only a salvation religion, it's a confessional religion. ... Each person has the duty to know who he [*sic*] is, that is, to try to know what is happening inside him, to acknowledge faults, to recognise temptations, to locate desires, and everyone is obliged to disclose these things either to God or to others in the community and hence to bear public or private witness against oneself.[6]

As the question of salvation is linked to the 'truth obligations' of belief, so confession, according to Foucault, is linked to the 'truth obligation' of self. Foucault states clearly that in Christian practice 'access' to God (truth) requires a 'disclosure of self'.[7] The Christian is obliged 'to say [these] things to other people', 'to tell' and 'bear witness'.[8] Christianity is seen to rest fundamentally on the act of speech, the verbalisation of truth. To speak is to believe and to speak is to know truth. Christianity is a religion of utter-ances, a submission into speaking, believing and acting.

Foucault first introduced his conception of Christianity as a 'confession' in the 1976 HS1, although he first announced his intention to explore this idea in 1970, a suggestion, according to James Bernauer, made by Ivan Illich.[9] In the fragmented HS1 Foucault attempted to demonstrate the way sex had been transformed into discourse, and the central place of Christianity within this history. The rigorous religious examination of sexual thoughts and actions in the act of confession were seen to transform Western society. In this work, and in his later lectures and articles, Foucault conveniently packages Christianity into a religion of confession, a religion with an obligation to speak, but ironically he failed to incorporate into this understanding his own theoretical interpretation of silence at the heart of the discursive argument in HS1.

Silence, as Foucault stressed, 'functions alongside the things said, within them and in relation to them within over-all strategies'.[10] There is an insepa-rable link between the operations of silence and speech. The attempt to understand Christianity in a singular trajectory of speech is therefore to operate on a diminished understanding of speech and silence. What Foucault in effect fails to develop is the implication of his view in 1976, that there is 'no binary division to be made between what one says and what one does not say'.[11] There is in his work an awkward lacuna between his conceptual organisation of speech and silence and his rendering of Christianity as a religion of confession.

Foucault's discussion of Christianity is therefore diminished by his over-dependency on confession as the central and most important tenet of the religion. If, however, he had been able to assimilate his theoretical work on silence into the discussion of Christianity, his 'religious question' would have assumed far greater clarity and importance. It would have enabled him, as I will illustrate, to hold together the diverse critical perspectives he made in the field of religion and theology. The failure to organise his work in this way transpired only to weaken his overall evaluation of religion and prevented the force of his repositioning of religious discourse from being fully realised. In order to unfold these tensions it is necessary first to demonstrate the significance of silence to Foucault's enterprise and then to show how a lack of theoretical clarity about silence results in a weakened understanding of Christianity as a confessional religion. Through this exercise we will be able to appreciate the nature of Foucault's discussion of Christianity from 1976 and open the way to see how his wider work seeks both to critically re-evaluate the religious space and to acknowledge its political efficacy.

Foucault and silence

Foucault's work originally came to prominence in France by recognising a 'silence', the 'broken dialogue' of the mad, who at the end of the eighteenth century were thrown into 'oblivion' with their 'stammered, imperfect words without fixed syntax' in a battle against the dominant reason.[12] In the dialogue between madness and reason Foucault attempted to articulate the 'archaeology of the silence'.[13] This exercise led Derrida, with equal brilliance and calculating strike, to question whether a history of 'silence' and unreason was possible.[14] It has never been fully appreciated that at the heart of this Derrida–Foucault debate is a fundamental ambiguity about the nature of silence. The lack of theoretical clarity behind the use of silence clearly leaves Foucault open to sharp critique from Derrida, but Derrida's own argument falls into the same obscurity about 'silence' as he fails to appreciate how the idea of silence operates in Foucault's discussion, subsuming the concept under his idea of 'unreason'. The difficulties within this debate can be seen when we consider Adam Jaworski's study of silence and sociolinguistics, *The Power of Silence* (1993). The Derrida–Foucault debate suffers from the same fate as research in sociolinguistics in its failure to sufficiently demarcate the theoretical boundaries of the concept of silence. As Jaworski indicates:

> Much work on silence lacks an underlying theory. This often leads to conceptual confusion and obscurity of the argument.[15]

Derrida challenges Foucault by asking: 'Is there a history of silence?' and

'Is not an archaeology, even of silence, a logic, that is, an organized language, a project, an order, a sentence, a syntax, a work?'[16] What Derrida's question does is reposition Foucault's work, whether or not it was intended, in terms of what Jaworski calls an 'essentialist' view of 'silence', by which Jaworski means a definitive ontological entity as opposed to the diverse operational nature of silence.[17] While Derrida's critique serves to clarify with some precision his 'master's' terms, it fails to appreciate, in this instant, the metaphorical and operational dimension of silence in a critique of unreason, and thus the power of Foucault's use of the word 'silence' is lost. As he never responded to Derrida's 1963 critique directly it is difficult to know exactly what he meant by 'silence', but the continuing use of the concept particularly in HS1 would seem to suggest his use of a non-essentialist view of silence.

Silence and unreason may not be literal philosophical markers but indicators of the 'marginal', to recall Derrida on a different note.[18] The voice of the mad, as is demonstrated in Dale Peterson's *A Mad People's History of Madness*, has been articulated at some level.[19] In the history of madness, it would appear silence is not so much outside reason, or holding no expression, but that which is unheard, crushed or denied validity in the dominant systems of power. Madness is not a 'silence' in itself but a position in society. In his 1976 study of sexuality Foucault is clearly able to demonstrate the link between that which is 'driven out, denied, and reduced to silence' without implying 'silence' as an essential state.[20] The problem is that the issue of silence is subsumed under the question of 'unreason'. There are fundamentally different objectives in the approach to this question and in the argumentation between Derrida and Foucault. Derrida's aim is to disrupt by presenting new questions in a hyper-rational economy of language, while Foucault seeks to disrupt the economy of madness historically. The wider argument has been explored cogently elsewhere by Boyne and it is not necessary to examine it further here, but the amount of slippage between Derrida and Foucault on this issue of silence reinforces Jaworski's analysis of the problems of obscurity in such discussions.[21] What does emerge from this examination is a need for clarifying how Foucault uses the idea of silence and a need for some framework to understand this concept.

By utilising Jaworski's study of silence I want to illuminate a number of features about silence in Foucault's work. What is particularly striking is that Foucault's brief remarks on silence in 1976, while lacking the more detailed analysis, closely follow the more extensive explorations of Jaworski on two fundamental points. First, Foucault and Jaworski agree on one basic and primary understanding of silence, as Foucault writes in 1976:

There is not one but many silences, and they are an integral part of the strategies that underlie and permeate discourse.[22]

While Foucault may appreciate this fact, he fails to indicate the range and specific nature of these silences. The research in sociolinguistics by Jaworski and others clearly indicates how the concept of silence varies according to 'gender, culture, and situation'; it is a 'very diverse phenomenon', which Jaworski seeks to place on a continuum of expression in interpersonal and macro contexts.[23] Jaworski supports this diversity by highlighting the problems of assuming an essentialist view of silence and appreciating the metaphorical quality of silence as substance and state.[24] In many ways it may seem unfair to demand such an ordering of silence in Foucault's work; nevertheless the weight that this concept assumes in his studies makes it an urgent task if clarity is to be achieved.

The second important connection between Foucault and Jaworski is the rejection of any binary opposition between silence and speech. As Foucault clarifies:

> There is no binary division to be made between what one says and what one does not say; we must try to determine the different ways of not saying such things, how those who can and those who cannot speak of them are distributed, which type of discourse is authorized, or which form of discretion is required in either case.[25]

Foucault's underlying agenda in 1976 is to formulate the 'repressive hypothesis' and show how a dominant discourse about sex is established in Western thought and in Christianity itself.[26] He is interested in 'silence' as a form of control within the discourse and he therefore draws an inseparability between speech and silence to enforce this position. Unfortunately Foucault does not extend this thought into his wider work, especially on confession and Christianity. By taking these two theoretical comments from HS1 and supplementing them with Jaworski's study on silence I will try to clarify Foucault's use of silence as a context for examining the discussion of confession.

Silence and oppression

Silence, as I have already indicated, assumes a central place in Foucault's conceptual geography. The predominant orientation, although not exclusively, is to view silence as a state of oppression and denial. It would be fair to say that Foucault's work began by listening to what was not heard, by the attempt to give the suppressed (the silent) a voice. His attempt to retrieve the 'silent' is a metaphorical device to locate and valorise the marginalised groups in society. It is this aspect which makes his work so accessible to feminists and gay theorists. The silence here is a negative state constructed

on the basis of what Foucault would later interpret according to the apparatus (*dispositif*) of power and domination; it is part of what Foucault calls
in 1976 a 'mechanism of exclusion'.[27] The theme of 'exclusion' underlies so
much of his work and not surprisingly surfaces on the key occasion of his
1970 inaugural lecture, where he examines the various 'prohibitions' against
speaking and the institutional power behind this silence.[28]

This recovery of the 'silent' is given more weight in the context of
Foucault's own personal experiences, especially if we consider Jerrold
Seigel's study of the relationship between Foucault's work and his homosexual identity. The silence and unacceptability surrounding homosexuality
in French society certainly plagued Foucault during his time at the École
Normale, with his attempts at suicide, his professional appointments and his
protracted time living and working abroad.[29] Foucault only began to talk
more publicly of his homosexuality towards the end of his life, and his
words to J.K. Simon in 1971 take on added significance if they are seen in
this context.

> On the other hand, there has been much less study of what has been
> rejected from our civilisation. It seemed to me interesting to try to
> understand our society and civilisation in terms of its system of exclu-
> sion, of rejection, of refusal, in terms of what it does not want, its
> limits, the way it is obliged to suppress a certain number of things,
> people,   processes,   what   it   must   let   fall   into   oblivion,   its
> repression–suppression system.[30]

Although Foucault connects silence to power, in the 'silent architecture' of
the prison and the 'silent precision of the human machinery' of women's
prison labour, his analysis remains restricted. What his work requires is a
discussion of silence to parallel his study of power, because it is precisely the
dynamic of silence, speech and power which at some level orientate so much
of his work, and in particular the discussion of Christianity.

Silence, power and Christianity

Foucault identifies Christianity (and in consequence religion) as a fundamental mechanism of power, a part of the institutional structures which
manipulate and control by silencing. The religious institutions are part of
the 'coercive technologies of behaviour'.[31] Although Foucault does not write
an archaeology of the Christian church, it is repeatedly seen to operate
alongside and within other regimes of power. There is for example a consid-
erable amount of supporting documentation interwoven into medical and
penal systems which derives from Christian perspectives.

In Foucault's study of madness the 'archaeology of silence' is permeated
by the historical deposits of Christianity. Religion, according to him,
enhances the 'constraints' of confinement; it 'safeguards the old secrets of

reason' and 'constitutes the concrete form of what cannot go mad'.[32] In one of Foucault's earliest works we find recognition of the complex alliances between medical and religious powers in the fight against heretics and the mad.[33] The same technology of power is replicated in the construction of the prison. Religion is seen as part of a wider disciplinary apparatus, developed from monastic models of ordered existence.[34] Silence was part of the disciplinary control found in religious exercises and incorporated into structures of penal practice. There was a distinct corrective function to be found in the use of silence, a procedure adopted in the silence and solitude of the cell.[35] Silence, as we shall see, does not operate alone; speaking and silence are inversely connected by the 'rules of exclusion'.

> I am supposing that in every society the production of discourse is at once controlled, selected, organised and redistributed according to a certain number of procedures, whose role is to avert its powers and its dangers, to cope with chance events, to evade its ponderous, awesome materiality.[36]

The church is for Foucault part of a network of institutions (an apparatus/*dispositif*) which seeks to control speech and silence. They form a political strategy in the creation of religious 'truth'.[37] Religious powers govern the individual self and nation-states through the operations of the said and unsaid; and it is precisely this mechanism of coercion which enables Foucault to develop his ideas of a 'political spirituality'.

The politics of silence

There is a fascinating link between the interrelationship of power and silence in the works of Foucault and Jaworski. Jaworski attempts to examine the place of silence in differing social contexts and, following Brummett's work in this area, sees silence in political discourse as a specific 'tool' or strategy. Silence in this sense can be used and enforced in different ways to create a series of different political situations. There may be a negative enforcement of silence on others as in the domination of political dictatorship or martial law, but silence may also be used by the dominant institution to create '*mystery, uncertainty, passivity* and *reliquishment*'.[38] Another interesting dimension to the use of silence in different social contexts is seen in Jaworski's outline of women's silence. There is a 'societal silencing of dominated groups' which Jaworski associates, using anthropological terminology, with groups which have a taboo or ambiguous status.

> My claim is that in sociolinguistic terms, when such groups are
> oppressed, one of the manifestations of their taboo status is that they
> become silenced.[39]

Foucault is making the same basic point of a correlation between exclusion
and silence. However, being silent and being silenc*ed* are two different things.
Jaworski demonstrates this by briefly outlining the evolution of women's
silence: historically women were/are silenced as a 'muted' and 'nameless'
group; women then broke off the silence by reclaiming their experience; but
significantly silence was still strategically used as a power-force against male
language. Jaworski particularly explores the silence found in women's literature, noting, for example, specific research on the use of silence in the work
of Virginia Woolf.[40] Although Jaworski does not extend his study to French
feminist writers, there is a continual struggle in this literature to find a voice
for women in a male language system. In a Lacanian system of male
language every utterance holds the intrinsic silence of women, who have to
find their own language, but who remain in part silenced.[41]

This brief overview of some of the issues of the politics of silence has
important implications for Foucault's work. Silence, like Foucault's concept
of power, is something that shifts and moves, it is not a static entity.

> Power must be analysed as something which only functions in the form
> of a chain. It is never localised here and there, never in anybody's hands,
> never appropriated as a commodity or piece of wealth. Power is
> employed and exercised through a net-like organisation.[42]

The word 'power' in this quotation could easily be supplanted by silence, in
so far as silence and discourse are strategically employed in power relations.
Silence moves around in very specific and localised ways as part of the
'multiplicity of force relations'.[43]

Silence, uncertainty and power

Although Foucault's work predominantly sees silence as a characteristic of
the oppressed and excluded, especially in his work on madness and the
prison, there are a number of places where he begins to appreciate the more
ambiguous nature of silence, which supports his more complex notion of
power relations. As in Jaworski's summary of women's experience, it is
possible to find a silence in Foucault's work which acknowledges the inverse
of the silencing power, a silence which is neither entirely negative or positive.

There are two facets to this position: first, the excluding powers of speech;
and, second, the power within silence or the power of anonymity. Here the
power is in naming, isolating and specifying those who were once happily
silent and free. Foucault in this sense refers to the 'discursive explosion' of
sexuality in the eighteenth and nineteenth centuries. As he evocatively writes,

with homosexuality in mind: 'It was time for all these figures, scarcely noticed in the past, to step forward and speak, to make the difficult confession of what they were.'[44] In this instance it is not silence but speaking which is the cause of oppression. To confess is to be controlled and to be silent is to remain free. Silence, like power, shifts in its strategic importance.

There is an ambiguous overlapping of speech and silence not only in terms of power but also in terms of Foucault's valorisation of those who were silenced. This silence was also for Foucault a source of inspiration. There was paradoxically a value to be found in the silence of the repressed; they were 'guardians of truth', but only in so far as they could be reclaimed.[45] This can be seen in Foucault's reclamation of the lives of the 'infamous' like Pierre Rivière and Herculine Barbin to their respectful places in history. In a 1977 foreword to an uncompleted anthology of such 'infamous lives' from history Foucault reveals his desire to give voice to the unheard:

> And I confess that these 'nouvellas', suddenly rising up through two and a half centuries of silence, stirred more fibre in me than what one usually calls literature ... .[46]

The silence of the infamous, like the 'sodomite friar', the 'deserting soldiers', 'scriveners' and 'vagabond monks', holds a dimension of mystery and insight. Their silence reveals something forgotten and secret, but, as Foucault makes clear, 'what rescues them from the darkness of night' is their 'encounter with power'.[47] They are rescued as exemplars of a struggle, a collision: 'they exist now only through the few terrible words which were destined to render them unworthy'.[48] In this retrieval of the 'infamous lives' from the neglected corners of history, Christianity is clearly established as one of the powers which not only restricts discourse but demands it in the confession.[49] This is a key transitional point in Foucault's understanding of silence which occurs in the mid-1970s and holds a close conjunction with his work on confession. Although Christianity is a dominant power controlling speech and silence, this does not exclude the possibility of Foucault viewing silence as a positive cultural ethos, as his interview with Stephen Riggins in 1982 revealed.[50]

Positive silence

A more positive and enigmatic silence can be found much earlier in Foucault's work in his adventure into the world of avant-garde literature, and it is therefore not singularly a feature of his later works. Silence during Foucault's literary period in the 1960s forms the labyrinths of discourse swirling off into voids and paradoxes. Such silences pervade the texts of exhausted language in Sade, Hölderlin, Artaud and Roussel, where language has been pushed to its limit, galvanised and stretched. This limit of language, as Foucault indicates in relation to Bataille, 'traces that line of foam showing just how far speech may advance upon the sands of silence'.[51] Foucault's admiration for Gustave Flaubert's *The Temptation of St Antony*, as Kitty Mrosovsky notes, also arises from the same 'love of works which suggest disjunction and silence'.[52]

The idea of silence in these literary texts subverts the dominant regimes and causes enigmas. There is a distinct destabilising in these works which wraps silence in a power of estrangement. The silence ruptures the dominant categories of reason, shatters language in its capacity to express, and evokes an esoteric arena. It was this dimension of silence which attracted Foucault and Blanchot to the positive aspects of religious silence and negative theology, even if they mistakenly identified discursive silence with a transcendent silence.[53] We can, however, begin to appreciate how Foucault can view certain religious experiences as constructive and recognise a potential for religious imagery and ideas to act as forces which disrupt the dominant regimes. This understanding will later open the way for Foucault to re-evaluate certain aspects of cultural silence and develop an aesthetic and ethical appreciation of silence. Silence operates, with speech, in numerous force relations, constantly shifting its position; it holds no essential quality.

Silence and speech

There is thus clearly a diverse range of inflections in Foucault's use of silence, ranging from an oppressive–dominant silence to a more positive enigmatic–aesthetic silence. In each of these positions there is an intrinsic relationship to power; silence acts with discourse (speech) in a series of strategic operations.

> Discourse transmits and produces power; it reinforces it, but also undermines it, renders it fragile and makes it possible to thwart it. In like manner, silence and secrecy are a shelter for power, anchoring its prohibitions; but they also loosen its holds and provide for relatively obscure areas of tolerance.[54]

In this text we see Foucault's inconsistent use of certain ideas in separating silence from discourse. In chapter 5 we shall see a return to the theme of silence in AK where Foucault attempted to place silence within discourse, which supports his non-binary theory of the said and unsaid. The terrain is, however, very murky and Foucault was never conceptually clear on his use of silence and discourse, leaving himself open to criticism, as in the case of Derrida. In order to avoid these confusions I have referred to silence and speech as mutual dynamics in the field of discourse; they form components of the wider concept of discourse.

What is of particular importance for our purposes is to see how these different strategic positions of silence and speech determine Foucault's assessment of Christianity. This understanding can only be demonstrated through an appreciation of the inseparability of speech and silence in the appraisal of Christianity. The speech–silence dynamic operates in such a way that both have an equally coexistent force in Foucault's assessment of the Christian tradition. The problem is that while Foucault is able to recognise the impossibility of developing a binary distinction between speech and silence in theory, he fails to carry forward the implications of this new perspective into his later work.

The centrality of the speech–silence dynamic to Foucault's study of Christianity can be seen in the way his 1976 HS1 appears to act as a subtle turning point in his approach to Christianity. In this work there is a distinct transition in Foucault's understanding of Christianity on the basis of speaking and silence. Up to 1976 Christianity is predominantly seen as an oppressive force which silenced others, but after 1976 Christianity is an oppressive force which demands an utterance. There is a shift from Christianity as an oppressive silencing power to a power which demands 'tell everything'.[55] These are in fact two aspects of the same thing, but presented, tactically, in the opposite form. In both instances the hidden aim of Christianity is to 'extinguish' the flesh and control, either through speech or by constraining speech (silence).[56] The significant point is that, in both silence and confession, religion remains for Foucault 'a constant principle of coercion', an oppressive mechanism of power.[57] Foucault's lack of consistency about the interrelationship between silence and speech means that the oscillation between these aspects of Christianity's strategic deployment of power is never fully appreciated. The submission into utterance is also the submission into silence of all that is not freely spoken. Foucault's 'religious question' was in part a response to this predicament, his earlier work on avant-garde religious discourse and the body rescuing the silenced aspects of the coercive religious powers.

What Foucault fails to make clear in his study of Christianity is the interrelationship between speech and silence as two forms of strategic power. Jaworski argues for such a 'complementary' understanding between silence and speech, and in appreciation of Tyler's work on the subject notes how 'the said and the unsaid are on a par with each other in the sense that all the elements of these two components are "reflexively determined" '.[58]

While Foucault rejects the binary opposition of silence and speech in 1976, there appears to be no sustained account of this position. By bringing together the broad scope of Foucault's use of both silence and confession we can begin to see the importance of his brief exposition on silence and speech. We can also begin to appreciate Foucault's challenge to the restrictions of religious discourse as reflecting simultaneously a critique of oppressive regimes (a technology of domination) and a rescuing of the silent and subjugated discourses in a more positive religious movement (a technology/government of self).[59]

Once we view Foucault's work in terms of these dynamics of silence and speech, and effectively reintegrate his 1976 theory of the said and unsaid, we can begin to appreciate how the fragments of his 'religious question' reflect different sides of a strategic struggle to reclaim the silent aspects of religion (the body and sexuality) and identify his attempt to expose the implicit polit-ical nature of all religious expressions. It also enables us to see how the strategic nature of religious discourse could be associated with both oppres-sive regimes and be positively re-evaluated as a creative political force. Foucault never made these overall connections principally because his discussion of religion and Christianity was always subsumed under his wider concerns with sexuality or governmentality.

The reintegration of Foucault's theory of silence provides a useful model for understanding the broad contours of his 'religious question', but it also makes it abundantly clear how his discussion of confession is severely restricted and diminished. In order to elaborate this point I want to finish this chapter by showing how and why speech/confession assumed a domi-nant function in Foucault's understanding of Christianity between 1976 and 1982. After outlining his discussion of confession and highlighting its central problems, I will go on to integrate the concept of silence. By bringing the concept of silence into the discussion of confession we will see how it sharpens the analysis of the politics of religious discourse.

The concept of confession

Silence is excluded in Foucault's discussion of Christianity because his prin-cipal aim in 1976 was to demonstrate how sexuality was put into discourse (speech). Christianity, according to Foucault, is the foundation stone of Western sexual discourse. Foucault illustrates this with a reading of Christianity from its acts of speech rather than through its oppressive silences.

> The Christian pastoral prescribed as a fundamental duty the task of passing everything having to do with sex through the endless mill of speech.[60]

Foucault at this point ignores his previous documentation of how Christianity was a silencing power and how this demand to speak relates fundamentally to the operation of silence. In fact, as we noted earlier, Foucault's argument opposes any idea that there was a silencing power in relation to sex; there was rather an explosion of discourse. It is at this point that he fails to integrate the non-binary understanding of speech and silence in discourse.[61]

The contradictions and the binary opposition between the said and unsaid are compounded by Foucault's selective and extremely sketchy outline of the confession in Christian history. In the 1976 work HS1 there is, as Bevis, Cohen and Kendall indicate, an 'essentialisation of Christianity' which ignores the intricacies of a complex theological tradition of reconciliation and justification.[62] There is also little appreciation of the 'jagged and disconnected' historical evolution of confessional practice.[63] Foucault's lectures and interviews do begin to appreciate this fact by differentiating between Tertullian's '*exomologesis*' (the dramatic recognition of the fact of one's status as sinner) and the fourth-century practice of '*exagoreusis*' (the disclosure of self in renunciation through obedience and contemplation), even if this is prone to simplification.[64] While it is important to realise Foucault's study of confession was to give an 'overview' of Christian history, he still tends to give more weight to the emergence of confessional practices in the Patristic period (to illuminate the origin of Christian confession) and the Lateran Council in 1215 (to demonstrate the legislative powers).[65] He ignores a vast number of theological intricacies by giving only passing mention to key historical events such as the Council of Trent and the Reformation.[66] In 1977 Foucault did suggest his later book on Christian practices would study the 'discursive procedures' of Christian confession 'from the tenth to the eighteenth century', and elsewhere he suggests that the reformed pastoral will be explored. Such hopes of a more comprehensive examination of Christian history never came to fruition and the unfinished project left many theological and theoretical problems, not least in the avoidance of the question of silence.[67]

Foucault's entire discussion of the concept of confession lacks sufficient theoretical weight from which to establish any coherent position. This can be seen in his discussion with a number of academics in 1977, where he is challenged by Jacques-Alain Miller about his very broad use of terminology in relation to confession and way the terms 'dissolve' under closer examination.[68] Foucault's response to Miller's argument is to acknowledge that his terms were 'meant to be dissolved' and he defends his 'very general definitions'.[69] Foucault had acknowledged the problem of using the term 'confession' (*aveu*), which he regarded as 'too broad'.[70] There are in fact a few terms he uses around 'confession' which complicate the meaning; for example, we find 'avowal', the 'ritual of avowal', 'direction of conscience', and 'examination of conscience', all used without any precision or detailed exposition.[71] There is also no adequate distinction between penal and religious confession.[72]

It soon becomes clear that Foucault is not attempting to establish a single 'framework' for confession, or 'reduce' confession and psychoanalysis to the same thing. Rather, he is strategically utilising 'confession' to exemplify a number of underlying practices. The utilisation varies according to the specific theoretical focus that dominates Foucault's work. The first exposition of 'confession' occurs in the context of sexuality and discourse (1976–7) and the second focus draws out the technology and governance of self (1980–2). This second focus merges into a third based on truth, power and the subject (1982). The discussion of confession on each occasion moves between these overriding concerns in a rather detached and awkward manner. However, on no occasion does Foucault integrate the question of silence; it is simply dropped from the equation.

In 1980 Foucault brought all these varied aspects of confession into the single framework of his genealogy of the modern subject. The Christian confession, albeit partial, was used to explore 'the strange and complex relationship developed in our societies between individuality, discourse, truth and coercion'.[73] Foucault's definition of confession was thus suitably broad enough to encompass 'all those procedures by which the subject is incited to produce a discourse of truth about his [*sic*] sexuality which is capable of having effects on the subject himself'.[74] Foucault's more extensive definition in HS1 had emphasized in addition the ritual basis of the discourse and the inherent power relationship in the process of disclosure.[75] Discourse and power are seen in this process as twinned 'procedures' in 'the extortion of truth'.[76]

Foucault's work on confession is therefore concerned with 'techniques for producing truth' in the modern subject and incorporates a whole range of discursive practices other than those loosely called 'confession'.[77] The difficulty, as Jeremy Tambling's own study of confession illustrates, is that Foucault has overburdened the idea of confession.

> There is no essential form of words or actions called 'confession'; there may be varied confessional practices; but even this term of course runs the risk, as I think it does even with Foucault, of essentialising the concept of confession, of making it a- or trans-historical, as though people were constituted by the inbred willingness to confess.[78]

If we accept that Foucault is not concerned with the Christian confession but with the techniques of 'truth' within Christianity, then his study is freed from being weighed down by specific chronologies of history; it is, as Cousins and Hussain indicate, to see Foucault's work as a 'case history'. Such case histories 'make a problem intelligible by reconstituting its conditions of existence and its conditions of emergence. This does not make them indifferent to evidence but merely means they handle evidence in a different way.'[79] Foucault 'makes use of "true" documents' from Christian history to bring about an new understanding of the religious 'subject'.[80]

The religious 'subject'

Foucault's fragmented work offers a kind of diagnosis of how a religious 'subject' is constituted.[81] The dynamics of power, truth and discourse (speech and silence) reveal the processes of 'subjectification' in religious practice.[82] The religious 'subject' is shaped by such mechanisms as confession; it orders, defines and controls. Foucault develops these ideas by unfolding a distinct play on the word 'subject', referring both to being 'subject to someone else by control and dependence' and a subject being 'tied to his [*sic*] own identity by a conscience or self-knowledge'.[83] (Foucault's work also allows for a third aspect of 'subject' as discipline, but this was not exploited in the same way.[84]) The central point of Foucault's work on confession is to demonstrate how religious discourse simultaneously forms a 'subject' (control, identity and discipline); it subjugates, subjectifies and forms a subject of knowledge. Religion, according to Foucault, creates 'subjects' through a strategic alliance of power, discourse and truth. Religion is caught in the inescapable politic of the 'subject'.

Foucault demonstrated this process of 'subjectification' by describing the confessional practice of '*exagoreusis*', a disclosure of self through renunciation, obedience and contemplation. He selectively utilised the work of a founding father of monasticism, John Cassian (*c.*365–*c.*435), in an attempt to demonstrate how in the monastic life there was an intensification of the processes of self-examination concerning sex. Foucault stressed the rigorous examination not only of actions, but 'thoughts and bodily movements day and night'.[85] There was a 'scrutiny of conscience' in order to extinguish all thoughts which prevented a closer relationship with God.[86] There was in addition a scrupulous expulsion of an underlying concupiscence; everything was examined from voluntary actions to involuntary nocturnal emissions. Foucault highlights the analogies of sorting grain, ordering soldiers and the checking of money from Cassian's *Conferences* (*c.*426) which demonstrate the careful process of 'discrimination' (*discretio*).[87] As Foucault emphasizes:

> This has nothing to do with a code of permitted or forbidden actions, but is a whole technique for analyzing and diagnosing thought, its origins, its qualities, its dangers, its potential for temptation and all the dark forces that can lurk behind the mask it may assume.[88]

The process imposed a 'truth' upon the individual; it was a 'subjectification' which produced a certain self-knowledge.[89] The 'truth' of self in Christianity was based on the personal scrutiny and control of the flesh/sex.[90] While Foucault clearly recognises this technology of self at the heart of Christianity, he fails to explore at this point the locus of power within theological doctrine which created this spiritual dualism. He shows no appreciation of how the regimes of 'truth' and 'power' operating in monastic life are implemented inside a political–theological ordering of spirit and flesh. This neglect of the relationship between religious doctrine and practice is one of the major weaknesses of Foucault's 'religious question' which I will explore later in chapter 6. At this point it illustrates how his theoretical critique of religious discourse suffers from inadequate theological reflection.

The broad contours of Foucault's genealogy of the modern 'subject' are once again undermined by the inadequacies of his consideration of the Christian confession. His lack of historical accuracy, the essentialisation of Christian ideas and his theological aberrations conspire to weaken his attempts to bring about the underlying analysis of the religious subject. The 'case study' approach offers a theory and an analysis without sufficient evidence. Foucault's work in this sense leaves us with a series of challenging questions about the religious subject without the formalities of systematic argumentation or any comfortable solutions. He simultaneously unearths and scatters the seeds for a new understanding of religion.

Integrating silence

The restricted scope of Foucault's work on religion means that the reader is always suspended in the question and the provocation without any of the comfort of detail and evidence. This means that any attempt to understand Foucault's 'religious question' requires a grappling with the sub-textual fragments in order to write in the spaces he left vacant. The dangers of misrepresenting Foucault have already been noted in the introduction and it is therefore important to read his 'religious question' by folding his own work back on itself, to fold text upon text. It is by following such a position that we can hope to integrate his work on silence into the discussion of confession and illuminate the wider strands of his work on religion.

The culmination of the confessional process was the confession to an external authority after the examination of conscience. This was an act of verbalisation to test and evaluate the quality and nature of the thought; it was for Foucault a kind of barometer of 'truth'. The process evaluated the resistance to verbalisation, the resistance to face the judgement of the superior. According to Foucault's reading of Cassian, the self-examination was subsumed under the 'obedience' of this act of verbalisation.[91] The speech act itself thus becomes the 'decisive element' for Foucault.

> It is the confession, the verbal act of confession, which comes last and which makes appear, in a certain sense, by its own mechanics, the truth, the reality of what has happened.[92]

The failure to establish the crucial non-binary link between speech and silence at this point of obedient verbalisation in confession diminished Foucault's appreciation of the said and the unsaid in religious discourse. For it was at this crescendo of the confessional process, the verbal act, that a whole set of force relations were set up in relation to silence. It is here that the multifarious nature of power invested itself into a series of multiple relations between both silence and speech. What is secret and silent becomes sinful; silence becomes a resistance to authority, but silence also becomes the very act of rendering to authority.[93] The ability to utter and extinguish is the mark of disposing of evil thoughts. However, in the very act of articulation there is a silencing, a rejection, of flesh. The priest listened in silence to the speech acts which would subsequently silence desire; Christianity demanded an utterance in order to silence. Paradoxically, in a non-binary system

Foucault's examination of the confession was also the archaeology of the silence.

Although Foucault never developed the link, the examination of confession (verbalisation) was entwined with his earlier ideas of silence. The Christian demand to 'dissociate', 'disinvolve', 'renounce' and 'sacrifice' the flesh is to silence the body in the very act of verbalising its reality. What is spoken is silenced. The verbal dialogue controls the body.

> The ascetic maceration exercised on the body and the rule of permanent verbalisation applied to the thoughts, the obligations to the body and the obligation of verbalising the thoughts – those things are deeply and closely related.[94]

What is also 'deeply and closely related' is the way silence (maceration) and speech (verbalisation) operate as political strategies in the organisation of 'truth'; what Foucault has managed to illuminate, albeit without conceptual clarity and at a marginal level of his work, is the way Christianity shapes and controls the self through the coercive forces of silence and speech. Christianity paradoxically constructs a self in the very sacrificing or silencing of the embodied self.[95] Foucault's lectures on confession end on this conundrum, a recognition of the complex political and historical forces which shape the 'truth' about the religious 'subject'.

> Even in these hermeneutical techniques derived from the *exagoreusis* the production of truth could not be met ... without a very strict condition: hermeneutics of the self implies the sacrifice of the self. And that is, I think, the deep contradiction, or, if you want, the great richness, of Christian technologies of the self: no truth about the self without a sacrifice of the self.[96]

The political force of religious discourse, in its power to silence and its power to demand an utterance, is the key theoretical operation on which Foucault's 'religious question' can be examined. Although Foucault inconsistently moved between silence (the unsaid) and speech (the said), his work as a whole constitutes a critical examination of both dimensions of religious discourse; it is a single critique with a two-fold edge. Foucault was insufficiently concerned with religion to bring together such an analysis, and it is the task of this work to attempt a textual reconstruction.

The recognition of the importance of silence and speech in Foucault's work provides a model to position the fragments of his 'religious question'. It enables us to draw a distinction between different groups of ideas on religion according to silence and speech. Foucault's early work, inspired by surrealism and the avant-garde, can be seen to rescue the body 'silenced' by religion. This group of ideas forms a critique of religion through what I have called a 'spiritual corporality'. However, his later work, post-1976, can be seen to redefine the 'utterances' of religion through the technology of self, a critique of religion which I have labelled a 'political spirituality'. These distinctions do of course collapse when the binary distinction between speech and silence is broken. It is in this sense that Foucault's critique of religion can be seen as a single entity.

The remainder of this work will seek to illuminate the two aspects of Foucault's critique of religion outlined above. In the next two chapters I will show how Foucault rescues the body silenced by religion through a 'spiritual corporality'. I will then reinforce this position by showing how his work challenges traditional religious epistemology in AK. Having established the basis of Foucault's early work as constituting a 'spiritual corporality' I will explore the tensions which develop in his 'religious question' between belief and practice in the mid-1970s. These tensions will eventually bring about the shift of emphasis from silence to speech as a tactical focus in his examination of religion. I will show in this respect how Foucault's later work on confession and governmentality can be seen as a 'political spirituality'. I will then finally make a brief return to the collapse of the binary opposition between speech and silence in order to show how his work forms a single critique of Christianity.

3 Surrealism and the religious imagination

> ... it is through the skin that metaphysics will be made to reenter our minds.
>
> Artaud [1932] (1988) 'The Theater of Cruelty', p. 251

Although Foucault had touched a number of religious themes in his *Historie de la folie*, such as Quaker spirituality and the religious suppression of madness, it was through the influence of surrealism and the avant-garde that he really began to grapple with religious ideas and the concept of God. Foucault's work at this time incorporated 'a certain use of vocabulary, of play, of philosophical experience' to open the silent enigmas of religious discourse, a style he would later reject when he, as Porter noted, 'abandoned his protracted war against everyday intelligibility and familiar intellectual forms'.[1] But these early works not only held an enigmatic style on the edges of religious discourse; they also evoked a fundamental 'religious question' in the suspension of traditional religious categories. Foucault joined with the surrealists in opening up the space of the Other in religion. He followed a critical perspective developed in French literature which rescued the body silenced and repressed by religion. This literary engagement gave voice to the unsaid and silent aspects of institutional spirituality and started to sub-textually build what I have called a 'spiritual corporality'.

Before his literary period in the 1960s Foucault had previously opened religious issues in his proposed 1958 course at the University of Uppsala entitled 'Religious Experience in French Literature from Chateaubriand to Bernanos'. The course, as Macey indicates, was never delivered due to Foucault's departure to Warsaw, but it does mark out some fundamental lines of interest in Foucault's work which are easily lost in the broader scope of his writing, and perhaps reflects some influence of the historian of religion Georges Dumézil, who had, according to Foucault, shaped his early study of madness.[2] How Foucault would have dealt with the strands of religious discourse in nineteenth- and twentieth-century French literature in his proposed course may never be known, but his subsequent engagement with aspects of this literary tradition do reveal some key aspects in the re-evaluation of religion in contemporary continental thinking.

Foucault and the 'spiritual'

The treatment of religious themes in the earlier part of Foucault's work is complicated by the assimilation of a diverse range of ideas within surrealism and the avant-garde, an intellectual climate which permeates his work in the 1960s through his involvement in such journals as *Tel Quel* and *Critique*. These journals brought an interdisciplinary approach to literature and literary theory and reflected, as Patrick ffrench's study of *Tel Quel* illustrates, the vicissitudes of contemporary intellectual debate in Paris in the early 1960s.[3] Foucault's immersion into this world constitutes a period of concerted literary interest resulting in a number of articles covering subjects from Robbe-Grillet and the *nouveau roman* (new novel) to Gothic and Sadeian themes, and a book-length study of the 'surrealist' writer Raymond Roussel.[4]

Foucault's involvement in the literary world of the 1960s also saw him chair a number of significant debates which were not only formative to the development of *Tel Quel* but provided revealing insights into the religious dimensions of modern French literature. In his opening comments for a debate on the novel in 1963 Foucault identified the central concerns in the literature of the 'new novel' (Robbe-Grillet) and surrealism as covering similar 'spiritual' issues, though it is important to realise he uses the word 'spiritual' cautiously.

> I was struck by the fact that, in Sollers's reading yesterday and in the novels of his that I've read, reference is constantly made to a certain number of experiences – experiences, if you like, that I will call, in quotation marks, 'spiritual experiences' (although 'spiritual' is not quite the right word) – such as dreams, madness, folly, repetition, the double, the disruption of time, the return, etc. These experiences form a constellation that is doubtless quite coherent. I was also struck by the fact this constellation was already mapped out in surrealism.[5]

The emergence of themes such as madness, dreams, unreason and the double evoked a series of religious and spiritual questions because they attempted to find an 'outside' to traditional rationality, an unencumbered, spontaneous state of mind, a reality 'beyond' conscious thought. It presented the question of how far the 'Other' could be viewed as religious or spiritual – it evoked the politics of religious discourse.

Foucault went on in his discussion of the literature to draw out the differences between *Tel Quel* and surrealism in their understanding of these so-called 'spiritual' experiences. The surrealists are seen to locate experience, as Patrick ffrench states, 'in a psychological space, positing a beyond', while *Tel Quel* sees these experiences 'as taking place within the space of thought seen as language'.[6] The different location of experience in surrealism and *Tel Quel* is grounded in a second major difference rooted in the conceptualisation of language: surrealism seeing language as an 'instrument' reflecting experience and *Tel Quel* validating language as a distinct process in itself.[7] ffrench's discussion of this debate captures precisely the tension between these two literary perspectives when he highlights how for *Tel Quel* it 'makes no sense to talk of a beyond, a non-linguistic space in which psychological operations could take place'.[8]

Foucault is obviously in agreement with Sollers and *Tel Quel* in the rejection of the assumptions of psychology in surrealism, as seen in the influences of Freud on Breton, but his alignment with *Tel Quel* is brief and complex. According to ffrench, the differences between Foucault's understanding of literature and that of *Tel Quel* is related to the influence of Maurice Blanchot, to whom *Tel Quel* had an ambiguous relationship.[9] There was a reaction by the *Tel Quel* group against the style and nature of Blanchot's questions about literature, which were more concerned with the limits and ontology of literature than the mechanisms of language.[10]

ffrench also entertains a second more striking difference between Foucault and *Tel Quel* which returns us to the question of 'spirituality'. In his 1963 essay for *Tel Quel* 'Language to Infinity', Foucault is concerned principally with the place of God's absence in the creation of literature. The death of God forms a key thematic in his discussion, influenced by Sade, Nietzsche and Bataille. The religious question, according to ffrench, is 'side-stepped' by *Tel Quel* 'in a more precise focus on the process of textual production'.[11] The shift of experience into language, as a process of thought in language, meant that in many ways *Tel Quel* circumvented the religious question in a narrative construction and presented, according to ffrench, a more 'scientific' agenda. It is this 'scientific' agenda which ffrench saw as separating Foucault from *Tel Quel*.[12] Foucault's understanding is therefore distinct from *Tel Quel* on the basis of his religious evaluation of literature and his concern with the absence of God.

Foucault's analysis of the differences between *Tel Quel* and surrealism and ffrench's distinctions between Foucault and *Tel Quel* are crucial coordinates in the assessment of Foucault's understanding of religion. They draw attention to strands of discourse which often remain obscure and marginalised. The introduction of the term 'spiritual' by Foucault always remains ambiguous. However, despite the uncertainty and problematic nature of this term, he still employs it to open debate and challenge the contours of its traditional location in religious discourse. In 1963 the 'spiritual' appears to be seen as a series of theorised 'experiences' at the boundaries of rationality, and later in 1984 he suggests it is a 'subject acceding to a certain mode of being and to the transformations which the subject must make of himself [*sic*] in order to accede to this mode of being'.[13] While the terminology is unable to sustain itself for Foucault, he does demarcate a region of 'experience' which is neither simply metaphysical nor psychological, but an immanent process of change on the edges of rationality, which perhaps involves an engagement with the excluded, the enigmatic and much later the politic of self. Foucault's use of the word 'spiritual' fundamentally creates a tension by locating the silenced events of dreams, madness, the play of language and, later, the political inside the framework of a more familiar religious context. Such a positioning of the term is problematic, but by examining Foucault's work on surrealism we can appreciate the radical critique involved in such an operation. What it reveals at this point is the fringes of a 'religious question' oscillating in certain parts of contemporary French literature, and Foucault's entertainment of this 'religious question'.

Foucault's interest in a religious question in French literature is reiterated in a 1967 interview with the Italian journalist Caruso when he acknowledges an unresolved tension in his passion for Blanchot and Bataille and his interest in Dumézil and Lévi-Strauss. Foucault believed that the 'unique common denominator' between these two positions of thought was 'perhaps made up of a religious problem'.[14] There is within this and other marginal statements a fascinating and unexplored dimension to his literary work, an aspect of his work which, as I have indicated elsewhere in relation to James Miller's 'narrative', can easily become distorted.[15] For it is through Foucault's encounter with avant-garde writers such as Blanchot, Bataille and Klossowski that the main thrust of his religious speculation in literature is constituted and where the ground of his religious perspective is established. There is, however, no direct symmetry between these thinkers and Foucault; rather, Foucault extends and adapts the work according to his own Nietzschean understanding of the death of God.

The surrealist legacy

Foucault's acknowledgement of a religious question in surrealist and avant-garde literature was a part of his own critical evaluation of Christianity. He placed the 'spiritual' in quotes and followed surrealism in destabilising religious thinking. This legacy of surrealism in his 'religious question' is in many ways filtered through the wider avant-garde literature of Blanchot, Bataille and Klossowski, all of whom had some relation to, but were distinct from, the main body of surrealism. Such a distinction reflects the precarious nature of distinguishing between the avant-garde and surrealism, which is largely a political division of ideas centred on an alignment with the main body of surrealism as captured in the work of the 'leader' of surrealism, André Breton, although even this definition is not entirely satisfactory.[16] The work of Blanchot, Bataille and Klossowski stretches beyond the concerns of surrealism. These writers are in consequence far more important to Foucault's 'religious question', and I will return to them, with specific reference to the surrealist icon the Marquis de Sade, in the next chapter.

Before we can embark on such an examination it is necessary to explore how surrealism altered the religious imagination in France and inspired later avant-garde writers to reclaim the 'spiritual' within such areas as the body. The examination of Foucault's response to surrealism is therefore crucial in showing how he built a framework for a 'spiritual corporality'. The surrealist cultural heritage allowed him to make three important moves in this endeavour: first, it enabled him to find resources to valorise the Other, to reconstitute the silence; second, it critically repositioned the language of 'spirituality' within a new politics of experience; and, third, in a complementary move to the second aspect, surrealism created the possibility for Foucault to locate the body at the centre of the 'spiritual'. In each case the 'spiritual' is awkwardly reshaped according to a non-binary opposition between the sacred and the profane. But more importantly the notion of the 'spiritual', in quotes, challenged the exclusive religious categorisation of experience.

By exploring the surrealist agenda we are able to demarcate the boundary of Foucault's own religious question and set the context for his more specific avant-garde adventure. It primarily enables us to see how the ideas of surrealism rather than the content of its religious themes brought about a re-evaluation of the 'spiritual'. I will therefore seek to show that although Foucault engages with the enigmas and ambiguities within surrealism, this engagement is principally an extrapolation of themes which link with his anti-humanist critique of philosophy and does not directly reflect his religious concerns. Surrealism, as we shall see, influences the broad trajectory of Foucault's work as a deposit of French culture, and in consequence it shapes the general contours rather than the specific details of his 'religious question'. The literary avant-garde would provide the specific issues of his religious engagement while surrealism provided the wider inspiration and groundwork for a 'spiritual corporality'. Surrealism in effect provided the tools to uncover the silent fragments of a coercive religious technology of confession.

Surrealist literature and the Other

The significance of surrealist and avant-garde literature in Foucault's 'religious question' needs to be initially understood in the context of the interplay of literature and philosophy in continental thought. Foucault's work, as with much of contemporary critical theory in France, is premised by greater fluidity of disciplinary boundaries than is familiar to the Anglo-Saxon world. Clare O'Farrell, in this respect, has highlighted the differences and problems of assimilating Foucault in the respective French and Anglo-Saxon literature.[17] The inclusion of literature and art into the space of critical reflection allowed Foucault to develop richer resources for his thinking and brought an imaginative quality to his writing, a strategy which opens concealed perspectives and allows for an uncovering of the unsaid of religious discourse.

Literature offered a transgressive space of reflection that was closed off to philosophy. It held the 'Other' of philosophy, the neglected dimension of the rational enterprise. Foucault's writing opens this subversive space, a series of labyrinths entangling thought, which seek through enigmatic language and oblique gestures to disrupt the rational subject and question the privileged centre of the Cartesian *cogito*.[18] The style of his writing becomes a part of the destabilising strategy; historiography is mixed with poetic elegance and oblique significations push the limits of thought. There is a distinct play with ambiguity in Foucault's early writing. This language takes on a new vitality as a positive force in his heterology (study of Otherness).

Foucault's literary influence enabled him not only to subvert philosophy but indirectly to create a sub-textual process to reorganise the 'spiritual'. By reclaiming the Other, the excluded or denied aspects of Western thought, he is drawn into the questions of the 'limits' of thought. Foucault attempted to reach outside the boundaries of conventional thought, to entertain the unthought, to transgress the limits of reasoning. The surrealist and later avant-garde thinkers were key facilitators in his entry into a dark hinterland of philosophical reflection; they offered ways to undermine the dominance of vision, to explore the absurdities of representation, to reach the point of death in language, and to listen to the screams of the body. These surrealist disruptions, the use of language, the enigmatic silences, the laughter and the attempt to disrupt rationality created a new space in thought. The understanding and interpretation of this new space of thought brought Foucault into the realms of a religious problem, the problem of the 'spiritual'.

The 'spiritual' appears to emerge at points of uncertainty, ambiguity or disruption as a conceptual zone for locating the undefined or conceptually unfamiliar. It represented the disputed territory of how intellectuals deal with not-knowing or mystery. A large part of continental thinking resisted an amalgamation with religious discourse by keeping the discussion within the boundaries of language, but in contrast surrealism had ventured more freely in the sphere of religion, borrowing and adapting religious vocabulary in the disruption of logic. The heterological dimensions of surrealism led Balakian to refer to the emergence of what she called a 'literary mysticism'. The ideas of the Absolute, the mysterious and the unknown predominated sufficiently in surrealism to elicit the misleading and obscure category of the 'mystical'. Balakian believes the surrealist poetic reaches towards 'a new philosophy of reality' in opposition to materialism. She writes:

> The tremendous mystical motivation beneath the surrealist texts is evident; and it is obvious that they are the product of a craving for the unknown ... .[19]

This religious understanding of certain aspects of surrealist activity is highly problematic in its dependency on a modernist agenda of mystical experience and in the way it confuses metaphysics with the limits of language. I will return to this issue of language and mystical experience in an examination of Foucault's AK in chapter 5. This linking of language and mysticism was, however, a dominant trope in much of the surrealist writing and relates to a fascination and preoccupation with spiritualist traditions, the occult and magic which circled the edges of surrealist activities. This particular orientation in the literature is picked up by Roger Cardinal in his study of Breton's *Nadja*; according to Cardinal, the concern with the altered perception of reality, or surreality, is 'intimately bound up with the question of the paranormal'.[20]

Surrealism, in its attempt to discover new sources of poetic expression and explore the unknown depths of language, was inspired, as Shamdasani has shown, as much by spiritualism as psychoanalytical ideas about the unconscious.[21] In the attempt to overcome 'all control exercised by reason' a whole realm of activities from 'automatic writing' (an unleashing of the spontaneous force of language) to hallucinations and magic were utilised. Anything that was perceived as breaking the mould of logic was brought forward for experimentation, and religious ideas permeated this quest.[22] Although Foucault would have been aware of the various occult and gnostic influences which intoxicated the work of writers like Antonin Artaud, and Alfred Jarry before him, these religious themes were never pursued. His utilisation of surrealist ideas remained at the level of a philosophical disruption of the 'spiritual' through its reclassification of religious ideas. His interest in surrealism therefore derived from a fascination not with its occult or quasi-religious experiences but with the technique of reordering experiences deemed to be 'spiritual'. It was a critical recognition of the exclusions made by religion in their system of value. In order to appreciate Foucault's selective utilisation of surrealism and the obscurity of his 1963 perception of surrealism and the avant-garde as sharing certain 'spiritual experiences', it is necessary to understand the wider intellectual inheritance of surrealism as a cultural precursor to the avant-garde and post-structuralist modern' thinking. I am in this sense seeking to take seriously Foucault's introduction of the notion of the 'spiritual' in order to establish the basis of a 'spiritual corporality' in his wider avant-garde work.

The surrealist inheritance

Surrealism, and its precursor Dadaism, arose in reaction to the turbulence of war and the machines of death. It was a literary movement and a 'community of aims' developed in the inter-war years which attacked conventional bourgeois society, both its logic and values.[23] The activities of the movement were diverse, ranging from Dada post-war reaction, anti-bourgeois comment, literary, artistic and political revolution, to a fascination and preoccupation with a variety of mental states in the creation of a new poetics and a new art form. The central feature of surrealism was the attempt to discover and bring about a new unrestricted way of thinking. There was a direct attempt to challenge the dominant logic and the understanding of the day – namely positivistic thought – in science and religion. There was a fundamental distrust of formal logic, which was seen to confine and imprison thought.[24] Within this scheme the surrealist also tried to break down apparent contradictions in the perception of reality, anticipating the challenges to binary logic of contemporary critical theory. The boundaries between the real and imaginary were rigorously challenged in the creation of 'absolute reality' or 'surreality'.[25] This assault on logic also had an institutional dimension in the attack on the church, the mental asylum, the academy and the family. Anything which was perceived as a 'straitjacket' of thought or desire was attacked.[26] One of the key characteristics underlying such a position was a respect for the 'marvellous', the mysterious and the unknown. As Breton wrote:

> Our brains are dulled by the incurable mania of wanting to make the unknown known, classifiable.[27]

The relation of thought to the unknown or to the unthought is the central feature of Foucault's rescuing of the Other, the silence in religious discourse. His entire work, according to many commentators, can be read in this sense as an exploration of the boundaries that demarcate the 'Same' and the 'Other' – the Same referring to the 'known, familiar or ordered' and the Other conceived as the 'mysterious unexplained "something" that lies outside and defines the limits of the known, that which is exterior and foreign'.[28] As O'Farrell quotes Foucault:

> [T]hought should not be directed towards establishing a kind of central certitude, but should be directed towards the limits, the exterior – towards the emptiness, the negation of what it says.[29]

Surrealism had shaken French literary and artistic culture and perhaps even burdened it with the inconceivable. The search for an alternative perspective had set the scene not only for a rescuing of the forgotten, but also, perhaps more importantly, for the re-emergence of liminality on the philosophical agenda and the development of a new religious problematic. Surrealism presented the possibility of incorporating the silence of religious discourse; it witnessed the birth of what Pefanis, following Bataille, calls the 'science of the heterogeneous'.[30]

If surrealism is envisaged as the emergence of a heterogeneous science, its relationship with contemporary French critical theory becomes much clearer. Wills has already made this point in relation to the specific question of language in his exploration of the work of Derrida and the surrealist Desnos. Wills' pioneering study confirmed

> the fact that both surrealism and recent critical theory have set themselves comparable tasks, however important the divergence might seem

from other points of view, namely to reassess the means by which language functions as a referential and representational system.[31]

Surrealism therefore not only enabled Foucault and the *Tel Quel* group to explore the labyrinths of language, but it also offered ways to think outside of formal logic, to transgress, and to think differently, the hallmarks of his thought. As Foucault, reflecting on his work towards the end of his life, states:

> There are times in life when the question of knowing if one can think differently than one thinks, and perceive differently than one sees, is absolutely necessary if one is to go on looking and reflecting at all. People will say, perhaps, that these games with oneself would better be left backstage; or, at best, that they might properly form part of those preliminary exercises that are forgotten once they have served their purpose. But, then, what is philosophy today – philosophical activity, I mean – if it is not the critical work that thought brings to bear on itself? In what does it consist, if not in the endeavour to know how and to what extent it might be possible to think differently, instead of legitimating what is already known?[32]

The attempt to 'think differently' meant that in the 1960s areas previously excluded or silenced from religion could be explored with new force. The 'spiritual' was freed to be both suspended as a signifier of mystery and reinvested with a more embodied value.

Foucault, surrealism and religion

Foucault's inheritance of the cultural phenomena of surrealism should not lead us to presume that his utilisation of this literary and artistic movement was free and wide-ranging. He approached surrealist literature in a very specific and selective manner. When he refers to surrealism it is difficult to ascertain which writers he characterises under this title and how he located them in the wider movement. In a special interview after Breton's death, Foucault acknowledged the important contribution of the surrealist leader in bringing together 'writing and knowledge' and opening up a space of 'experience' in contemporary thought. He conceded in the interview that 'we are now in the hallowed space left behind by Breton'.[33] Despite these acknowledgements Foucault makes little reference to Breton in his work and saw many of Breton's discoveries as preceded by Goethe, Nietzsche, Mallarmé and others. Surrealist literature, for Foucault, was in many senses a 'disguised' and impure experience of the register of death, of unthinkable thought, of repetition and of finitude, manifest more clearly in the works of Kafka, Bataille and Blanchot.[34]

Foucault had a stronger association with writers on the fringes of surrealism. While Breton is largely ignored by Foucault, figures like Bataille and

Artaud, who had a more distant relationship with the movement, receive closer attention. The separation of Bataille from surrealism reflects the trend in French critical theory to diminish the surrealism associated with Breton. In fact all the major surrealist thinkers who interest Foucault reside on the boundaries of surrealism rather than existing comfortably inside it. On the whole he rejected the more psychological and spiritualist aspects of the movement. In this respect we may note that he did not respond to Pierre Janet's exploration of Roussel's 'ecstatic' writing experience, but concentrated instead on the nature of his 'secret' and the labyrinth of his language. In general, Foucault's utilisation of surrealism is very much in conjunction with *Tel Quel*, not only in following 'dissident' or 'tangential' writers of surrealism but, as ffrench makes clear, in 'adopting some of the strategies of a radical movement'.[35]

Foucault's selective engagement with surrealism, the inheritance of 'strategies' rather than involvement with specific ideas, confirms his lack of interest in the subsidiary religious features of the movement. There is no direct assimilation of the surrealist overt attack on the institutional representation of religion and no exploration of spiritualist and occult themes. Foucault is rather drawn to the writings of Artaud, Magritte and Roussel as ways to disrupt the philosophical subject and undermine rationality through the imaginative play of language, thought and perception. His lack of concern with the broad scope of surrealism and the specific religious tropes of the movement is clearly demonstrated by his consideration, or lack of consideration, of Artaud. Artaud in this sense provides a useful point of focus to explore the 'spiritual' concerns in Foucault's assessment of surrealism.

Foucault and Artaud

Antonin Artaud (1896–1948) is one of a list of literary names which is introduced in MC in a lineage of the mad poets, those at the threshold of the void of madness and creativity. The line of writers, which also includes Nietzsche, van Gogh, Hölderlin and Nerval, is, as Hayman notes, unlikely to have emerged without the '*poètes maudits*' of Artaud's essay 'Van Gogh, the Man Suicided by Society'.[36] There is very little discussion of Artaud's work by Foucault; he stands rather as an icon of madness, 'the absence of the work of art'.[37] This abbreviation of Artaud supports Goodall's analysis of the 'mythologisation' of Artaud by French critical theorists and philosophers, a process which neglects the key features of writers to support the anti-humanist position.[38] We may note in this respect how Foucault completely neglects Artaud's gnostic, occult and apocalyptic fantasies found in such works as 'The New Revelations of Being' and 'To Have Done With the Judgement of God'.[39]

The wider Artaudian influences on Foucault's history of madness have been appreciated for some time: Hayman has noted the 'narrative' is 'strikingly

Artaudian'; Susan Sontag also observed the close alignment; and, as Barber has indicated, Foucault's understanding of madness directly parallels Artaud's understanding of the 'madman' as someone 'society does not want to hear, and whom it wants to prevent from speaking intolerable truths'.[40] Artaud's influence on Foucault, as with surrealism at large, is principally in providing the contours of a new philosophical perspective. He first provides a revolutionary context for rewriting history and reappropriating knowledge and, second, valorises the body in the historical scheme. In many ways Foucault's work appears to complement Artaud's Research Bureau state-ment for surrealism envisaged as a perspective which would 'unlevel' thought. Artaud's vision developed a revolution of all states of mind and all human activities, a revolution that would bring about a Nietzschean-like 'devaluation of values' and 'a depreciation of the mind', and, more specifi-cally for Artaud, 'an absolute and perpetual confusion of languages'.[41] It was about not beliefs or formulas but a certain 'order of repulsions' and a 'reclassification' of life.[42] Foucault's work can clearly be seen in these broad terms, and although there are few signs of any surrealist religious themes in his work, it reveals the context of his critical suspension of certain experi-ences such as madness and unreason in the 'spiritual'. The 'spiritual' was being used to demarcate a new politics of experience outside the traditional dualist and hierarchical categories of religion. It was a term which valorised the excluded. There was a valuing of the silenced and marginalised experi-ences of Western thought by paradoxically recognising and rejecting a traditional register of religious value.

Foucault's work is also influenced by Artaud's 'spiritual' reordering of the body. The articulation of the body was a key theme in Artaud's work, from the screams and cries of his poetry and prose, through the rewriting of history from the perspective of bodily fluids in the life of Emperor Heliogabalus, to the shocks of the theatre of cruelty, there was a reorienta-tion of thought from the body which Foucault assimilates.[43] The full force of Artaud's visceral language is appreciated by Foucault as a new literature written at the point of finitude:

> [I]n Artaud's work, language, having been rejected as discourse and re-apprehended in the plastic violence of the shock, is referred back to the cry, to the tortured body, to the materiality of flesh.[44]

Artaud provides Foucault with the possibility of an embodied language which is a crucial determinant in his later re-evaluation of religion and the development of a 'spiritual corporality'. Artaud's critique of religion is fired by an embodied passion and forms part of what Naomi Greene sees as Artaud's 'metaphysical revolution', a reordering of spiritual concepts into the body.[45] This can be seen when Artaud took editorial control of the third issue of *La Révolution surréaliste*, which he entitled '1925: End of the Christian Era'. In this edition Artaud made a vehement attack on

Christianity in his 'Address to the Pope', condemning the promotion of souls to the neglect of the body. In reference to the Pope he wrote:

> In the Name of Family and Country you urge the sale of souls, the unrestricted grinding of bodies. ... The world is the soul's abyss, warped Pope, Pope foreign to the soul. Let us be immersed in our own bodies, leave our souls within our souls. We don't need your enlightening razor edge.[46]

While Foucault's work does not hold the same quality of vehement attack on Christianity, it constitutes the same fundamental reappraisal of the body and carries forward the spirit of Artaud's 'metaphysical revolution'. Foucault's work on the death of God and his genealogical studies are grounded not only in a Nietzschean critique of religion but also in a reclamation of the body articulated powerfully by Artaud. In Foucault's 1975 study of the prison we see how he repositions the soul on and in the body in ways similar to both Artaud and Nietzsche; the language of the soul in the prison regime constituted as a series of 'inscriptions' on the body.[47]

The 'spiritual' in this ordering of the soul and body is reorganised according to a critique of the values of Christianity. While Foucault avoids any direct discussion of Artaud's religious themes, he does entertain its broader dimensions. The lack of reference to the more traditional religious ideas is important because it reveals how Foucault dismissed religion as part of the oppressive structures of the Same. In his work there was no need to demolish religious thinking. Rather his work builds on the assumptions of a deceased religious order. It assumes the death of God. Foucault carries forward Artaud's 'metaphysical revolution' by tactically reusing or recycling the remnants of religious discourse. The notion of a 'spiritual corporality' is not therefore an acceptance of religious values but a radical disruption of its exclusions. It opens up the space of the Other in religion, the neglected and silenced aspects of the religious institution; in this case, the body. The 'spiritual' becomes part of a political remapping, religious understanding, a redefinition of values. It territorially reclaims the value of the Other.

A non-religious mystery

It is important to remember that Foucault's recognition of a 'spiritual' dimension to surrealism is made cautiously, and certainly does not constitute the main solution to demarcating what is Other or unknown. In the onslaught of philosophical critique and the play of language to reclaim the Other of thought, he prefers to hold ambiguity, enigma and mystery without reference to religious ideas. His recognition of the inadequacy of the word 'spiritual' to refer to the surrealist concerns can therefore be seen as reflecting the tension of reading the 'unknown' or 'mystery' in religious terms. Despite the fact that religious and psychological registers of experience run through surrealist literature, it is significant that Foucault rejects these traces in his own understanding. It would be a mistake to read his engagement with surrealism in religious terms, precisely because the recognition of the 'spiritual', in quotes, is a rejection of traditional religious understanding. Foucault wants to acknowledge a new space of thought created by a radical critique of rationality and certainty which is outside of the wider surrealist fascination with religious ideas. The surrealist attempt to posit an unknown often attached itself to a religious or occult framework, or other ideas which control the unknown, which in effect reduces and contaminates any illusory purity of thought. Georges Bataille captured this tension when referring to the poetic image.

> The poetic image, if it leads from the known to the unknown, attaches itself however to the known which gives it form, and although it tears the known and life apart in this rupture, it holds fast to it.[48]

Foucault does not position the 'unknown' in a religious domain; it exists in its own space of philosophical critique, in a space of disruption. He refuses to locate the new space of thought except in very general categories, such as the Outside, the Other or, more infrequently, the 'spiritual'. His reluctance to adopt religious terminology can be seen in his engagement with Magritte and Roussel. These studies confirm the non-religious provocation of mystery which seeks rather to challenge philosophical certainty. Foucault becomes fascinated with representation, similitude and secrets which collapse and cause disruption. These form a complex boundary in the politics of knowledge and illuminate the arena of uncertainty and mystery on which religious discourse had previously held a monopoly. Despite his use of the term 'spiritual', Foucault does not equate any of these conundrums of Magritte and Roussel with religious language. They remain part of philosophical discourse. In order to demonstrate this point it is necessary to consider briefly Foucault's discussion of these two surrealist thinkers.

Magritte and Roussel

Foucault's work on the Belgian surrealist painter René Magritte (1898–1967) – an essay principally exploring the painting *Ceci n'est pas une pipe* ('This is Not a Pipe') – and his book-length study of the obscure 'surrealist' writer Raymond Roussel (1877–1933) map a territory of deception, enigma and mystery. These are evoked by creating tensions in thought/perception (Magritte) or investing autonomy in language (Roussel). The avoidance of religious language to describe their work shows how Foucault's interest in the secret and the cryptic existed adequately inside the boundaries of language and representation. His work on these thinkers holds no transcendent referent, develops no confusing allusions to the language of Pseudo-Dionysius and creates no critique of religion by adopting the concept of the 'spiritual'. Such an approach makes Foucault's use of the idea of 'spiritual' more intriguing and shows the polemical nature of depicting the Other.

Foucault was interested in Magritte's work because of the way it revealed the Other. There was little concern in Foucault's essay to locate this Other. Rather he celebrated the tricks and play of Magritte's puzzles. Magritte's work utilized words and images to challenge the understanding of art and the arbitrary nature of the sign. He was not so much an artist as 'a thinker who communicated by means of paint'.[49] He was interested in the dynamic of representation in the visual arts and used words to disrupt the process of signification. For Magritte, 'images, ideas and words are *different* determinations of a *single* thing: thought [*la pensée*]'.[50] It is precisely this that interested Foucault in his own study of the 'order of things'. There was a rupture in the certitude of the sign, the image and the mental assumption which displaced the order of thought.

Magritte's work *Ceci n'est pas une pipe* (1926) intrigued Foucault. It disrupted the equation that the image of a pipe refers to the common object we know in everyday life as a pipe. For Magritte the image of the pipe is itself; it does not require any objective referent in order to provide meaning – it is purely arbitrary. Foucault seizes this idea because it offers an opportunity for opening up a different order of value from formal logic and rationality. As he writes about Magritte's painting:

> The operation is a calligram that Magritte has secretly constructed, then carefully unraveled.[51]

The calligram, initially associated with Apollinaire, is a poem in the shape of the poem's theme, but *Ceci n'est pas une pipe* is clearly not a calligram. However, despite this fact, Foucault uses it as a way of reading Magritte's painting. For Foucault it holds the characteristics of the calligram in disrupting the conventional relationship between language and image. In the calligram the 'gazing subject' becomes a 'viewer' not a 'reader'. One thing is hidden in the other. In Magritte's work there is a series of negations, where the 'gazing subject' is transported, if not thrust, into a world of representation and similitude.

Foucault's enthusiasm for Magritte's valorisation of the Other often meant he distorted Magritte's own intentions. In the complex hinterland of images, words and things, Foucault believed that Magritte had separated similitude (appearance) from resemblance (likeness of the original), which Magritte had disputed in his letter to him.[52] Foucault's language is here confusing for, as Jay notes, in his earlier work *The Order of Things* these terms had a slightly different meaning.[53] But by rescuing the idea of the similitude the external referent is lost and Foucault is able to entertain the 'deceptive' process which he had previously stated was seen as tinkering on the edges of the visionary and mad.[54]

Resemblance makes a unique assertion, always the same: this thing, that thing, yet another thing is something else. Similitude multiplies different affirmations, which dance together, tilting and tumbling over one another.[55]

Clearly Foucault is more interested in utilising Magritte for his own purposes of illustrating a particular 'disorder', what he calls 'heterotopias', as opposed to Utopias, which 'secretly undermine language'.[56] Foucault's language is playful and very clever. He refers to Magritte's 'infinite games' and 'secret constructions' to be 'unraveled'.[57] Magritte 'mines' and 'excavates', old pyramids become molehills about to cave in, and supporting pegs are being eaten away by termites.[58] Everything collapses not surprisingly into a 'silence', but not the 'silence' of religious discourse.

Foucault's introduction of the idea of 'silence' is a kind of sleep or dream from which words arise. By juxtaposing Magritte's painting *L'Art de la conversation* (1950) with *Ceci n'est une pipe* he saw discourse as being 'reabsorbed into a silence [of the stones]'. Foucault, as we shall see in his discussion of Blanchot in the next chapter, was intrigued with the 'silence' from which words emerged, the sense that words 'come from elsewhere'.[59] Here we see again the sense of speech and silence forming a unity. The idea of language holding an exteriority was also what interested Foucault in Roussel's work. Roussel, along with Artaud, signified for him the emergence of a 'new mode of being of literature', a literature at the very limit of existence, 'where death prowls' and where 'thought is extinguished'.[60] The tensions and enigmas of the Otherness of language at this point make it possible to see how tempting it was for Foucault to easily slip into religious analogies and raise the question of whether such experiences could be understood, however unsatisfactorily, inside the 'spiritual'. His work holds a 'religious question' in so far as it raises these problems.

Foucault's fascination with Roussel, a relatively unknown French writer rescued by the surrealists, was not, however, based on any conception of the 'spiritual'. Roussel rather held for him the fundamental anxiety of language, a work built on secret constructions and devices.

In Roussel's work, language, having been reduced to powder by a systematically fabricated chance, recounts interminably the repetition of death and the enigma of divided origins.[61]

Foucault was particularly interested in the posthumous work by Roussel *Comment j'ai écrit certains de mes livres* ('How I Wrote Certain of My Books'), which revealed the secret key behind Roussel's lifetime work.[62] The work explained the techniques or devices behind his prose. It uncovered the way language was made to function according not to imaginative expressions but to machine-like productions.

The subtlety of the devices in Roussel's work is lost in English translation, for the process was to create a novel by rearranging letters and words. This began by taking a sentence at random and changing the meaning of the sentence by altering one letter in a word, taking words which had the same sound but not the same sense and extending puns and creating prepositions. The language took on a life of its own like a series of telescopic extensions as each sentence emerged from the words and letters of the former sentence, a party puzzle of language. Unlike automatic writing it is a conscious process exposing the limits of language.

The life is drained out of language as it is pushed to formulate itself in its arbitrary and absurd manner. Roussel also revealed that his work *Impressions d' Afrique* ('Impressions of Africa') could be understood if the reader started with chapter 10 and read the second half of the novel first. However, Foucault notes that here there was also the possibility in the end that we were being deceived by the idea there was a secret. In Roussel's work any secure ground was continually being removed from beneath one's feet.[63] The register of language was made to suffer in Roussel; it was 'anxious and animated', 'extinguished and then brought back to life by the marvellous void of the signifiers'.[64] The 'void', however, always remains, in Foucault's appreciation, inside the 'game of significance', the 'misery and the celebration of *signifier*'; it never shades off into a serious consideration of the occult or the 'spiritual'.[65]

Magritte and Roussel provided Foucault with a world of unsettled representation, secrets and disruptions. He may have misunderstood Magritte and generously read Roussel in his 'very personal' connection with the work, but both, as Almansi points out in relation to Magritte, were 'heroes' of the Other.[66] They were allies in Foucault's attempt to destabilise dominant forms of thought and perception. The striking feature of this very powerful entertainment of paradox, mystery and enigma by Foucault is the way he resisted any attempt to align these two thinkers inside the 'spiritual' frame of reference. The question therefore remains as to why he regarded the work of surrealism as depicting experiences which could be understood as 'spiritual', in quotes. The work of Magritte and Roussel certainly appears to exist in the 'constellation' of dreams, madness, unreason and repetition which Foucault had in passing located in the 'spiritual'. What is clear from the examination of Magritte and Roussel is that he was not consistent in his use of the term 'spiritual' to represent the surrealist work. So why did he formulate surrealist experiences and those explored by *Tel Quel* as 'spiritual'?

'Spiritual' quotes

The answer to the question of the 'spiritual' can be found in Rudi Visker's fascinating study of Foucault's quotation marks. The use of quotation marks, as Foucault stated in his work on sexuality, 'have a certain importance'.[67] They are a key dimension to Foucault's critical work. As Visker explains:

Foucault's quotation marks are an exemplary expression of a model of critique which runs throughout his entire *oeuvre*.[68]

The quotation marks form part of a 'philosophical problematic', an attempt to deal with the material limitations of the text, the tension between what Visker calls the 'internal' and 'external author'.[69] Although Visker does not deal with the peripheral issue of the 'spiritual', it is clear that the location of this idea in quotation marks, like that of human 'sciences' and 'sexuality', is an attempt to indicate an 'impossibility' of the discipline or idea.[70] In this sense, by developing a constellation of ideas under the term 'spiritual', Foucault is rejecting the categorisation while using its external force to draw attention to a previously conceived arena of experience. The quotation marks demonstrate his ambivalence with religious ideas and theological registers. It confirms how his reading of surrealism, selective as it is, cannot be seen as supporting a religious understanding as such. He rejects the surrealist preoccupation with traditional religious categories and seeks to create a new space for demarcating the Other of thought. He specifically rejected ideas of spiritualism and mysticism. When challenged by the Marxist Eduardo Sanguinetti during the 'Debate on the Novel' for *Tel Quel*, he pushes the conceptual frontiers by stating:

> There is an ongoing effort, fraught with difficulty (even, and especially, in philosophy), to determine what thought is without applying the old categories, by attempting to bypass this dialectic of mind once defined by Hegel.[71]

Foucault's depiction of the 'spiritual' and his own selective engagement with surrealism reveal the complex boundaries involved in examining his own 'religious question'. There appear to be two inseparable strands to his encounter with surrealism: first, an avoidance or rejection of the specific religious themes; and, second, a general reclassification of thought. On the one hand Foucault wants to separate the enigmatic and mysterious from the religious domain by acknowledging the awkward nature of the 'spiritual' and rejecting its traditional organisation of experience, and yet, on the other hand, he seeks to retain the 'spiritual' by 'contaminating' it with an embodied register. Religion is therefore both affirmed and negated simultaneously in the idea of the 'spiritual'. The 'spiritual' is introduced into the discussion as a mark of value, an intensity, without 'spirit'.[72] Foucault could have simply jettisoned the religious register of the Other as unimportant. What is significant is that by using the term 'spiritual' he acknowledged some value in disrupting or unlevelling thought. Throughout his career he reintroduced the word 'spiritual' to break the exclusive boundaries of religious discourse in terms of the valuing of the body and later in terms of its political location. The 'spiritual', in quotes, formed the critical edge of his 'religious question'.

Surrealism and the emergence of the 'spiritual' body

Surrealism provided Foucault with a platform to reorder religious discourse, to destabilise confidence in the dominant order, to discover the boundary or the edge of thought. The appropriation of surrealist literature is therefore a tactical alignment with a movement which revolutionalised thought and cleared the landscape of preconceived registers. The surrealist literature in this sense provided a framework for Foucault's avant-garde adventure into religious thinking, by providing the intellectual ground for creating religious subversions. The religious ideas about the body in avant-garde thinking, found in the work of Bataille and Klossowski, are to some extent born out of and fed by the transgressions of surrealism.

Surrealism created a new philosophical context to break the stranglehold of traditional thought; it provided the knife to cut the eye. This surrealist metaphor from Dali and Buñuel's 1928 film *Un Chien andalou* ('An Andalusian Dog') is a poignant register of the anti-ocular discourse in the work of Foucault, a theme explored by writers such as Jay, Certeau and Flynn.[73] Surrealism, according to Dali, attempted to 'destroy only what it considers to be shackles limiting our vision'.[74] Such a limited vision was seen to operate in religion. In this respect there was a deliberate undermining of Western Christian experience in the surrealist attack. Artaud's film *La Coquille et le Clergyman* ('The Seashell and the Clergyman') explored a priest's sexual obsessions and the hypocrisy of the church. In Buñuel's film *L'Âge d'or* ('The Golden Age') the skeletons of bishops were portrayed on coastal rocks. These images were part of a series of religious subversions which can be seen to go back to the work of Alfred Jarry, in such plays as *Caesar Antichrist* (1895), and to the attacks on Christianity by Nietzsche and Sade. It is no surprise that in the works of Sade, and some surrealists, priests and those in religious orders are some of the main protagonists in the sexual adventures. These figures are introduced as part of an attack. They constitute a repulsion towards the dualism and binary constructions of body and soul in Western Christianity.[75] Surrealism, as we have seen in relation to Artaud, rescued the body and unleashed the censorship on philosophical and religious discourse. It took Christianity into a dark and 'perverted' zone; it inserted the 'spiritual' into the messy (w)hole of the flesh.

The relocation of the body and the sexual into the religious domain was a tactical deployment of surrealism, but it was only in the work of Bataille and Klossowski that Foucault unlocked his own 'religious question'. It was these writers, coupled with Foucault's understanding of language in the work of Blanchot, who brought him more immediately into the realm of religious ideas. A new ontology of language, eroticism, transgression and the Nietzschean thematic of the death of God was eventually brought together by Foucault in the 1960s to develop a 'spiritual corporality', a critique of religion which valorised the body. The idea was born in surrealism and matured by Foucault's engagement with the avant-garde. The shared icon of both these groups was the Marquis de Sade. It is this figure who orders Foucault's religious subversions. Surrealism and the avant-garde brought Foucault's 'religious question' to the erotic body, the erotic body of 'man'; it gave voice to the 'silence' of religious discourse.

4   Male theology in the bedroom

> The fact that 'God is recognized to be dead' cannot lead to a less decisive consequence; God represented the only obstacle to the human will, and freed from God this will surrenders, nude, to the passion of giving the world an intoxicating meaning.
>
> Bataille [1939] (1985) 'The Sacred', p. 245

The central features of Foucault's 'spiritual corporality' emerged from his literary engagement in the 1960s with the avant-garde literature of the period. At this time his work constituted, as he described in *The Order of Things*, an 'open site' in which 'many questions are laid out on it that have not yet found answers'.[1] This experimentation with questions 'currently in vogue' involved a significant and yet neglected religious dimension.[2] There was an extraordinary interweaving of literary theory, philosophy and theology forming a complex tapestry of ideas. While the literary and philosophical features have been isolated and examined, there has been little exploration of the scattered and often obscure religious strands of the work. Hidden in the diverse fragments of his avant-garde studies Foucault began to articulate a series of religious ideas concerned with the death of God and sexuality. It was this discourse which rescued the body silenced by religion.

There are two important features in Foucault's religious engagement with the avant-garde material which I want to examine. First, I want to explore his development of a 'corporal' religious understanding based on the work of the eighteenth-century aristocratic writer the Marquis de Sade. In Foucault's literary work there was a complex integration of themes forming a new embodied religious discourse around the awkward figure of Sade. Sade formed the avant-garde platform on which to entertain an embodied religion at the site of a dead God. The location of religion in the 'corporal' emerged from Foucault's recognition that the space left by the death of God opened up new questions about the body. It is in this sense that I refer to Foucault's work as holding a 'spiritual corporality'. His work is a 'spiritual corporality' rather than a 'corporeality' because, as I pointed out earlier in the introduction, the former indicates *only* 'of the body'. The death of God extinguished the dualistic opposition (corporeality) between body and spirit.

I continue to refer to the 'corporal' as 'spiritual', in quotes, because of Foucault's suspension of traditional religious values and the specific emergence of the body after the death of God. His work can be seen as reflecting a 'spiritual corporality' in so far as it brought together the surrealist critique of religion and the embodied ideas of Sade and the death of God.

The prioritisation of the body in Foucault's religious question highlights a second important feature of his engagement with the avant-garde in the 1960s: his failure to recognise the gender-specific nature of his work. Foucault followed the avant-garde writers in bringing together issues of religion and sexuality with no critical understanding of the sexual politics of gender identity. The centrality of the misogynist works of Sade to Foucault's 'spiritual corporality' and Foucault's lack of concern for the plight of women in such work brings this question of gender into even greater focus. As many recent feminist commentaries on Foucault make clear, his gender-blind analysis is cause for much concern and deliberation.[3] The tension in some feminist engagements with Foucault is based on the fact that he offers useful models of analysis in relation to power and the social construction of identity, but simultaneously undermines the humanist platform on which the emancipatory politics of feminism is built. Lois McNay does suggest that Foucault's later work on the self is more congenial to a feminist perspective, but she clearly recognises the 'inadequacies in his treatment of gender issues' and the male norm of his work on the body.[4] There is an assumption in Foucault's work that references to 'man' and 'sexuality' refer to a universal subject. The 'corporal' (and the 'spiritual') appear to lack specific sexual and gender orientation.

In this chapter I want to bring together these two features of Foucault's avant-garde religious sub-text by critically assessing the development of his 'spiritual corporality' from a feminist perspective of gender identity and exploring the male norm of Foucault's 'body'. Such a critique will involve taking the gender-blind language of 'man' and 'sexuality' in Foucault's work as referring to 'male' sexuality, even though he assumed a universal subject. In order to emphasise this reading I will at times employ the literary transgression strategy of placing the word 'male' in parentheses. This experimental strategy will reveal how the religious discourse of the death of God/man and the issues of a 'spiritual corporality' hold the basic rudiments of a male theological model. In this sense I am suggesting that by owning the male perspective of Foucault's religious question we can find a valuable resource for contemporary debates in gender and religion. It is to recognise how his 'spiritual corporality' can be read in a gender context.

There are, however, a number of difficulties in isolating a specific 'male' perspective from the basis of a gender-blind universal subject in Foucault's work. The universal subject to some extent obscures both male and female sexuality in so far as it lacks any sexual and social location. To some extent the non-sexual body and the generalised idea of sexuality in Foucault's work distort a 'male' position by their lack of specificity. This is not to presume an essential 'male' perspective can be isolated but to recognise, following recent studies on the social construction of masculinity, that Foucault's work holds a particular undeveloped 'male' discourse.[5] Foucault in this sense writes not so much from the position of a male norm as from the position of a certain culturally 'undifferentiated' male perspective. In this chapter I will hope to locate aspects of this 'male' perspective in its social context.

In order to illustrate the complexity of ideas behind this gender reading of Foucault's 'spiritual corporality' I will follow a number of stages of elucidation. I will first critically assess the historical background to Foucault's work on Sade. This will enable me to show how he incorporates an inherited Sadeian male model into his 'spiritual corporality'. I will then detail the specific coordinates of Foucault's 'spiritual corporality' through the themes of language, the death of God/man and sexuality, and entertain the male perspective behind these ideas. It is important to remember that in this discussion I am not attempting to incorporate the growing literature on masculinity but rather seeking to detail the fragments of Foucault's own work which can illuminate this debate.[6] I am in effect attempting to do no more than to draw out Foucault's 'spiritual corporality' in the light of gender identity.

Foucault and Sade

Although Foucault never wrote any single book or article specifically on Sade, the prominence of Sade to his thinking can be seen in the numerous allusions and references he makes to him throughout his writings and interviews up to 1976. For the purposes of summary we can divide Foucault's work on Sade into four phases.

First, the presentation of Sade in the *Histoire de la folie* in 1961. Sade is portrayed here, following a number of surrealist rehabilitations, as a figure who was a victim of confinement and a voice of unreason. Sadism was seen to be born out of the fortress, the cell, the cellar and the convent, 'the natural habitat', according to Foucault, 'of unreason'.[7] The experience of Sade at the end of the Classical age is seen as a major cultural shift, 'one of the greatest conversions of Western imagination'.

> Sadism appears at the very moment that unreason, confined for over a century and reduced to silence, reappears, no longer as an image of the world, no longer as a *figura*, but as language and desire.[8]

The second phase of Foucault's work on Sade is seen in the numerous references in writings and interviews between 1962 and 1970. This is the phase determined by Foucault's interest in the avant-garde and out of which is developed a series of themes around Sade and the death of God, which emerged principally from such writers as Bataille. It is this phase of work on

Sade which will predominate in this chapter as it forms and underpins the 'religious question'.

The third phase in Foucault's work on Sade can be seen in the occasional references in interviews between 1971 and 1975, which reflect a more cautious tone and acknowledge the importance of Sade with less dramatic force. Foucault qualified his interest in Sade in a 1973 interview by firmly locating his interest in him as a distinctive figure in the history of Western thought.

> I don't make Sade out to be a god, and I don't make him the prophet of our age; my interest in him has been constant principally because of the historical position he occupies, which is at a point of transition between two forms of thought.[9]

This was one of the most consistent views Foucault held on Sade, arising in his work on madness and carried through into his work *The Order of Things*. Foucault's assessment of Sade in the mid-1970s does go through a shift in emphasis and he does seem to modify his earlier enthusiasm.

The final phase of his remarks on Sade can be seen in his 1976 *History of Sexuality*, where, as James Miller points out, Foucault 'ventures a criticism' of Sade by questioning the idea of sovereign right in his final chapter 'Right of Death and Power over Life'.[10] Foucault's work on the dynamics of power had led him to reassess the 'unlimited right of all-powerful monstrosity'.[11] He wrote criticising Bataille and Sade:

> We must conceptualise the deployment of sexuality on the basis of the techniques of power that are contemporary with it.[12]

This discussion of Sade constitutes the last of any significance, and few references to Sade can be found from this time onwards. The shift of focus away from Sade seems to be partly related to the diminishing influence of the avant-garde on Foucault's work and the move to a new series of concerns about subjectivity, power and the technologies of the self.

Biographers such as James Miller have attempted to explain Foucault's interest in Sade and the changes in 1976 in terms of his private life and his experiences in the gay sadomasochistic scene in California. While such accounts put forward fascinating, and even plausible, hypotheses, the details remain largely built on speculation.[13] It is easy to equate Foucault's interest in Sade with such sexual practices, but this does not explain the interest in Sade by French surrealists and avant-garde writers throughout the twentieth century. As we shall see, in the light of Sadeian scholarship in France, it is important not to give undue personal and psychological significance to Foucault's work on Sade without taking account of the cultural context of France.[14]

In order to appreciate the context of Sade in France and to understand the theological model that arises in conjunction with works by the avant-garde, we need to explore two interwoven interpretative strands of thought: first, we need to appreciate the nature of Sade in the context of French avant-garde thought; and, second, we need to highlight the problematics of the discussion of the body and theology from the perspective of Sade's writing. These issues can be brought together by providing some background to the Marquis de Sade himself and considering some of the feminist accounts of Sade and Foucault.

The interpretation of Sade

The Marquis de Sade (1740–1814) is clouded in the veils of historical uneasiness and, as Gallop has so persuasively demonstrated, contemporary interpretative lenses.[15] In one historical reading, Sade represents the dark side of the Enlightenment, the rational enterprise taken to its most macabre and extreme. According to Adorno and Horkheimer, Sade is the 'logical negative outcome of the Enlightenment'.[16] His works demonstrate a rationalisation of Nature unconstrained by any moral categorical imperative, the rational opposite of the Kantian edifice. It is in the light of such extremes that Blanchot sees Sade's work as 'the most scandalous ever written'.[17] The reactions indicate how we now hear, as Said states, the words 'de Sade' as a particular 'event'.[18] The 'event' is built up through the layers of commentary and social affect that accumulate around the figure and the work, preventing any uncontaminated reading. It is necessary in this respect to give a brief overview of the person Bataille called 'the most subversive man who ever lived'.[19]

Sade was born into an aristocratic family in pre-revolutionary France. His military career, in which he achieved the ranks of Captain, Lieutenant-General and Colonel, ended after a number of incidents involving excessive sexual behaviour. The most significant of these were the Marsailles events of 1772, where Sade and his valet, Latour, were accused of acts of poisoning and sodomy (then a crime punishable by death) during one particular orgy. Sade managed to escape trial and prison for a number of years and the charges were dropped. He was, however, eventually convicted for 'debauchery and excessive libertinage' in 1777 and kept in prison by a *lettre de cachet*, a special act of the King which meant that a prisoner could be kept indefinitely without trial and sentence. This particular sentence of Sade had been brought about by the influence of Sade's mother-in-law, Madame de Montreuil.[20] Sade spent a total of twenty-seven years in prison. It was this situation which created the stimulus for his major writings. The initial thirteen years of imprisonment included a period in Bastille, where he wrote his famous novel *The One Hundred and Twenty Days of Sodom*, a work cataloguing the sexual and criminal events in Siling Castle over a four-month period.

After the French Revolution in 1789 Sade was released but continued to write many other challenging works, including his 1795 work *Philosophy in the Bedroom*, an account of extreme acts of sexual initiation interlaced with philosophical attacks on the existence of God. All of his novels consist of this strange mixture of sexual pursuit and vehement theological assault. This sexual and theological aggression is held together in such a way as to make the orgasm a statement of atheism, where each excessive act becomes a provocation against God's existence. In the style of many rational Enlightenment arguments against God, Sade wrote:

> Would this all-powerful God permit a feeble creature like myself, who would, face to face with him, be as a mite in the eyes of an elephant, would he, I say, permit this feeble creature to insult him, to flout him, to defy him, to challenge him, to offend him as I do, wantonly, at my own sweet will, at every instant of the day?[21]

Sade was eventually imprisoned again in 1801, this time for obscene litera-ture, principally his novels *Juliette* and *Justine*. He was to spend the remainder of his life in prison, where he died in 1814, leaving behind a huge corpus of literature that was to be distorted and reinterpreted beyond recog-nition.

The crimes of violence and sexual assault against women have, not surprisingly, been cause for much criticism, especially from feminist writers. The radical feminist Andrea Dworkin sees Sade as 'the world's foremost pornographer' and she strongly attacks the literary and artistic interest in Sade as evidence of a 'woman-hating culture'.[22] While Dworkin is correct in the assessment that the crimes and the victims almost become 'invisible', her analysis fails to address the complex cultural significance of Sade in France, and why Jane Gallop can justify her own feminist interest in Sade's work.[23] This is not to diminish the central force of Dworkin's argument, but to show that the works of Sade are filtered through a specific historical evolution and tactical illumination of misogyny (and arguably at times misandry). The literary significance of Sade means that writers such as Simone de Beauvoir engage with Sade as a specific cultural figure in French thought.[24] Feminist interest in Sade often views his work as promoting an awareness of crimes against women, as in Angela Carter's *The Sadeian Woman* (a work regarded by Dworkin as 'pseudofeminist'), and Luce Irigaray, as Gallop demon-strates, 'considers Sade valuable inasmuch as his work lays bare "the sexuality that subtends our social order"'.[25]

In the 1960s, when the *Tel Quel* group and Foucault addressed the issue of Sade's writing, Sade was hidden and concealed, even distorted, in the strands of literary discourse; 'de Sade' had become an 'event' outside the actual texts. This transformation of Sade is clearly documented by Carolyn Dean in her excellent examination of the notion of self in modern French thought.[26] There was in effect a reconstruction of Sade as victim and humanitarian revolutionary against the forces of repression. Dean shows how desire is located at the centre of a 'cultural subversion' which mutated the figure of Sade from monster to victim.[27]

Sade had undergone an earlier rehabilitation through medical and literary writers at the end of the nineteenth century. The Sadeian 'event' was perhaps most powerfully constructed by the Austrian clinician Richard von Krafft-Ebing in his 1886 *Psychopathia Sexualis* when he took Sade's name to pathologise certain sexual activity under the term Sadism, alongside the later writer Leopold Sacher-Masoch (1836–95), from whom he derived the term Masochism.[28] The debate then centred on whether non-procreative sex was necessarily pathological. This question over the pathological nature of non-procreative sex was put forward by the French physician Pierre Janet in the foreword to a French edition of Krafft-Ebing's work. The link between repression and perversion was soon established in these psychiatric debates; unnatural religious and moral constraints were seen to result in more extreme acts of behaviour.[29]

The greatest transformation of Sade occurred in the inter-war years, mainly due to the influence of surrealism, and Apollinaire in particular, who published newly discovered manuscripts of Sade. Apollinaire even suggested that Sade's character Juliette represented a 'new woman', but this was only within the constraints of a male perspective.[30] In the bloody aftermath of the First World War Sade was a prophetic figure for the surrealists. They viewed him as a man misunderstood and driven to sadistic fantasies due to imprisonment. There is here, as Dean notes, a powerful separation between the man Sade and his literary works. The surrealists 'normalized Sade' by viewing his fiction as the 'very force of his reason'.[31] Andrea Dworkin is correct to see in many of these writings a situation where women did not count, where they were simply figures of surrealist fantasy. The surrealists created a mythology of human (though obviously male) liberation around Sade and, according to Dean, this would form the 'interpretative norm for the generation of avant-garde thinkers to come'.[32]

The avant-garde writers continued the move to 'normalise' Sade by attempting to understand the nature of the extreme writing, and to provide an explanation of his motives. This hermeneutical shift occurred alongside, and extended beyond, the main surrealist literature from the 1930s through to the 1950s, in the works of Bataille, Blanchot and Klossowski. The 'textual network' of Bataille–Blanchot–Klossowski is closely analysed by Gallop, who sees the work as forming the contemporary reading of Sade in the 1960s.[33]

Although the conceptions of Sade in Bataille, Blanchot and Klossowski are interlaced, their readings of Sade differ in the ways they understand and interpret the work. Bataille focuses on the limits and impossibility of Sade's work, a feature of Klossowski, who extends these issues into religious questions about God's existence and the tormented soul. Blanchot concentrates on the Hegelian dialectic and the nature of Sade's writing. All of these writers, as Dean notes, attempt, unlike the surrealists, to explain the 'compulsion' Sade had to write.[34] They were attempting to explain the locus of Sade's writing. In the search to find some underlying rationale the avant-garde writers put forward, amongst other suggestions, a number of religious explanations. Sade's work was seen to hold attacks on theology and hidden gnostic themes. It was these avant-garde religious interpretations of Sade which led Foucault to explore his own 'religious question'. And while Foucault did not wholeheartedly accept the avant-garde religious interpretations of Sade, they would shape his 'spiritual corporality' and, unfortunately, also reinforce a gender-blind analysis.

Klossowski and Bataille

The theme of theology and the body in Sade's work was developed initially by the writer and artist Pierre Klossowski, a man who, like Bataille, had earlier in life entered monastic orders and who later developed an interest in eroticism. Blanchot, as Macey notes, saw Klossowski's work as 'a mixture of erotic austerity and theological debauchery'.[35] Foucault was deeply impressed by Klossowski's work, and although he never took up the latter's interest in gnosticism, the theological tone of the work has clearly infiltrated his overall model of religious reflection.[36]

In a series of articles in the 1930s Klossowski rejected the atheistic quality of Sade and attempted to devise a reading based on Manichean gnosticism and the Carpocration cult of orgasm.[37] The original purity of the soul was found through the Carpocration doctrine of non-resistance, based on a peculiar reading of Matthew 5:25–6, 'Agree with thine adversary quickly'. Through such immersion into the world of darkness the creator would restore the human being back to the rightful place with God.[38] The soul attempts to extinguish its sense of separateness from the divine by repudiating God's existence and its own immortality, and in the end the soul returns to God by exhausting its own alienation.[39] According to Klossowski, Sade's work held a similar theological perspective. 'The libertine's atheism', as Dean, commenting on Klossowski, points out, 'is not a denial of God but an angry attempt to force God to manifest himself [*sic*]'.[40]

Klossowski's essays were collected in his 1947 work *Sade My Neighbour*, probably the most well-known study of Sade. However, as Gallop has shown, Klossowski modified his work and played down his earlier gnostic excesses in the 1967 edition.[41] Although Klossowski's later work loses its gnostic overtone, the paradoxical process of redemption continued in the idea of 'integral monstrosity'. The idea of 'integral monstrosity' is based on the establishment of integrity in the (male) outrage against normative reason and God. The value system is turned upside down in what Klossowski sees as an 'inverted monotheism' at the heart of Sade's work. Perverse actions become moral imperatives against a normalising authority. The 'key sign' of such thought is the act of sodomy, homosexual or heterosexual. Sodomy

breaks the institutional control over the body which propagates the preservation of the species and becomes a moral testimony to the death of God.[42]
Klossowski sees the Sadeian pervert as attacking the controls imposed on
the body and simultaneously extinguishing the ego-identity.

> The language of institutions has taken over this body, more particularly
> taken over what is functional in '*my*' body for the best preservation of
> the species. ... 'I' then do not possess '*my*' body save in the name of
> institutions; the language in '*me*' is just their overseer put in me.[43]

Many of these ideas resurface in Foucault's later work on 'docile bodies'
in his study of the prison, but what is significant in the 1960s is how
Klossowski's obscure work forms a backdrop to an emerging theological
sub-text in Foucault's writing. Klossowski's examination of Sade establishes
the interrelation of the language of bodies and God's existence.[44] What
again is so absent from this discussion is the awareness of gender identity.
There is a persistent and inaccurate assumption that references to the body
or sexuality implied both male and female. Klossowski's work brought
together a cultural package of powerful images which fascinated Foucault,
but Foucault's subsequent religious question failed to grasp the male and
misogynist quality of the 'corporal' redefinition of religion. There was no
recognition that the theological 'debauchery' and anger was male.

Klossowski's religious reading of Sade and the breaking of traditional
(male) binary opposition between body and spirit was continued by Bataille.
It was Bataille, as Jane Gallop has documented, who was to have the
greatest influence on post-war readings of Sade in France. In Gallop's disen-
tangling of the inter-textual matrix surrounding Sade she clearly indicates
the impact of Bataille.

> A reader of Sade, exposed to the atmosphere of modern French
> thought, cannot escape being infected by Georges Bataille.[45]

Bataille, described by Richman as 'one of the most elusive figures of French
intellectual life', was interested in religion from the perspective of anthropology and the history of religions, influenced predominantly by such
figures as Émile Durkheim and Marcel Mauss.[46] He was a co-founder in
1937 of 'The College of Sociology', a non-establishment group of intellectuals who sought to explore the sacred in a community of active
participation and moral social awareness. As Richardson points out, they
took up Marx's challenge in the *Theses on Feuerbach*: 'Philosophers have
hitherto only "interpreted" the world; the point, however, is to "change"
it.'[47] Under such objectives they declared their work 'Sacred Sociology', but
due to the war it only lasted until 1939.

Throughout his work Bataille was interested in what he called the 'inner
experience' of religion, rather than in its diverse forms of expression.[48] In

his later work *Eroticism* in 1957, strongly influenced by Sade, he links the
workings of Christian religious experience with erotic impulses through the
anxiety of death and discontinuity. Death is, paradoxically, the continuous
aspect of being, while life, because of death, is discontinuous.

> We are discontinuous beings, individuals who perish in isolation in the
> midst of an incomprehensible adventure, but yearn for our lost conti-
> nuity.[49]

The desire in eroticism is to find continuity in the face of discontinuity, and
thus in erotic activity there is a 'dissolution', a nakedness, where the orgasm
becomes the 'little death'.[50]

> The whole business of eroticism is to destroy the self-contained char-
> acter of the participators as they are in their normal lives.[51]

The sexual act thus involves a 'violation' of the other's state of self-posses-
sion and, echoing Sade, Bataille sees eroticism as existing in the same
domain as violence. (This is a view also found in Andrea Dworkin's work
Intercourse, but with very different implications.[52]) Bataille seems to be
unaware of the fact that in eroticism the so-called 'violation of self-posses-
sion' can be a mutually agreed adventure and an 'affirmation' (not violation)
of the other; whereas in an act of violence the action is usually based on a
conflict of interest. The preoccupation with 'violence' reflects a specifically
Sadeian male thematic, and it is this limited male identity which pervades
the work of the avant-garde writers and Foucault.

Eroticism is different, according to Bataille, from the simple physical
sexual act because it brings into play the whole problem of existence; it is a
philosophical and theological issue.[53] The erotic expresses a condition of
being related to the problems of discontinuity which is overcome in the
sexual relationship. Religious behaviour perpetuates the same dynamic of
sexual interaction in its attempt to overcome the isolated discontinuity of
being with a sense of continuity. This dynamic is seen at different levels in a
variety of religious practices and beliefs. In religious acts of sacrifice, for
example, the participants share a feeling of continuity by witnessing the
death of a discontinuous being.[54] In the absence of a specific religious
object, like sacrifice, the sense of continuity in death or the beyond is experi-
enced through certain practices which break the sense of discontinuity.
Bataille places mystical experiences in this category.[55] Eroticism is a religious
question, and 'God', as Foucault quotes Bataille, 'is a whore'.[56]

When Foucault takes up Bataille's argument, as Richardson identifies, he
dramatically shifts the context of the latter's discussion and introduces the
idea of the death of God with a reading of Bataille's idea of transgression
and the limit. Richardson's criticism is direct, when he writes:

It is not so much that one can say that Foucault is in disagreement with Bataille, but that what interests him belongs to a different discourse.[57]

Foucault's 'spiritual corporality' is principally built through his commentary on Bataille's work, but the rearrangement of ideas produces a slightly different sound. In Foucault's work, as we shall see, there is a bringing together of issues concerned with language, the death of God/man and sexuality around the figure of Sade. Foucault in this sense relocates Bataille's religious concerns within a wider cultural context. What Foucault carries forward from Bataille is a relationship between sexuality and religion derived from a Sadeian male thematic, a thematic of death, violation and aggression.

This outline of the cultural context of Sadeian scholarship in French avant-garde thought enables us to see the complex and often confused ways in which Sade becomes the screen upon which a constellation of contemporary issues are projected. The experimental literary and philosophical debates smother the texts of Sade and have led to scathing criticism by such writers as Annie Le Brun. In her extensive introductory essay for the French edition of Sade's collected works, Le Brun argues that Bataille, Blanchot, Klossowski and their followers have completely distorted Sade in the process of abstract theory and linguistic analysis. Her critique also extends to Foucault:

> Nothing in the whole of Sade had ever walked into this hall of half-measure. How could anyone still take Michel Foucault seriously, referring, in his *Madness and Civilisation*, to 'Sade's calm and patient language'?[58]

Le Brun exposes the way Sade is tamed and filtered by the avant-garde writers. Andrea Dworkin would agree with Le Brun about the way real physical events have been ignored in the theory surrounding the excessive writing of Sade, although she would dispute her underlying motive in rescuing the surrealist indulgence in such writing. It soon becomes clear that Sade is caught in a number of political struggles. As Carolyn Dean states:

> Thus, while there is no 'correct' reading of Sade, no Sade to 'get right', there are clearly more or less valuable readings of his work. Of course, those readings are less about Sade than about the politics or the fantasies of the people who read him.[59]

Foucault's 'spiritual corporality', based on Sade, is therefore caught in a multilayered interpretative matrix shaped by French artistic and literary culture. This history is not, however, an excuse for uncritically adopting Sade. If anything the history of Sadeian scholarship confirms Dworkin's critique of the artistic and literary interest in Sade as reflecting a 'woman-hating culture'. Sadeian scholarship can, however, be valuable, as I intimated earlier in relation to Gallop and Irigaray, not only in revealing the agonies and pains of a misogynist social order, but also in highlighting the violent and oppressive constructions of male identity. The use of Sade, as Dean acknowledges, reflects the 'politics' and 'fantasies' of the reader and not 'de Sade' (whoever he may be).

Foucault, male sexuality and the Sadeian body

The diverse readings of Sade reveal a profound tension in his location in Foucault's 'spiritual corporality'. Sade, on the one hand, allowed avant-garde writers and Foucault to find a more embodied reflection of religion through sodomy and sexual excess. But, on the other hand, these reflections were undermined by misogynist attitudes. The embodied enlightenment of religion is therefore constructed at the cost of women. There is a funda-mental alienation and obliteration of women (and to some extent men) in the rescuing of the (male) body in Foucault's work. In approaching Foucault's 'spiritual corporality' I want therefore to show how the specific 'politics' and 'fantasies' in his reading of Sade hold a specific male religious quality. Sade enables Foucault to rescue the male 'spiritual' body according to a specific (and limited) construction of male sexuality. Foucault is in this sense operating on a culturally constructed avant-garde Sadeian male paradigm to reinstitute the (male) body into religion. It is, however, not the *only* male paradigm. What I am calling the Sadeian male paradigm is a male sexual construction built on the themes of death, domination, sodomy, pain and 'theological' anger (an anger towards the restrictions imposed on the male body by traditional Christianity).

These negative themes of the Sadeian male paradigm have led feminist writers like Somer Brodribb to dismiss Foucault's work.[60] She writes:

> Foucault is preoccupied with the precarious nature of being, with the seed of death in life, and he chooses annihilation as the foundation of his particularly masculinist metaphysics.[61]

Foucault's 'spiritual corporality' can clearly be seen as a 'masculinist meta-physics'. The themes of Foucault's religious question are inescapably wrapped up in a male perspective. This does not mean we have to reject such work. It rather means we can understand Foucault's 'spiritual corporality' inside a male context. Such a strategy is to follow Bartkowski in seeing Foucault as one of the men responding to Hélène Cixous's statement, in a significant footnote to her central French feminist essay 'The Laugh of Medusa', that 'men still have to tell us about their sexuality'.[62] By locating Foucault's 'spiritual corporality' in a male context of Sadeian scholarship we can establish the connection between religion and gender. It will enable us to see the preoccupation with the issues of death and annihilation as distinct, although not exclusive, male concerns.[63]

Language, God and sexuality

Foucault's 'spiritual corporality' is unfolded through a triangulation of issues held together on the basis of the Sadeian male paradigm. Sade was the violent foundation stone of the avant-garde challenge to religious values but Foucault repositioned this work according to his own contemporary interest in language, the Nietzschean thematic of the death of God/death of man, and sexuality. These strands are brought together in Foucault's study of Bataille in 1963 when he writes:

> Perhaps the importance of sexuality in our culture, the fact that since Sade it has persistently been linked to the most profound decisions of our language, derives from nothing else than this correspondence which connects it to the death of God.[64]

The sentence conceals the dense interweaving of issues which have little meaning or validity outside the reified atmosphere of avant-garde discourse on Sade which I have outlined above. In order to clarify the underlying triadic basis of Foucault's 'spiritual corporality' we can present the work as shown in Figure 4.1.

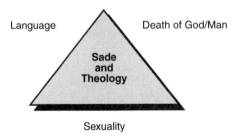

Figure 4.1 Foucault's theological model in the 1960s

Foucault's 'spiritual corporality' in the 1960s

If Foucault's 'spiritual corporality' is based on a Sadeian male paradigm, then it is possible to see how the coordinates of this discussion reflect hidden issues about male identity. Although Foucault is unaware of the gender-specific nature of his work, by reclaiming the male perspective we can see the discussion of language, the death of God/man and sexuality as reflecting certain 'anxieties' in male identity.[65] I will examine each of the coordinates of Foucault's 'spiritual corporality' in turn and not only show how he repositions religious discourse but also reveal the hidden anxieties of male identity held in each thematic.

Language

Foucault's understanding of the nature of language in the 1960s is influenced, on the one hand, by the waves of structuralist theory and, on the other hand, by Blanchot's enigmatic theorising about the link between language, death and negation. These issues of language form the central platform from which Foucault builds his own theology of language; for the nature of language is determined by God's existence and disappearance in Western consciousness. Many accounts of Foucault's work *The Order of Things* (OT) examine the idea of successive epistemes (the discursive relations that through history give rise to different forms of knowledge) and the evolution of language, without considering how dependent they are on the notion of God.[66]

In Foucault's OT the basic pattern of the historical analysis of language (Renaissance period–Classical age–Modern period–decline of the modern edifice) is grounded on two major considerations of the position of God in human thought. At the beginning, Foucault describes the Renaissance world as one where language is a sign of the reality of God. As Kearney explains, and the exclusive language is important: 'The world was deemed to be a Divine Script authored by God Himself for man to read.'[67] Everywhere there were marks and signs of God's existence. Language was seen as part of the 'similitudes and signatures' of nature to be studied and explored. Foucault recreates a mythic atmosphere of the Renaissance, rather than factually representing it, in order to portray a world of 'resemblance' where words (God's words) and things were one.

> There is no difference between the visible marks that God has stamped upon the surface of the earth, so that we may know its inner secrets, and the legible words that the Scriptures, or the sages of Antiquity, have set down in the books preserved for us by tradition.[68]

Foucault goes on in his mythical construction to use the biblical imagery of Babel from the Old Testament to show how the 'transparency' between words and things came to an end with the breaking of the alliance of God and 'His' people. This relationship is preserved only in fragmentary form in Hebrew, in order to show 'it was once the common language of God'.[69] There still remains a connection to God's original word but 'primal visibility' is lost. In the Classical age a gap emerges which creates the space for the emergence of 'representation' in language.

> And though God still employs signs to speak to us through nature, he is making use of our knowledge, and of the relations that are set up between our impressions, in order to establish in our minds a relation of signification.[70]

Once there is a space between words and things through the process of representation, human beings begin to read and interpret the world without God. The Classical age, as a result, becomes the time when, in the absence of God, human beings begin to name, classify and order things, as we see established in Galileo, Descartes and Darwin.

Foucault then goes on to describe the final transition to the Modern period in which Sade is a central figure, as Don Quixote was in the transition between the Renaissance period and the Classical age. Sade exists at the transition point from the Classical to the Modern period, where language is exposed to the tension between 'simple' representation of sexual acts and the limits of representation in attempting to portray desire. Sade's writing shifts between these two poles of thought: one where there is a 'meticulous ordering' and Law behind every sexual act, a feature coterminous with the Classical age; and another pole where there is a continual stretching of the limits of language, with, as Foucault wrote, 'the obscure and repeated violence of desire battering at the limits of representation'.[71] In this situation language turns on itself and opens up strange and complex enigmas.

> After [Sade] violence, life and death, desire, and sexuality will extend, below the level of representation, an immense expanse of shade which we are now attempting to recover, as far as we can, in our discourse, in our freedom, in our thought. But our thought is so brief, our freedom so enslaved, our discourse so repetitive, that we must face the fact that that expanse of shade below is really a bottomless sea.[72]

What emerges in this new phase is an uncertain space where words recover an 'ancient, enigmatic density', not like the Renaissance period, but one where 'language may sometimes arise for its own sake in an act of writing that designates nothing other than itself'.[73] As Foucault saw in the works of Mallarmé and Nietzsche, what was speaking was nothing other than the word itself, the vibration of its 'enigmatic and precarious being'.[74]

This theo/ontology of language is explored with specific reference to Blanchot in Foucault's 1966 essay for the journal *Critique*. In this discussion of Blanchot's 'thought from the outside', Foucault sees Sade as the first in a line, through Hölderlin, Flaubert and Nietzsche, to shed light on a language without subjectivity or an objective referent.[75] Language ceases to be simple representation of thought and assumes a quasi-religious function in holding its own mystery and enigma. In the next chapter I will explore this feature of language in Foucault and Blanchot and show how it is confused with the religious language of Pseudo-Dionysius. The influence of Blanchot is central in the development of Foucault's religious question of language. This point is underlined by Timothy Clark when he stresses how Blanchot's 'radical notion of writing' puts into question a whole series of religious ideas.

> Blanchot eschews the dominant subjectivising and historicising approach to literature and renders it the field of a life-long meditation on the borders of philosophy and religion ... .[76]

But it is not the transformation of language by Blanchot alone that initiates Foucault's own religious question. What is also significant for Foucault's 'spiritual corporality' is the centrality of 'God's disappearance' or the 'death of God' to the positivity of language, and the curious place Sade occupies in this development.[77] Although Sade's vehement attacks on God's existence are not explicitly mentioned, they are nevertheless intrinsic to the discussion. When language loses its theological reference, the language of desire assumes a powerful unrestricted force which ruptures language itself.[78] In Sade theological and sexual language are fused together, a relationship that Bataille was to explore in his 1957 work *Eroticism*, which Foucault would closely draw upon in his own essay on Bataille in 1963.[79] When language is taken out of the restrictions of theology it finds not only its enigma but the force and passion of unrestricted desire. There is a joining of the erotic and the religious.

Foucault reveals the inadequacy of language to hold and express desire. There is something which exceeds language in Sade, where man is faced with a desire outside rational categorisation. Language, according to the theory of the French avant-garde, is faced with its self-referential and limited capacities. In this situation there is a tension in the Sadeian male desire for mastery and domination. As Gallop suggests in her radical positioning of the body, there is always something which exceeds the philosophical discourse, which is never contained in rational categories.[80] There is in effect an experience of mental 'impotence' with language to function according to the male desire for order and control. In this situation men are faced with the problem of 'how to speak' and 'write' with uncertainty, with a language which turns back on itself and turns man back to his finite body. This uncertainty and vulnerability of male expression begins to open up other areas of male experience outside the Sadeian paradigm. We may note, for example, how the recent work of James Nelson has shown the need of men to learn to think not only with the erect phallus but also with the flaccid penis. Foucault's 'spiritual corporality', while prefiguring contemporary debates on the body and religion, is therefore restricted not only in its lack of gender specification but also by its failure to register the diversity of male experience.[81]

The death of God and the death of man

The unification of (male) sexuality and theology through the new ontology of language is extended in Foucault's discussion of the death of God and the death of man. These themes which dominated the literature in the 1960s were not new; as Descombes notes, the death of God/man was prefigured by Alexandre Kojève's lectures on Hegel in the 1930s.[82] It was from these lectures that Sartre built his humanist atheism where man replaced God in the creation of an 'inverted theology'.[83] This 'theologizing of man', as Foucault put it in his own reaction to Sartre, was not the only response to the death of God.[84] The death of God assumed a different form in the anti-humanist literature of the 1960s, where it was coupled with the death of man in the critique of subjectivity.[85] The attack on God is linked to the attack on man, opening a new space of reflection where, as Foucault put it, the death of God and the last man are 'engaged in a contest with more than one round'.[86] When this struggle is read in terms of a gender-specific discourse, as opposed to the language of the universal subject, we can see how the absence of a male theological authority figure and the destruction of a dominant discourse about the male subject raises questions and anxieties about male identity. After the death of God and the death of man the body and sexuality assume a priority which destabilises male identity.

There are two dimensions to Foucault's discussion of the death of God: the first explores the relationship to sexuality in terms of Bataille and Sade; and the second which has received more consideration, deals with the more specifically Nietzschean emphasis found in OT, where Foucault links the death of God to the death of man. The importance of Nietzsche has been adequately explored elsewhere.[87] It is, however, the combination of Sade and Nietzsche, two great figures of the death of God, as they are disseminated into the French literary and philosophical circles, which forms Foucault's 'religious question'. The dead God of Sade is joined with the dead God of Nietzsche to create a new theological territory constructed on (male) sexuality.

The central emphasis given to the Nietzschean idea of the death of God is seen in Foucault's short 1966 interview 'What is Philosophy?' In this interview Foucault isolates the different notions of the 'death of God' in writers such as Hegel, Feuerbach and Nietzsche. While in Hegel and Feuerbach reason and man's conscience replace God, in Nietzsche the death of God signified the end of metaphysics, but this was not just a matter of man taking the place of God but the opening of an 'empty space'.[88] This is crucial in understanding Foucault's Nietzschean interpretation of the death of God and the way he links this to the death of man.[89]

> Rather than the death of God – or, rather, in the wake of that death and in theprofound correlation with it – what Nietzsche's thought heralds is the end of his murderer; it is the explosion of man's face in laughter ... .[90]

The 'death of man' has its own distinctive literary and philosophical tradition, established before structuralist theory. It is therefore important to see Foucault's concern with the death of man as a specific strand of discussion within a wider tradition.[91] In OT he sees the Modern period as defined by the creation of 'man', what he calls, in his analytic of finitude, the 'empirico-transcendental doublet'.[92] This is where 'man' becomes both the subject and object of 'his' own knowledge.[93] Foucault's use of the term 'man', as Schrift has clearly illustrated, should be seen in a technical sense to refer to the Kantian summation of all knowledge under the question 'What is man?'[94] Foucault, as Schrift goes on to show, links this to Nietzsche by showing how the 'death of man' is the death of the 'last man', and that the '*Übermensch*' (the superman) is a new being not defined in terms of Kantian anthropology or subjectivity.[95] The language of 'man' obliterates the gender question and conceals the more awkward question: what is male identity after the death of God and the death of man?

In one of the first attempts to link Foucault and theology, James Bernauer attempted to build a theology out of Foucault's notion of the 'death of man'. Bernauer argued that the death of God paralleled the divinisation of man, as seen in the work of Sartre, and that by breaking the privileged position of 'man' an opening was made for the possibility of new conceptions of God.[96] Bernauer's study left open the possibility of a wider theological engagement with Foucault. When we bring the issues of language and (male) sexuality to Bernauer's discussion we can see how new conceptions of God are to be found in Foucault's 'spiritual corporality', in the questions of the body, sexuality and gender. In this sense Nietzsche and Sade form a unity in understanding the death of God in this 'spiritual corporality', within which the interrelation between the death of God, the death of man and the body is crucial. God, as Irigaray has suggested, provides a symbolic framework for gender relations.[97] When God dies there is a loss of authority. In a similar fashion, when the notion of man is questioned, there is a loss of ontological stability. When theology and anthropology have provided a conceptual matrix to assert the power and domination of man, the collapse of such a structure threatens the whole of male identity and precariously throws man back to the reality of his own body. At this point in Foucault's 'spiritual corporality' the death of God is coupled with an explosion of desire according to a Sadeian male paradigm of death, discontinuity and isolation. Brodribb dismissed these male issues as 'masculinist metaphysics', but they seem to reflect something fundamental about the anxiety of male identity in the face of the death of God and the death of man. There seems to be a fundamental question in the social construction of male identity about continuity, power and extinction. It is interesting in this respect to note how Hugh Pyper sees the preoccupation of the Old Testament writers with male inheritance as an anxiety about fathers and the preservation of the male lineage.[98] When the traditional frameworks of male authority are threatened, the question of sexuality assumes priority. The death of God in Foucault's 'spiritual corporality' brings religion back to the awkward space of the body.

Sexuality

Although Foucault does not offer any answers to the predicament of the death of God and the death of man, he does provide his readers with a direction; he presents the 'open site' from which new possibilities may emerge. The situation is made clearer when we consider Foucault's thoughts about the disappearance of the author.

> It is not enough, however, to repeat the empty affirmation that the author has disappeared. For the same reason, it is not enough to keep repeating (after Nietzsche) that God and man have died a common death. Instead, we must locate the space left empty by the author's disappearance, follow the distribution of gaps and breaches, and watch for the openings that this disappearance uncovers.[99]

If Foucault feels it is not enough to leave the empty space of the death of God, what, we may ask, is left by the death of God and the death of man? Foucault's answer to this closely follows Bataille in the way it is linked to the question of (male) sexuality.

Language, the death of God and sexuality are interwoven threads in Foucault's theological model. When language is no longer a simple referent to God, when the idea of God and the idea of man disappear, there is an anxiety and crisis about the nature and limits of existence. These ideas come together in Foucault's essay on Bataille in 1963.[100] In this piece he outlines the predicament of the death of God and how the situation since Sade has brought about the emergence of sexuality at the limits of existence. At the limits of existence there is the possibility of transgression. Foucault, as Richardson notes, extrapolates the idea of transgression from Bataille's work on society, where transgression completes and transcends the taboo, to create an elusive and enigmatic notion. Transgression, Foucault argues, is to be seen not as black to white, or prohibited to lawful, but as a 'spiral' which constantly 'crosses and recrosses', the point where everything is always, following Blanchot, 'contested'.[101] The idea of 'spiritual corporality' is one such contestation. Foucault sees transgression in this sense not as negative but as something which affirms the limits of being.[102] This concept of 'limit' is important in the way he joins together, using Sade, the idea of the death of God and sexuality.

God's existence, Foucault argues, provided a limit to the apparent limitless nature of being. When God is killed, the limits of existence are broken and the individual is apparently liberated, but the individual is also brought back to the limits of existence in the face of what is 'impossible'. Sade's work is an impossible book; it exists at the limits of what can be written.[103] The death of God thus created possibilities but also 'impossibilities in which it entangled thought'.[104] As Foucault points out, the death of God is not a statement of the non-existence of God but 'the now constant space of our experience' where we face the limits of our existence.[105]

By following Bataille's idea that religion and sexual eroticism are grounded in the same experience, Foucault believed that the limit God had once provided could now be found in sexuality. Sexuality, especially since Sade, is demarcated by limits: the limit of consciousness in face of unconscious desire; the limit of law in the light of universal taboos; and the limit of language in its incapacity to express desire.[106] These limits mean it is still one of the few areas, 'in a world which no longer recognises any positive meaning in the sacred', where profanation and desecration can occur.[107] Sexuality thus becomes an act where the 'absence' of God is manifest. Foucault sees Sade's work as representing the precise point where the language of (male) sexuality emerged out of the death of God.

> From the moment that Sade delivered its first words and marked out, in a single discourse, the boundaries of what suddenly became its kingdom, the language ofsexuality has lifted us into the night where God is absent, and where all of our actions are addressed to this absence ... .[108]

Sexuality and the death of God are thus intrinsically connected, tied together at the limits of human thought. According to Foucault, in (male) sexuality we face not only the absence of God but also our own death.[109] The body and God are thus fundamentally fused together in the realisation of the finitude of human life. This problematic of the finite nature of existence is taken up in a different context in Foucault's OT. Here Foucault saw the modern creation of the figure of 'man' as born out of the realisation of finite existence. The body, desire and language are discovered at the limits of existence, at death.[110] At the limit, at the point of transgression, a discourse silenced by religion is opened up and the space for a 'spiritual corporality' emerges.

Rescuing the (male) body

Foucault's 'spiritual corporality', as Gallop has shown, holds a desire to 'mess up philosophy'. It attempts, like surrealism, to 'contaminate' religion by subverting the ideology of respectable subjects.[111] The adoption of a Sadeian male paradigm challenged not only the traditional male division of the body and mind but also the religious division of body and spirit.[112] While Sade's works are outrageous and extreme, they provide the uncomfortable background with which to understand the atrocities in thinking and acting against women and men which formed male sexuality and its relationship to God and the death of God. Sade provided the platform to break the constraints of Western Christianity.

However, despite its value in rescuing the male body silenced by religion, Foucault's adoption of a Sadeian male paradigm still held a number of profound tensions. His 'spiritual corporality' operated on models of isolation, distrust and anxiety. It excluded the positive quality of relationship and failed to appreciate the diversity of masculinities and sexualities. It also ignored the interrelated question of women's sexuality. These tensions demonstrate the problems of translating Foucault's universal subject into a gender-specific language. The limits and constraints expose the undeveloped male discourse and the lack of concern for women in such an analysis. While Foucault's 'spiritual corporality' holds the body in theory, his work never follows through the implications of such ideas. The spiritual body in Foucault remains 'a fragment of ambiguous space'.[113]

These tensions in Foucault are reflected in Jane Gallop's later work *Thinking Through the Body*, where she argues that male European philosophers have failed, despite some recognition, to allow the body to be 'a site of knowledge'. Male European philosophers continued, according to Gallop, to contain the body in a rational scheme of male order and control.[114] As Gallop states:

> The tension between a desire for neat order and the specific details that seem outside any order enacts one of the central Sadian conflicts: the conflict between rational order, that is, 'philosophy', and irrational bodily materiality. Sade's work seems to be a long, concerted effort to bring Philosophy into the Bedroom, that is, to subsume the body, sexuality, desire, disorder into categories of philosophy, of thought.[115]

Foucault's Sadeian male paradigm brought religion into the bedroom, but it was restricted by the failure to explore the hidden anxieties and uncertainties of the male order it propagated. In introducing the body into his work, Foucault recognised neither the oppressive Sadeian basis of his expressions, nor their sexed nature. Nevertheless, while his 'spiritual corporality' never recognised the fundamental question of gender identity, it did indicate how the 'spiritual' becomes located in the 'corporal', how naked bodies inform religious thinking. Despite opening this space, however, Foucault missed the opportunity to show how male and female bodies could become organs of religious belief – perspiring, excreting and coming with revelations of God's absence.

5   Mystical archaeology

> One might assume that it [thought from the outside] was born of the mystical
> thinking that has prowled the borders of Christianity since the texts of the
> Pseudo-Dionysius ... .
>
> Foucault (1966c) 'Maurice Blanchot', p. 16

The embodiment of religious discourse in Foucault's 'spiritual corporality'
brought together several themes in literature and theology. It reflected his
engagement with a number of contemporary issues about the nature of
language and eventually led him to entertain a 'religious' problem at the
heart of language itself. In Foucault's 'spiritual corporality' language and
the death of God were seen to be central to developing an embodied religious perspective. This link between theology and language continued to
arise at the margins of his work when in 1966 he made a minor allusion in
his essay on Blanchot and the 'thought from the outside' to the work of the
Christian mystic Pseudo-Dionysius.[1] This linking of the ontology of
language with religious ideas was reinforced when Blanchot, in his own
essay on Foucault, established a relationship between Foucault's negative
language in AK and negative theology.[2] Although these reflections have
little significance in relation to Foucault's wider contributions, they do
present some central issues in understanding his critique of religion. The
brief remarks are also significant in so far as they have led to the misleading
assumption that there is a 'mystical discourse' within Foucault's work.[3] The
linking of the obfuscating languages of contemporary continental philosophers with mysticism is, however, not new, as recent studies of Heidegger
and Derrida illustrate.[4] The links are based primarily on the way the
language of these writers is seen to fold back on itself, hold obscurity,
contain paradoxical, suggestive or negative features, which in consequence
push the boundaries of reflection towards the question of a religious epistemology.[5]

The juxtaposition of language and religious experience, as we noted
earlier, was part of a wider experimentation at the limits of language in
surrealism. There are, however, great dangers in confusing 'styles' of
thought in Foucault with the models of religious transcendence developed

in surrealism or the avant-garde.[6] Foucault was an atheist and his 'religious question' was principally a critique of religious 'transcendence'.[7] His 'religious question' sought to bring religious discourse into this world, into the world of the body and of politics. The ideas of a 'spiritual corporality' and a 'political spirituality' are thus attempts to critically relocate spirituality in an immanent human process.

In this chapter I want to show how the associations between Foucault's AK and the mystical discourse of Pseudo-Dionysius are misleading. I want to show that even though the ideas of 'negation' may hold intriguing parallels, they are fundamentally different in Foucault's work and those of Christian mystics such as Pseudo-Dionysius. Foucault's negation in AK is to clear human thought of secondary constructions in order to reveal the primacy of discursive practice, whereas Dionysius sought to move beyond all thought and discourse to ascend to the primacy of God. The complexities of these texts should not hide the profound historical and intellectual differences. This comparison will also illuminate how Foucault's work opposes traditional theological understanding and provide a backdrop to underpin his critique of religion. It will demonstrate how his 'religious question' is fundamentally a question of religious immanence.

The Archaeology of Knowledge

AK is a difficult text, and in order to understand how it is linked with a mystical discourse we must first examine its complex use of language and the problems of interpretation it presents. Sheridan in this respect notes the 'austerities' and 'aridities' of the work, and Kusch, who offers one of the most illuminating accounts, acknowledges its ' "sober" nature'.[8] The nature of the text has meant it has had a restricted appeal and the responses to it are, not surprisingly, varied in their attempts to position adequately the work within Foucault's overall programme.[9] As Kusch has shown, interpretations of AK are based largely on the individual disciplinary perspectives and intentions: the philosophical readings emphasising the phenomenological context (Dreyfus and Rabinow); the aesthetic view highlighting its paradoxical and poetic dimensions (Deleuze/Megill); the biographical literature positioning the work in a life and thought that had brought Foucault to Tunisia (Eribon/Macey/Miller); the historians of science, perhaps registering its central concerns, detailing the prescription for a new methodology (Gutting/Kusch); and others, for various reasons, capturing its models for liberating thought (Major-Poetzl/Bernauer).[10] These wide-ranging responses reflect the different textual and theoretical approaches to Foucault's work, and when trying to position AK we are left with a rather puzzling vortex.

One of the central tensions arising from the various discussions of AK is whether Foucault was creating a parody or attempting a serious methodological study to elucidate his previous archaeological examinations. Megill, who believes AK is 'the most consistently misread of all Foucault's writings', develops a reading of the text from Margaret Rose's work on parody and a Nietzschean aesthetic, arguing that those who fail to see the parody will gain little from the work.[11] He writes:

> One notes a peculiar unimaginativeness in many of Foucault's readers, that they seek to constrain within the boundaries of methodology something so obviously antimethodological.[12]

The so-called 'turn' to genealogy has raised questions about the effectiveness of the archaeological inquiry, and as Lemert and Gillan suggest, it is not clear whether this was a methodological inquiry to be strictly applied.[13] There are aspects of the work that clearly lead to parody and paradox, but such accounts fail to recognise the context of Foucault's discussion in the debates of the history of science, as commentators such as Gutting and Kusch demonstrate.

Foucault's methodological concern in AK involves 'clearing' the ground of the history of science, from the dominant *Annales* school in France to epistemological thinkers such as Bachelard and Canguilhem. It seeks to challenge dominant methods in the history of ideas. To position AK singularly as parody is a failure to see the intricate, and often complex, levels of discussion in the work, which Sheridan saw as appealing to 'a small body of specialists'.[14] When such specialists in the history of science, such as Martin Kusch, locate AK in the context of such debates, we see the necessity of taking this work seriously on its own terms.

A closer examination of the intentions behind Foucault's 'methodological experiment' supports Kusch's position. It is possible to identify in Foucault's text a determined effort to offer an alternative methodology for the history of science, and a very specific struggle to devise a distinctive approach from, as he writes, 'the enterprise to which I have devoted myself for so many years, which I have developed in a somewhat blind way'.[15] Foucault throughout AK cross-references his work and amends previous ideas. His manner is self-effacing as he 'stumbles', 'gropes' and writes with 'a rather shaky hand' in an attempt to define the 'particular site' of archaeology.[16]

The work for Foucault remains incomplete and at the 'rudimentary stage of mapping'.[17] His archaeological approach is not a completely watertight system, but rather written to overcome 'certain preliminary difficulties'; it is an 'initial approximation'.[18] He does not regard his project as offering a 'rigorous theoretical model' or even a theory in any 'strict sense of the term', but hopes to 'have freed a coherent domain of description' and thus to have 'opened up and arranged the possibility' for a theoretical model.[19] This tension within the work is replicated throughout the later sections of the study. He 'regrets' failing to offer a complete theory, which would require further development of the work before completion, but, importantly, he does envisage a time when such a complete theory would arise with more careful analysis.[20] These concerns are not those of a writer who is just playing with the parody of antimethodology, but those of one who seriously wants to disrupt and change the history of ideas by offering a different method. Foucault may have later changed his view about such a project, but in 1969 his intention, partly in response to questions in *Esprit* and *Cahiers pour l'analyse*, is to offer a coherent position of his work to date.[21]

Foucault's AK does hold some curious paradoxical aspects, not least the construction of an elaborate theory, of magnificent technical proportions, to deconstruct theories in the history of ideas. He is not only indulging in the avant-garde playground; he has very specific reasons for introducing this elaborate scheme of discourse. It is a necessary procedure to break the humanistic and subjective continuities of the history of science. It was an exercise he needed to follow because of his 'suspicion' of the 'unities of discourse'; the end result indeed leaving him with uncomfortable feelings.

> I have tried to reveal the specificity of a method that is neither formalizing nor interpretative; in short, I have appealed to a whole apparatus, whose sheer weight and, no doubt, somewhat bizarre machinery are a source of embarrassment.[22]

Megill and others are right to identify features of parody in AK, but they remain contributing factors to Foucault's wider aim. Despite the tensions, Foucault is struggling to offer an alternative way of thinking. Such thinking will involve paradox and take him to the edges of thought, theory and language. It will, perhaps, mean he will fail to offer any coherent system of thought, but this does not diminish his struggle,[23] a struggle that involves, as Miller points out, carefully distancing himself from the 'structuralist camp'. Despite these careful negotiations the 'structuralist atmosphere' still imposes certain theoretical demands on the work, and in this sense Ray is correct to note that the later move to genealogy does not diminish the significance of discourse, but 'lets go of the structuralist preoccupation with its rules' which characterises AK.[24]

The new 'site' that Foucault is trying to explore in AK is defined by what he refers to as the 'exteriority of its vicinity', a phrase that recalls his earlier work on Blanchot about the 'thought from the outside'.[25] Foucault wanted to find a language without subjectivity, without humanistic constructions.

> From the moment discourse ceases to follow the slope of self-interiorizing thought and, addressing the very being of language, returns thought to the outside ... it becomes attentiveness to what in language already exists, has already been said, imprinted, manifested – a listening less to what is articulated in language than to the void circulating between its words, to the murmur that is forever taking it apart; a discourse on the

non-discourse of all language; the fiction of the invisible space in which it appears.[26]

Although, as Macey argues, Foucault in AK is beginning 'to move away from the Blanchot-like contention that "language-is-all" to a broader notion of discourse', the connection to Blanchot, as we shall see, still remains strong.[27] Foucault carries through earlier literary influences that had preoccupied him through the 1960s into AK. The history of science is brought into the 'labyrinth' of language and is forced through the 'underground passages' to the 'invisible space' from which all discourse emerges.[28]

Foucault's project is therefore highly problematic and not surprisingly entered into with 'a rather shaky hand'. He is faced with two tasks in the attempt to establish critically archaeology as a method against other forms of inquiry: first, rejecting previous methodological approaches, of which he shows a 'close awareness'; and, second, establishing the new ground for his own theory.[29] The two tasks in effect become one, with, as Kusch notes, 'two steps', a positive and a negative one.[30] The process of rejecting dominant theories and outlining a 'site' within thought which attempts to let discourse speak, as if from the 'outside', draws Foucault into a language which evokes an 'elusive Other', an idea predominant in certain strands of continental philosophy which has distinct religious overtones.

Foucault directly addresses the contemporary issues within the historical study of the sciences, and meticulously separates his archaeological method from associations with earlier conceptions. Such is the subtlety of his method, its undercutting of previous conceptions of thought, that he repeatedly puts forward ideas and rejects them in case confusion arises with archaeology. It is precisely this 'conceptual clear-out of notions', as Macey refers to it, that forms the 'negation' that is so keenly noted by theologians.[31] Before Foucault can explore the rise of new concepts in the history of science, such as 'discontinuity', 'rupture', 'threshold', 'limit', 'series' and 'transformation', which create new and exciting procedural issues, he has to carefully rid thought of the assumptions inherent in historical and philosophical inquiry.[32] He even acknowledges that ridding thought of certain ideas will be 'irritating', 'unpleasant', 'provocative' and 'unbearable' to many who want to retain the comfortable and pleasant characteristics of humanistic and subjective approaches.[33] The previous ways of thinking are so seductive and tempting that many shades and forms will return. By employing the negative – by showing precisely what archaeology is 'not' – clarity will hopefully be developed. Foucault outlines his approach clearly from the beginning:

> But there is a negative work to be carried out first: we must rid ourselves
> of a whole mass of notions, each of which, in its own way, diversifies
> the theme of continuity.[34]

Bernauer, reading Foucault's AK principally through the position of his
later 'Discourse on Language' (1970), shows persuasively the attempt to free
thought from certain constraints and the desire to awake from the 'anthropological sleep'.[35] The proliferation of the negative in this strategy attempts
to demarcate a new space for thought, a space which puts discourse, and
more specifically the 'statement', at the centre of the analysis. Once the
negative assumes such an importance inside a text, especially when there is a
move to step outside the conventional patterns of thinking, the theological is
evoked. This entry into the theological territory of negation is, as Bernauer
noted, fuelled by brief associations made by Foucault with the writer and
literary critic Maurice Blanchot.[36] Such passing allusions leave the doors
open to wild distortions.

The Foucault/Blanchot enigma

The references by Foucault and Blanchot to negative theology are found in a
few lines of mutual veneration in 1966 and 1986 respectively. However, these
revealing passages say more about the contemporary significance of negative
theology and its primary exponent, Pseudo-Dionysius, to the avant-garde
world, rather than indicating a full appreciation of the theological issues
involved. The references to negative theology attempt to capture, as with
Heidegger and Derrida, the 'mystery' of thought, the enigmatic play of
language and the struggle to push the boundaries of logic by referring to a
theological tradition which has ironically more to do with Neoplatonic
'unity' than post-structuralist 'dispersion'.

The theme of negative theology is introduced, not surprisingly, in
Foucault's reflections on Blanchot's 'thought from the outside', a thinking
without subjectivity, which we mentioned earlier. The references to Blanchot
take on an added significance when we consider, as Deleuze correctly
emphasises, the fact that Foucault has not 'disguised' his close association
with Blanchot's work.[37] Interlacing his own ideas with the work of
Blanchot, Foucault wrote:

> It will one day be necessary to try to define the fundamental forms and
> categories of this 'thought from the outside'. ... One might assume that
> it was born of the mystical thinking that has prowled the borders of
> Christianity since the texts of the Pseudo-Dionysius: perhaps it survived
> for a millennium or so in the various forms of negative theology.[38]

Foucault's suggestion that he and Blanchot open a trajectory of thought
in line with mystical texts is music to the ears of theological engagement.

The suggestion does seem to hold a magnetic possibility of transforming Foucault into the distorted face of 'postmodern' mystic, but such suggestions are premature and misplaced. In the very next sentence Foucault extinguishes the idea, with lines that are echoed in AK and which hold the same force of negation:

> Yet nothing is less certain: although this experience involves going 'outside of oneself', this is done ultimately in order to find oneself in the dazzling interiority of a thought that is rightfully Being and Speech, in other words, Discourse, even if it is the silence beyond all language and the nothingness beyond all being.[39]

Foucault at this point rejects the 'mystical' association because it holds certain assumptions about the individual and God which contravene his own understanding. The mystical experience is seen to step outside the self in order to reinstate the very nature of self in relationship to God. It is anchored deceptively in an idea of self–God rather than in Discourse. (This distinction is crucial in the comparison between Foucault and Dionysius, and I will explore this issue later in more detail.) The 'thought from the outside' was for Foucault very difficult to represent, because, as he states: 'Any purely reflexive discourse runs the risk of leading the experience of the outside back to the dimension of interiority.'[40] Similar arguments are found in AK, where Foucault attempts to prevent thought from re-entering the domains of prescribed thinking and subjectivity.

Despite Foucault's rejection of negative theology, Blanchot, twenty years later, picked up the idea in his own tribute to Foucault, this time with direct reference to Foucault's AK.

> Read and reread *The Archaeology of Knowledge* ... and you will be surprised to rediscover in it many a formula from negative theology.[41]

Blanchot's comment kept alive this spurious association with negative theology and mysticism, and it has slowly, despite its brevity, assumed some force on the edges of Foucauldian scholarship. It is important to note in this respect that while James Bernauer's work on Foucault and negative theology develops ideas of mysticism, they are to a large extent separate from any intrinsic link between AK and negative theology. Bernauer's work constitutes a secondary elaboration of Foucault's ideas, an application of Foucault's death of man to theology, which is very different from the mystical identification James Miller establishes in his 'narrative' account of Foucault's life.[42] The aim of this chapter is not to exclude Foucault's work from assisting theological reflection but to clearly separate that discussion from any confusion, partly created by Foucault and Blanchot, that Foucault's AK is a text which somehow stands in the tradition of Christian mysticism.

Foucault and Pseudo-Dionysius

In order to test the validity of the link between Foucault and negative theology in AK, as suggested by Foucault and Blanchot, I propose to make a detailed comparison between Foucault's AK and Pseudo-Dionysius' *Mystical Theology*, which will inescapably involve, as Paul Rorem makes clear, an examination of Pseudo-Dionysius' earlier work *The Divine Names*.[43] Such an examination will clear the ground for the dialogue between Foucault and religion by exposing the problems inherent in such an exercise and clarifying the possible areas of intersection. The study will also help to evaluate whether Foucault can justifiably be associated with Christian mysticism. Finally, by focusing on the epistemological gulf between Foucault and Pseudo-Dionysius, I will highlight the dangers of any uncritical application of such a fascinating marriage with theological discourse. It should of course be stated that Pseudo-Dionysius, influential as his work was, represents only one strand of the Christian mystical tradition. My focus on Pseudo-Dionysius is based on the fact that he is specifically mentioned by Foucault in his discussion of Blanchot; but it also reflects a distinctive intellectual tradition of Christian mysticism which can usefully interact with continental philosophy. The following comparative exercise is therefore limited to one particular tradition and can only raise a series of epistemological problems which may or may not be relevant for a different understanding of mysticism.

Before we embark on such an exercise, a number of methodological problems present themselves on the boundary of interdisciplinary dialogue. Any comparative exercise holds within it the intentions and political dynamics of two distinct areas of thought being brought together to serve a wider interest. There is a danger of prioritising one text over the other and, with texts from different historical periods, falling into anachronistic interpretations. We need to ask: whose face is lost and gained in the process?

The exercise also faces the precarious mirrors of a self-reflexive activity. How far do we use Foucault's archaeological method in the comparison between a twentieth-century French text and a late fifth-/early sixth-century Greek text? Any pretensions to construct a meta-interpretative framework are quickly sucked into the vacuum of relativity. Foucault's AK exposes the problems of disciplinary assumptions and the hidden criteria of historical and philosophical research. Does the exercise involve utilising humanistic conceptualisations, implicitly adopting continuities which hide the real ruptures between early Christian thought and post-structuralist Parisian intellectual reflection? Many of these questions extend beyond the nature of this inquiry and we must proceed cautiously into the comparative terrain.

One of the most pressing issues is the relationship between anachronistic fallacy and institutional validity in comparing Pseudo-Dionysius and modern continental philosophers. Foucault raises the issues around this question in his reflections about the basic unit of his archaeological method, the 'statement'. In exploring the nature of the statement, its 'special mode of existence' (the enunciative function), Foucault examines the 'conditions and limits' of a statement, such as the 'repeatable materiality', which explores the authority and order an institution gives to a statement regardless of its 'spatio-temporal localisation'.[44] Foucault also examines what he calls the 'field of stabilisation' imposed on a statement, which makes it possible, 'despite all the differences of enunciation, to repeat them in their identity'.[45] Some sentences remain the same but the 'statement' changes. Foucault refers, for example, to the sentence 'dreams fulfil desires', which, although it may have been repeated for centuries, 'is not the same statement in Plato and in Freud'.[46] The 'conditions of use and reinvestment' change the statement. This a vital point in regard to the constitution of negative theology; for example, how has the statement of 'negation' been changed and modified, even manipulated, between early Christian thought and modern philosophy? Foucault, examining the final condition for a statement, could be talking about any theological statement, not least 'negation', when he writes:

> Instead of being something said once and for all – and lost in the past like the result of a battle, a geological catastrophe, or the death of a king – the statement, as it emerges in its materiality, appears with a status, enters various networks and various fields of use, is subject to transferences or modifications, is integrated into operations and strategies in which its identity is maintained or effaced.[47]

Concepts and ideas are constantly changing their meaning and applicability throughout history. Such an instability, as Grace Jantzen's Foucauldian reading of the history of Christian mysticism reveals, is also evident with the idea of 'mysticism'.[48] This shows the enormous problems of myopia in comparing two texts with different epistemological foundations and different discursive formations.

In order to establish a comparative framework between Foucault and Pseudo-Dionysius, I propose, after an initial examination of the differing aims and purposes, to hold the divergences and differences, by focusing principally on the metaphorical language and isolating one strand of Foucault's text which acts as an analytical key to open the fundamental characteristics of each work. This analytical key is found in the group of ideas around secrecy, hiddenness and the concept of 'silence'. By examining the ideas around 'silence', it will be possible to bring to light three major questions in the comparative exercise, namely the issues of transcendence, unity/difference and the question of the human/subject. These questions show how the primary differences between 'silence' are worked through at other levels within each work, exposing the disparity between a discourse on God and a discourse on Discourse. It is precisely the relation between these two discourses which forms the final question as to whether Foucault's AK constitutes a negative theology or a mystical text.

Foucault's archaeological project

It is vital in any comparative assessment to understand the ground from which a work organises itself, its epistemological foundations and purposes. Once we embark on such an exercise it soon becomes apparent that Foucault's AK and the works of Pseudo-Dionysius could not be further removed. They are in fact so diametrically opposed as to offer in each form a negation of the other! As Foucault is passionately opposed to ideas of Unity, Cause and Transcendence, so Pseudo-Dionysius is ardently a Neoplatonist defender of such ideas. Foucault and Pseudo-Dionysius may hold a superficial similarity, a mystique of the author and the obscure language of negation, but the ground from which they operate is so different as to make one wonder why such a comparison, beyond the generalisations of history, is made at all.

We have already noted how Foucault in AK is attempting to challenge theories in the history of science, and it is now important to explore how the work seeks to carry out its objective and construct a new approach. Foucault's overall aim is to 'uncover' and explore the 'consequences' for historical knowledge of such new principles as 'discontinuity, rupture, threshold, limit, series, and transformation'.[49] In consequence, he is opposed to the unities of thought such as the book, the author and the *oeuvre*, which constantly impinge themselves on historical work. The attempt to move beyond this requires a number of careful strategies, and within a few pages the nature of Foucault's task becomes apparent. He seeks, for example, to 'uncover', 'suspend', 'question', 'disconnect' and 'renounce', 'define', 'interrogate', 'break up' and 'replace'.[50] And later in the work he refers to 'attacking', 'unravelling' and the attempt to 'invert arrangements' and 'usual values' in order to 'practise a quite different history'.[51] Foucault's historical work required this excavation of ideas.

> We must question those ready-made syntheses, those groupings that we normally accept before any examination, those links whose validity is recognised from the outset; we must oust those forms and obscure forces by which we usually link the discourse of one man [*sic*] with that of another; they must be driven out from the darkness in which they reign.[52]

Foucault moves away from unifying concepts to a new phenomenologically determined position. He continually refers to his method as one of 'analysis' and 'description', but these are very distinct procedures. In the attempt to avoid misunderstanding, he points out that 'the analysis of discursive formations is opposed to many customary descriptions'.[53] It follows the phenomenological features of avoiding interpretations, establishing 'no hierarchy of value', and preventing any proposals for a 'real' or essential meaning by holding to the central feature of 'differences'.[54]

Foucault develops a new vantage point, what we have previously referred to as a kind of Heideggerian 'clearing'. The debt of modern French philosophy to Heidegger has previously been well documented by Descombes and elaborated with specific relation to Foucault by Dreyfus and Rabinow. The effects of this influence are particularly manifest in AK.[55] Although Foucault's project is more localised than Heidegger's 'destruction' of the history of Western ontology, similar processes of 'shaking off' previous ways of thinking are in operation. However, it is interesting to note that Heidegger, like Kant before him, did not view his project as simply negative, but as a positive recognition of 'limits'.[56] Foucault does at one point seem to suggest that he is not completely rejecting other methods in the history of science, but rather establishing their constraints and assumptions. When exploring the various unities in the history of ideas, for example, he seems to soften his approach.

> They [forms of continuity] must not be rejected definitively of course, but the tranquility with which they are accepted must be disturbed ... .[57]

The fundamental phenomenological aim of AK is to move from unifying concepts to a process of open analysis and description.

> Archaeology describes discourses ... .[58]

Once we have established that archaeology is an analysis and description of discourses, we have to ask what specifically about discourse is being analysed and described. The focus of the descriptions is the 'groupings', 'relations' and 'rules' of the emergence of 'statements', which Foucault calls 'discursive formations'.[59] The important factor is that continuities, syntheses and unities of thought 'do not come about of themselves, but are always the result of a construction'.[60] Foucault attempts to establish a phenomenological reduction by carefully examining the discourse and 'bracketing out' other categories in the history of ideas. His work therefore seeks to establish the statement's 'existence and the rules that govern its appearance'; he seeks in effect the 'rules of formation'.[61] These 'rules' must not be understood in the strict sense; rather they refer to patterns of relation between statements which establish certain constructions, and, in consequence, they are open to change.[62]

The descriptive work is therefore about 'mapping' and 'surveying' a whole dispersion of statements. Such an exercise can identify a number of forms within discourse without prejudging historical situations.[63] Foucault, grounded in the central spatial metaphor of his work, refers to the 'regularities', 'multiple relations', the 'relations of resemblance, proximity, distance, difference, transformation' and, finally, the 'discontinuities, ruptures, gaps' and 'redistributions'.[64] While he acknowledges that discourse has its 'own forms of sequence and succession', it is important to note that the 'practice' of discourse is determined by a whole series of complex relations between institutions, and involves a whole array of economic and social processes, what he calls 'non-discursive practices'.[65]

The fundamental task of Foucault's archaeology is the attempt to create a free space to observe 'statements', to allow them to be held in their moment of 'irruption' and 'occurrence' without fabrication.[66] His aim is therefore to hold 'dispersion' and 'discontinuity' without any 'reduction' to a 'pre-established horizon'.[67] As he writes in response to his imaginary inter-locutor:

> It is a discourse about discourses. … It is trying to deploy a dispersion that can never be reduced to a single system of differences, a scattering that is not related to absolute axes of reference; it is trying to operate a decentring that leaves no privileged centre.[68]

Such a procedure, as Bernauer emphasizes, positively promotes 'difference' at the centre of thought. According to Foucault, reason and history are created, as are we, through difference, which the history of ideas attempts to avoid.[69]

Foucault writes from a post-Enlightenment, post-Heideggerian and post-Freudian platform, and his critique is shaped by these very contours. The shift from a technical methodological treatise in the history of science to one that, as Louth has argued, arises from the context of liturgy in the early Christian church requires a huge adjustment.[70] In the writings of Pseudo-Dionysius we enter a very different atmosphere shaped not by Bachelard, Canguilhem and Blanchot but by Plato, Plotinus and Proculus. Such writers from antiquity would not occupy Foucault until his later work on the history of sexuality, when the rigours of the archaeological method had faded.

Pseudo-Dionysius

Pseudo-Dionysius' work *The Divine Names* (hereafter DN) is, with the summaritive text *The Mystical Theology* (MT), a 'systematic consideration' of the names for God.[71] It is constructed out of the Neoplatonic framework of Plotinus (AD 205–70), a triadic and hierarchical structure of the One, Intelligence and the Soul.[72] These are linked by a huge process of emanation and return, a movement from the One to the multiple at the base of the 'chain of being'. This should not necessarily be seen as a spatial reference, although it is often perceived in this way.[73]

In Plotinus' scheme there was a 'flight from the alone to the Alone', a kind of 'homecoming', from the multiple to the One through the chain of being.[74] Pseudo-Dionysius' work is based on this structure with an inter-weaving of biblical inspiration and liturgical practice. Dionysius embeds within the Neoplatonic framework his belief in a 'revealed and yet transcendent' God.[75] It is this tension that creates the perplexing quality of the Dionysian corpus and of Christian thought in general. God transcends knowledge and yet is knowable through revelation in scripture and worship, a paradox that utilises negation in order to sustain itself. Dionysius, using 'only what scripture has disclosed', 'affirms' (cataphatic theology), in hierarchical order, the Unity and Trinity (*The Theological Representations*), the conceptual names (DN) and the perceptible and multiple symbols (*The Symbolic Theology*) of God in the Platonic process of 'emanation'.[76] He then in the process of 'return', moving back to the Unity of the One, 'negates' (apophatic theology) the previous affirmations, forming a crescendo at the end of MT in the denial of negation (DN and MT).[77] The primary aim of this process is for the Soul (Mind) to find union with God by moving through the various intermediary stages, a process of intellectual 'purification'.

> The fundamental goal of the Dionysian journey and the Dionysian corpus is ... to pass beyond sense perception and contemplative conceptions in order to be united with God beyond all knowledge.[78]

The idea of negation in Dionysius is grounded in this very process of reaching towards God; affirmation and negation maintain the central idea of God's supreme transcendence. The 'key concept' of the Dionysian epistemological and theological system is, according to Rorem's extensive commentary, found in this idea of 'transcendence', and is expressed by Dionysius at the beginning of DN.

> And if all knowledge is of that which is and is limited to the realm of the existent, then whatever transcends being must also transcend knowledge.[79]

God transcends human knowledge in Dionysius' system, and this categorically implies that revelation, which is expressed in human constructs, must be simultaneously affirmed and negated. The negation in Dionysius is grounded in a preservation of God's supremacy not in a concern for Discourse as in Foucault.

The initial outline reveals the different levels of negation operating in Foucault and Pseudo-Dionysius. What is particularly illuminating is the way the primary concepts of Discourse and God interplay within a language of negation. This 'parallel' sequence of negation finds support in Kirsteen Anderson's discussion of the religious perspectives in a number of French Protestant thinkers (Barthes, Camus, Ponge and Sartre). She highlights the way 'mid-twentieth-century awareness projects onto language issues which previously were theorised around the concept of God'.[80] This intriguing suggestion opens up the question of the relation between God and Discourse and creates the danger, so pervasive in many contemporary discussions of mysticism, that 'parallel' structures and similarity of 'issues' imply a shared object. This is a premature association, for the same gesture in one culture can have a very different meaning in another. The projection of theological issues onto language is possible in the early work of Foucault because of the way, in his exploration of discourse, 'language arrives at its own edge'.[81] At the edge of language or the edge of thought itself, we start to fumble, fall, bruise ourselves, we enter the labyrinth and become entangled in paradox, parody and negation. But the negation to find the edge of language rests on fundamentally different metaphorical registers and conceptual models to the negation in Pseudo-Dionysius which seeks to find God.

Silence and the secret enigma

In order to embrace the issues more clearly, I want to show the fundamental differences between Foucault and Dionysius by focusing on the issue of 'silence'. The concept of silence and the way it operates is of a very different order in the two works. The trajectory of this inquiry into silence is once again taken from Foucault's 1966 text on Blanchot, where the issue of negation and negative theology first arises. In his exploration of Blanchot's work, Foucault sees language as reaching its edge and entering 'a void that will efface it'. He continues:

> Into that void it must go, consenting to come undone in the rumbling, in the immediate negation of what it says, in a silence that is not the intimacy of a secret but a pure outside where words endlessly unravel.[82]

Written only a few years earlier than AK, these comments on Blanchot clearly resound in the later methodological work, reflecting Foucault's preoccupation with the conundrum of language and its limits in the 1960s. The procedure of negation in AK cannot be understood without reference to the Blanchot text. It is hard to believe that Foucault could have employed the extensive levels of negation in AK without having in mind what he had written with regard to Blanchot, a fact that would seem to be confirmed by Blanchot's own comments about negation and AK. In the model of negation Foucault suggests, the silence is linked to the jointly tied ideas of 'secrecy' and 'hiddenness', and it is the quality of this relation which determines the very nature of silence. The nature of silence is qualitatively different in the works of Foucault and Dionysius because of the way they respond to the idea of secrecy and hiddenness within this concept.

The concept of silence is central to understanding the work of the early Foucault, a point confirmed by his research assistant François Ewald.[83] The idea takes on an added significance when we explore the etymological root of the word 'mystical' to which Foucault's archaeology has been compared. The word 'mystical' is originally found in the pre-Christian context of the

Mystery religions, where it was associated with the secret rites of initiation. The word derives from the Greek verb meaning 'to close', and more specifically, as Louis Bouyer's examination reveals, 'to close the eyes'.[84] In the early church, as Bouyer goes on to show, the word 'mystical' is found predominantly in relation to the interpretation of scripture and liturgy. This view of the 'mystical' pertains in the works of Dionysius and receives specific mention in the textual notes to prevent confusion with the modern understanding. The Colin Luibheid translation of MT qualifies the term *'mustikos'* as meaning 'something "mysterious" or secret or hidden'.[85] Paul Rorem in his own commentary also places emphasis on the 'hidden'.[86] Clearly Dionysius is not referring to the modern psychological conception of mysticism, which, as Grace Jantzen so persuasively shows, derives from William James.[87] Jantzen, in her later work, *Power, Gender and Christian Mysticism*, also demonstrates how mysticism is socially constructed, evolving through different historical periods according to power and gender.[88] This work enriches our discussion by showing how any interrelation between Foucault and mysticism holds within it specific assumptions and forces which 'reinvent' the 'mystical' in accordance with the dynamics of institutional power and gender assumptions. The reinvention of mysticism in relation to the reified notions of contemporary philosophy implicitly reawakens certain religious notions according to the values and assumptions of post-structuralist thought.

By focusing specifically on the texts of Foucault and Dionysius through the issue of silence and secrecy, I wish to shift the discussion to the question of the dynamics of negation in relation to Discourse and God, which I regard as distinct from, although related to, the politics of 'who counts as a mystic'. This shift is supported by the understanding of *'mustikos'* in Dionysius' MT as 'mysterious', 'secret' and 'hidden' and the specific use by Dionysius of the word 'silence'.[89] Foucault, who does not use the word mystical in AK, does use the word 'silence' about twenty times (*'le silence'* or *'le mutisme'*), and in conjunction with this term employs the idea of 'secret' and 'hidden'.[90] It is also important to note, as we have seen in chapter 3, how Foucault is fascinated by the ideas of secrecy in the work of Raymond Roussel and René Magritte. The close relation of Foucault's studies on these two surrealist thinkers (1963 and 1968 respectively) to AK (1969) shows the importance of these works for understanding Foucault's use of silence and his early interest in the limits of thought.[91]

Dionysius negates every conception of God in the attempt to preserve the Transcendent reality. God is ungraspable, and as the language fades Dionysius is forced to use the third person pronoun (it) in repeated succession as the final signifier for the reality beyond all knowledge. At the point of exhaustion, in the final movement, as language reaches its edge, Dionysius is forced to recognise yet another limitation and falls into negating negation.

There is no speaking of it, nor name nor knowledge of it. ... It is beyond assertion and denial. We make assertions and denials of what is next to it, but never of it, for it is both beyond every assertion, being the perfect and unique cause of all things, and, by virtue of its pre-eminently simple and absolute nature, free of every limitation, beyond every limitation; it is also beyond every denial.[92]

Dionysius masterfully creates a mystery beyond all human images and conceptions, even beyond the negations. He carefully deconstructs thought and leaves, as Rorem concedes, 'only silence'.[93] The skill and force of the work builds on the basic premise of Transcendence to undercut and devalue the human capacity to understand God in an intellectual rather than erotic or emotive mysticism. In adoration of God, Dionysius creates a dominant and subservient mechanism which positions a powerful mystery outside of everything. The mystery is unattainable in its entirety and assumes its power by its very hiddenness.

Dionysius' system in fact only works on the grounds of a faith which holds a central affirmation in the crowd of negations. Without the centrality of faith the negations would be meaningless. This idea is effectively captured in the image of the sculptor in Dionysius' MT.

We would be like sculptors who set out to carve a statue. They remove every obstacle to the pure view of the hidden image, and simply by this act of *clearing aside* they show up the beauty which is hidden.[94]

In Foucault's work there are no 'hidden images' to be discovered, rather continually shifting sands which form different patterns. This is a key difference in understanding the silence or hidden mystery in Foucault and Dionysius.

Foucault on the whole presents a critical perspective of silence as a mechanism which distorts by preserving hidden assumptions. There are basically three ways in which he strategically uses the idea of silence in AK: first, as a means to reject the underlying assumptions in the history of ideas; second, to bring the analysis of history back to discursive events; and, third, linked to this, as a way of preventing misconceptions of archaeology, and the 'statement' in particular, as a hidden or secret discourse or event. In other words, silence for Foucault is a way of tactically repressing the hidden assumptioms of knowledge.

In Dionysius the 'hidden silence' orientates every other reality. Foucault, working from a very different perspective, is critical of such silent assumptions in the history of ideas, which he sees determining the reading of history and the understanding of reality.[95] The history of ideas seeks to find a 'deeper level', creating a silent undercurrent.[96] Foucault rejects the silences and hidden origins in their preservation of the controlling unities within thought and cautions against the view 'that beyond any apparent beginning, there is always a secret origin – so secret and so fundamental that it can never be quiet grasped in itself'.[97] Although this is a critique of the history of ideas, it indicates how Foucault is suspicious of any *a priori* assumptions outside the phenomenon of discourse.

Foucault is in this respect very careful not to mislead the reader into thinking that archaeology is a secret discourse below the manifest. In one of many corrections against the false conception of archaeology, he writes:

> We do not seek below what is manifest the half silent murmur of another discourse ... .[98]

The tension within Foucault's discourse is to be found at the level of presenting a series of ideas which act to transform previous perceptions. There is a kind of 'knowledge', as in Dionysius, in forgetting or rejecting knowledge, the process which creates the necessity for negation.[99] The different types of 'knowledge' and the process of negation show the acute significance of the problematic of translating Foucault's work from the French. The English translation uses the single word 'knowledge' with Foucault's words *'connaissance'* and *'savoir'* in brackets. The distinction is introduced by Foucault in his revision of *The Birth of the Clinic*. *'Connaissance'* refers to a kind of disciplinary knowledge, what Bernauer usefully translates as 'cognition', and *'savoir'* refers to the conditions of knowledge which makes *'connaissance'* possible.[100] There are two levels of thought, as Bernauer notes, a kind of conscious conceptual level and an unconscious, preconceptual level.[101] The idea of silence swivels on this distinction in Foucault's AK.

Foucault does not want to give the idea that his work is yet another secret formula or unity underpinning thought (Megill's idea of parody), and he therefore provides a number of careful qualifications for his idea of the 'statement'. Acknowledging the paradox, he rejects that the statement evades the verbal performance and resides hidden. While it is not given in the same way as grammatical or logical structure, it is not a secret entity. 'The statement is neither visible nor hidden.'[102] It rather holds a 'quasi-invisibility': it is 'implied, but never made explicit'.[103] The problem of perceiving the statement as another unity is transcended by viewing it as 'characterising' the fact of 'givenness' and 'the way' a statement is given, 'not what is given in' the statement. In order to recognise the statement a new level of awareness or 'attitude' is required.[104] The key to this safeguard against secrecy and the creation of another unity is the desire to preserve the phenomenology of discourses by avoiding interpretations.[105]

Foucault refuses to accept the 'silent monuments' preserved in history and seeks to bring the analysis back to a phenomenological perspective, to the surface of events, to discourse.[106] The aim is 'not to neutralize discourse' or 'reach what remains silently anterior to it' but to allow discourse to 'emerge in its own complexity'.[107] Foucault's aim is not therefore to document the 'history of the referent'; it is not to grasp the 'object' or 'thing' presented. What he seeks is not the object outside discourse, but 'the regular formation of objects that emerge *only in* discourse'.[108] Silence, secrecy and hiddenness in this perspective all hold a very negative quality in contrast to the positive dimension of silence and the hidden in Dionysius. However, Foucault's view of silence is far more complex than this initial outline indicates and is not limited to this negative understanding. There is a subtle shift, only on a few occasions, when Foucault reaches the 'edges of language', when a silence emerges which is a 'positive unconscious of knowledge'.[109] At this edge, silence is 'not the intimacy of a secret but a pure outside where words endlessly unravel'.[110] This occurs at the level of what Foucault calls the 'prediscursive' or 'preconceptual'.

> Behind the visible façade of the system, one posits the rich uncertainty of disorder; and beneath the thin surface of discourse, the whole mass of a largely silent development [*devenir*]: a 'presystematic' that is not of the order of the system; a 'prediscursive' that belongs to an *essential silence*.[111]

The idea of an 'essential silence' (*essentiel mutisme*) is extremely problematic and it is difficult to know precisely how Foucault uses this term. Such an idea does not rest easily inside an archaeological methodology. In chapter 2 we noted how there is some conceptual confusion in Foucault's understanding of silence, and at this point it is important to remember that he does not see this silence as exterior to discourse. Silence is rather somehow implicit within discourse at a 'prediscursive' level. As Foucault makes clear, the 'prediscursive is still discursive'.[112] This is crucial for distinguishing between Foucault and Dionysius. In Dionysius' view there is something 'beyond words', something outside human understanding.[113] In Foucault, however, we exist in a set of 'multiple relations'; there is no inside or outside, rather the labyrinth of language.

> We do not live inside a void that could be coloured with diverse shades of light, we live inside a set of relations that delineates sites which are irreducible to one another and absolutely not superimposable on one another.[114]

This is not to say, as some critics of post-structuralist thinking argue, that there is 'nothing but' language, but that the world is shaped by a set of discursive structures.

In AK Foucault gives priority to the discursive event and the relations with what he calls 'non-discursive practices', such as institutional, political and economic factors within and surrounding discourse.[115] Theological conceptions, like ideas of the void, are caught in a whole set of discursive relations and cannot be extrapolated in order to write a 'history of the referent'.[116] In his attempt to hold the phenomenological dimension, Foucault would have to identify the underlying discursive 'rules' which determined such ideas as 'God' or the 'mystical'.[117] Theology, as the comparison with Dionysius reveals, is held within the limits of discourse and is built on the assumption of certain unities and transcendental ideas. The theological negations in Dionysius are built upon an epistemological foundation that Foucault opposes in his archaeological method. Foucault breaks up fixed conceptions into a network of relations. To apply a definitive historical category to the process of breaking down unities, in the hope that Foucault will be finally positioned, is to dream of a sieve holding water.

Transcendence, unity and the human subject

The tensions and epistemological frictions between Foucault's AK and the works of Dionysius are evident from the different development of the idea of 'silence'. The apparent similarity in language and mystery of the respective texts is shown to move in a different orbit. In conclusion to this chapter, I would like to reinforce these fundamental differences by identifying three central ideas from Dionysius' corpus which provide further evidence of the problems of positioning Foucault within the former's 'mystical' context. In this assessment a number of implicit oppositions can be identified. It is these oppositions which show how Foucault's work not only holds a distinct epistemological framework but positively undermines the Dionysian mystical edifice and traditional theology as a whole. Foucault challenges theological thinking by moving from a discourse of religious transcendence to one of radical immanence. It is precisely this move which brings us to the heart of Foucault's religious question.

Transcendence and the metaphor of space

We have already noted how the idea of transcendence is a key factor in the Dionysian scheme where there are continual references to the 'transcendent Cause' and the 'Transcendent One'.[118] Although Foucault is working within a different discursive field, the opposition to the 'transcendent' is equally applicable to theological modes of thinking which have so powerfully shaped Western thought. The critique of 'transcendence' is, with the idea of the subject, a major axis of AK and Foucault seeks to undermine its predominance in the history of ideas. In a Heideggerian phenomenological tone Foucault repeatedly attacks *a priori* forms of knowledge and the 'historico-transcendental thematic'.[119] He wants to free thought from those restrictive unities which secretly control our historical and philosophical perception.

A creative study by Michael Sells into the nature of mystical languages points out that a 'formal approach' to the tradition of apophasis (negation) could be broad enough to include a whole range of texts.[120] It is clearly possible, as Sells shows, to 'extend' apophasis as a technique and identify 'comparable elements' with such fields as psychoanalysis, but this is not 'the same thing' as classical apophatic mysticism.[121] Sells, while recognising that his proposal 'is not a formula', attempts to identify a number of features of apophatic discourse in the West. Although there are problems with such a 'formal description', it is striking that Sells places great emphasis on the 'radical dialectic of transcendence and immanence' at the heart of what he labels 'languages of unsaying'.[122] The differences between Foucault and Dionysius are clearly manifest at this crucial point.

The rejection of models of transcendence can also be seen in the different function and structure of metaphor in Foucault and Pseudo-Dionysius. They are both grounded in opposing models of metaphorical reality, the latter based in the fixed Ideas and Forms of Plato and the former immersed in the changing dispersions of a 'post-structuralist' discourse. While the metaphors function in Foucault's work to displace certainty, the metaphors in Dionysius have a more objective function to secure the reality of a transcendent God.[123] The difference emerges in the displacement which occurs between metaphors of 'light' and 'space'.

Megill, following Derrida's own critique, argues that Foucault was unable to escape the logocentric metaphors of light. He highlights the way Foucault's use of visual and spatial metaphors are still grounded on the ideas of 'darkness and light', which Derrida regarded as 'the founding metaphor of Western philosophy as metaphysics'.[124] The predominating metaphor of light is clearly revealed in the Platonic scheme of Dionysius. In *The Mystical Theology* (MT) such metaphors of light/knowing and darkness/unknowing reach, as Rorem notes, a 'peak', and are twisted with such oxymorons as 'brilliant darkness'.[125] Dionysius' MT also builds on metaphors of height, movement and ascent in conjunction with a wider Neoplatonic framework.[126]

Although this fundamental relationship between the logocentric metaphors of Western philosophy would bring Dionysius and Foucault into a closer relationship, it is important to realise that there is a fundamentally different emphasis given to the 'spatial' metaphor in Foucault as opposed to the 'light' metaphor in Pseudo-Dionysius. While Megill shows the usage of visual and spatial metaphors in Foucault's early work, the specific link to the logocentric metaphor of light is not fully substantiated. The documentation of the visual metaphor has been explored in recent Foucault scholarship by Certeau, Jay and Flynn in their studies of the 'gaze', the metaphor often causing self-disruption, but the spatial metaphor remains more open.[127] There is an intrinsic bias within the logocentric critique to understand 'space' in visual terms instead of registering the relation of the metaphor to physical sensation, to a tactile experience. This particular nuance of 'space' is often neglected and can position Foucault's work slightly differently. The logocentric categorisation of visual and spatial metaphors into the dominant idea of light also blurs the specific differences, modifications and ruptures within the 'light-centred' tradition that Megill adopts in his reading of Foucault. In this sense the archaeological method can be played back against logocentric evaluations in highlighting the controlling determinants of such an historical assessment; it, in effect, blankets the entire tradition and fails to allow the archaeological dispersion and irregularity of any metaphorical usage.

The spatial metaphor is an important metaphorical variant, even if it still remains within a singular tradition of light. The differing metaphorical structures operating in Dionysius and Foucault confirm this differentiation. Dionysius' metaphors of light and ascent determine a singular direction of thought towards an Ideal form, while, as we shall see, Foucault's spatial metaphors help to break up singular constructions by creating something which is fluid and constantly interacting.

The importance of space in Foucault's work can be seen in the earlier 1967 lecture 'Of Other Spaces'.[128] Foucault places emphasis on the 'form of relations among sites', sites which were 'defined by relations of proximity between points and elements', described formally, according to him, as 'series, trees and grids'.[129] This is precisely the type of analysis that Foucault uses in the description of statements in AK and which opposes the celestial hierarchies of Dionysius.

By lifting the metaphors from Foucault's AK we can very quickly see the way space is employed and how the idea of movement across surfaces is conveyed. The unity of discourse is determined not by the stability of the object but by 'the space in which various objects emerge and are continuously transformed'.[130] It is the creation of the discursive space which is central to Foucault's enterprise, and these spaces are created by the relationships between statements. The description of statements involves a whole array of spatial metaphors: Foucault refers to 'surfaces', 'networks', 'domains', 'regions', 'distribution', 'proximity', 'nexus', 'web', 'map', 'sites', 'grid', 'constellations', 'positions' and 'configurations'.[131] We are presented with a kaleidoscope of statements, different patterns forming in relation to the numerous positions of each statement.

Although employed in very different ways, the images in Foucault's work are found scattered throughout 'post-structuralist' discourse and the deconstructive interplay of language. It is the proximity and relationship of language on a surface which is central to wider 'post-structuralist' debates in religion. Don Cupitt, for example, picks up this theme in his image of the pond skater which he introduces in a work exploring Derridean ideas. He writes explaining the title of his book *The Long-Legged Fly*:

> I take the pond skater as an image of religious thought in an age of thoroughgoing reductionism. It is light, resourceful, fastmoving and well able to survive. The tendency in many quarters is to reduce reality to, or model reality as, no more than a field of vibrations or differences: packets of wavelets in the texture of space-time, ripples of sensation on

the surface of the human body, patterned pulses in an electrical circuit, a sideways play of signs.[132]

Theology, for Cupitt, must be 'horizontal', and this clearly demonstrates the paradigmatic shift from Dionysius' metaphorical structure to those found in contemporary forms of discourse.[133] The ideas may be bound in a logocentric prison but the existence within these walls has a profoundly different effect upon the understanding of life. This shift in metaphoric structure reflects Foucault's opposition to traditional theological models and the move to reposition religious discourse in the 'spaces' of the body and the political rather than in the transcendent hierarchies of Dionysius. Foucault's AK breaks the mould of traditional religious discourse and seeks to map a new space of 'religious' thinking.

Unity/difference

Dionysius' corpus is interwoven with the basic Neoplatonic conception of the One.[134] Although Dionysius talks of difference in the Godhead as Trinity and the nature of difference in God as 'providentially available to all things', these are technical variations from an image of simplicity, truth and unity at the centre of all things.[135]

> The reality is that all things are contained beforehand in and are embraced by the One in its capacity as an inherent unity.[136]

The dominance of this theme of the One creates a striking dissonance with Foucault's register of 'differences'.[137] The good has a single cause for Dionysius and evil numerous causes. Evil is associated with 'inharmonious commingling of discordances'.[138]

> Evil things are not immobile and eternally unchanging but indeterminate, indefinite, and bearing themselves differently in different things.[139]

The epistemological gulf between Foucault and Dionysius is again revealed in this opposition of unity and difference. It exposes the association of 'difference' with 'evil' which has undermined the heterology within society and created an intolerance of the Other within Western thought, not least seen in relation to women, 'race' and ethnicity, and to homosexuality. Although the language carries a slightly different emphasis, the references to God as the 'same' in Dionysius and Foucault's challenge to ideas of the 'same' in OT are not unrelated factors.[140] The desire to preserve Oneness and Unity in Dionysius is contrasted with Foucault's retrieval of 'differences' and the valorisation of what is 'different'. Dionysius has to carefully and tactically bring multiplicity back into the One, while Foucault creates multiplicities, differences and dispersions. In Dionysius there is a single

Truth but for Foucault there are multiple truths created in a fluid movement of discourses.[141]

In opposition to the history of ideas, which attempts to dissolve contradictions, archaeology aims to describe the 'different spaces of dissension'.[142] Foucault wants to hold ruptures and contradictions within thought in order to break the controlling unities, in contrast to Dionysius, who attempts to overcome differences in the One. Foucault, as we shall see later, 'disperses' theology into the space of the 'Other', the forgotten dimensions of religious discourse. He is concerned with what he calls 'heterotopias', a space outside all others, the 'Other space' or 'counter-sites'.[143] The key aspect of a heterotopia is the quality of a 'hidden exclusion', sacred or forbidden, as in his examples of brothels and Jesuit colonies in South America.[144] Foucault's religious question can be seen as an attempt to enter the 'heterotopias' of religion and in the process destroy the boundaries between the sacred and profane.

Human/subject

A central polemic in Foucault's AK is to challenge the tendency in modern thought to ground understanding in a 'transcendental subject' and a 'psychological subjectivity'.[145] Foucault was heavily critical of the ways humanism, anthropology and psychology had introduced the idea of the 'sovereignty of the subject' into modern thought and sought through his archaeological method to undermine such modes of thinking.[146] He had previously shown in OT how psychoanalysis, linguistics and ethnology had 'decentred the subject' and announced his, now famous, declaration of the 'death of man'.[147] Foucault concludes his 1966 work OT with the powerful image of the sea erasing the face of 'man'. The theme is recalled at the end of AK in a statement he realises some will find difficult to hear.

> Discourse is not life; its time is not your time; in it, you will not be reconciled to death; you may have killed God beneath the weight of all that you have said; but don't imagine that with all you are saying, you will make a man [*sic*] that will live longer than He.[148]

Foucault's language of negation is introduced to partly counteract the 'sovereign subject' in the history of thought. The idea of the 'subject' is a modern construction which has no parallel in the work of Dionysius. As we previously noted, the specific definitions given in the footnotes of the English edition of Dionysius' work caution against translating the idea of the 'mystical' into the terms of the modern subject. This caution needs to be extended to other ideas and sequences of thought, especially 'negation'.

Dionysius uses negation to put the human being in correct perspective against the background of his Christian and Neoplatonic belief in the ultimate transcendence of God. The negation is introduced to deal with the dichotomy between God and humanity. Foucault is not working within this trajectory of thought. In his work the negation is introduced to separate certain constructed unities in human thought from the multiple relations of discourse. While Foucault aims to reach a kind of phenomenology of all thought by returning to Discourse, Dionysius recognises the limits of 'discursive reasoning' in the face of God's transcendence.[149]

In one sense Dionysius appears to offer a more radical negation. He explores different ways of talking about God and then surmounts them all. Foucault is only content to negate those conceptions which diminish the importance of discursive relations with all their irruptions and dispersions, although he realises the tensions in such a study. He does not devalue the human being against an idea of God; he devalues the 'transcendental subject' against the multiple discourses human beings create. Foucault remains within the human realm of discursive relations because he is suspicious of any transcendent unity which restricts and confines humanity. It soon becomes clear, in this sense, that it is Foucault who offers the more radical model because he suspends the certainty of the referent and remains with the uncertainty of the network of statements. Dionysius was concerned with how we think about God and Foucault about how we think; both ran into the complex labyrinth of discourse and negations, eventually disappearing at different points into different types of silence. For Dionysius this silence was in the face of a transcendent God, and for Foucault, who extinguishes the 'subject', the silence was at the limits of discourse.

The archaeological method, in its attempt to follow through issues in the 1960s about language and discourse, brought Foucault's work into a confrontation with a 'religious question' at the boundaries of language and 'silence'. This 'religious question', however, arose not from adopting a mystical language of negation but from suspending the heart of traditional religious discourse. Foucault's AK is opposed to the theological thinking of Dionysius and opposed to the traditions of Western theology. But Foucault did not simply dismiss religion in his wider work; rather he developed a critique of religion through his 'spiritual corporality' and, as we shall see, in a 'political spirituality'. What he presented was a sub-textual critique of the epistemological foundations of religious thinking.

6 Body and belief

> It would be wrong to say that the soul is an illusion, or an ideological effect.
> On the contrary, it exists, it has reality, it is produced permanently around,
> on, within the body by the functioning of power that is exercised on those
> punished – and in a more general way, on those one supervises, trains and
> corrects ... .
>
> Foucault (1975a) *Discipline and Punish*, p. 29

In the 1960s Foucault's 'religious question' could be understood as a critique
of religion developed in terms of a 'spiritual corporality', but this perspective gradually faced some tensions and began to change its emphasis in the
1970s. The issues of a 'spiritual corporality' were still present but they were
slowly sublimated into a wider historical and political framework. This was
brought about by the gradual shift towards a new critical perspective in
Foucault's 'religious question'. The results of this shift meant that the ideas
of a 'spiritual corporality' were no longer interpreted in the context of
language, the death of God and Sadeian erotics (religious ideas) but rather
reconstituted according to a new conceptual apparatus of discipline, domination and control (religious practice). There was a shift of emphasis away
from a purely discursive spiritual body to a more inclusive non-discursive
analysis of the mechanisms and technologies of power. In this process we
also see the move from reclaiming the unsaid and silent in religious
discourse to an examination of the inseparable components of the manifest
and spoken. The body still remained the principal focus of Foucault's 'religious question' through the adoption of a Nietzschean genealogy, but it was
relocated and redefined in terms of power and governmentality. These ideas
gradually evolved in the late 1970s to form a 'political spirituality'. However,
in the early part of the decade there was much more ambivalence in
Foucault's work about the relationship between the body, belief and religious practice.

In Foucault's 1975 work *Discipline and Punish* (DP) the spiritual is redefined through a discussion of what he calls the 'modern soul', the surface
of disciplinary practices which shape the body. In this interconnection of
body and soul Foucault continued to suspend the traditional coordinates of

religion by challenging the dualistic ontology. This critique is developed by focusing not on belief but on religious practice. This proves to be a very confused aspect of Foucault's sub-text and the subsequent discussion of Christianity in his *History of Sexuality*. There is little appreciation in Foucault's work of the inseparability of religious ideas, practices and the surface of the body. He assumes that aspects of religion can be explored by isolating the social manifestations of religion without considering how theological ideas have informed the social context. The fragmentary exploration of religious themes means that while Foucault maps the soul onto the body by considering monasticism and religious discipline, he fails to ground the work in the underlying power of theological ideology.

Belief and practice

The location of the archival process in the body dominates Foucault's work and has produced a whole corpus of secondary literature, particularly from the field of sociology.[1] While this work has powerfully illuminated Foucault studies, there continues to be little appreciation of the complex religious dimensions involved in this exercise. It is possible to identify two main aspects to the question of the body in Foucault's religious excursions: first, the question of religion as a social phenomenon; and, second, the philosophical-theological question of embodied thinking.[2] The first dimension is captured in the work of the sociology of religion and developed cogently by such writers as Bryan Turner. Turner uses Foucault's work to devise a 'materialist' sociology of religion grounded in Foucault's 1975 assertion that the question of the body must precede questions of ideology.[3] Foucault's methodology enables Turner to show how religion cannot be 'divorced from questions of the body'. As Turner later explains:

> The object of these investigations is the emergence of discursive and non-discursive practices by which the human body is organised and controlled within the social space.[4]

There is no doubt that from 1975 Foucault's principal concern with religion is as a social practice. He is, for example, not principally concerned with questions of soteriology or doctrine. We have already seen in chapter 2 how his later work on Christianity focused on its confessional rather than its salvific dimensions. In 1982 he made the distinction between Christianity's preoccupation with the 'history of beliefs' and the 'history of real practices', a strategy through which he deliberately extracts belief in his later discussion of the 'technologies of self' in Christianity.[5] This prioritisation of practice over belief is highlighted by Nancy Fraser in her appraisal of the modern modalities of power in Foucault's work.

Foucault's genealogy of modern power establishes that power touches people's lives more fundamentally through their social practices than through their beliefs.[6]

There is, however, a tension in Foucault's later work on Christianity when belief and social practice are separated so absolutely, for religious belief informs practice. Foucault was very much aware of this fact when he saw that the 'conditions and rules of behaviour for a certain transformation of the self' rested on a view of salvation.[7] His earlier literary experiments had presented a more cohesive view by positioning 'belief' within the body, the space left by the 'death of God' re-emerging in the sexual body. This embodied reflection challenged the binary opposition of belief and practice and opened the possibility for a creative relationship in exploring belief as shaping the body. It was, as some French feminist writers have indicated, to recognise the importance of the 'symbolic' order in shaping the 'social realities'.[8] This interrelationship is developed by Foucault in his idea of the 'soul', and it reveals the second aspect of religion and the body in his work: the philosophical-theological question of embodied thinking. My aim here is not to undermine Foucault's work on social practices and the work of sociology but to show the broader scope of his enterprise, and to appreciate the wider development of his own 'religious question' in the 1960s which gave birth to an embodied belief in his 'spiritual corporality'. The striking aspect of Foucault's later work is precisely how his theological sub-text of embodied belief indirectly permeates his historical and social analysis and the tensions displayed between belief and practice.

Foucault's dilemma in DP is whether the analysis of the body stops at a description of the location of body in the religious space (sociology/practice) or whether one examines the religious rationale behind the time–space location of the body (theology/belief). This tension is never resolved by Foucault because he never fully explored the shift he made between the religious sub-text of the 1960s, the embodiment of belief, and the description of the body in the social space. These two operations are similar to that developed by Paula Cooey in her own study of the body and the religious imagination, where she makes the distinction between the body as 'artifact' and the body as 'imagining subject'.[9] In Foucault's work this distinction is never made clear and the two levels of discourse are simultaneously fused and confused in the genealogical emphasis on the body.

These tensions between belief and practice were witnessed in chapter 2 in the analysis of silence and speech in the Christian confession. In the course of Foucault's study of the confession it became clear that his neglect of the theological underpinnings of salvation resulted in a partial and inadequate understanding of the dynamics of the Christian technology of self. The central problem arises from his attempt to extrapolate a technology of self from the question of belief, to suspend his work of embodied belief. Foucault's study was therefore restricted by a lack of appreciation of theological doctrine in the social processes of confession, and a failure to appreciate fully how theological ideas covered body surfaces. His lacuna in overcoming the binary opposition between speech and silence is mirrored in the continual binary opposition between religious ideas and religious practice. What he fails to realise is that when theology is located in the body a description of social practice directly becomes a statement of embodied belief.

Foucault was of course not a theologian and sought rather to approach Christianity in DP and in the later studies of sexuality through its institutional manifestations and the social organisation of the body according to space and time. He attempts to stay within the boundary of the social phenomenon of religion by examining the power structures and the architecture of Christianity. This position would have enabled a clarity to emerge in understanding the organisational parameters and the effects on controlling the body, but Foucault undermines this analysis in DP by introducing a different discourse on the inseparability between concepts of the 'soul' and the body, between theological belief and the manifestation of the body in space. There are in fact two different theoretical assumptions operating in DP. At one level Foucault attempts to look at the social religious body without reference to religious belief, but holds onto certain underlying concepts which link the body *to* belief. It would appear that he is struggling to separate a social analysis of the religious body from his 1960s insights which developed the interconnection between body, language and belief. What I am suggesting is that, as with the later discussion of confession, the examination of monasticism and Puritan spirituality in DP suffer from a failure to integrate fully the key insights of the 1960s that linked the body to belief. The ideas of embodied belief from the 1960s were carried into DP but were subsequently submerged in the attempt to isolate the social aspects of religion from a philosophical-theological perspective of the body. We may represent the tension diagrammatically as in Figure 6.1.

Foucault never sufficiently develops his study of religious belief in terms of the body to make his later work on the social practice of monasticism and confession fully coherent; in consequence two types of analysis collide in a revealing way. The key aspects of his 1960s theological sub-text of religious embodiment remain latent while the social and historical analysis of Christianity emerge as a central thematic of his study of sexuality. At the point where Foucault's work on Christianity becomes more prominent, he attempts awkwardly to drop the avant-garde themes of spiritual embodiment and refocus his work into a more socio-political analysis. Such a move neglects the crucial insights of a 'spiritual corporality' and makes way for the emergence of a 'political spirituality'. But this shift causes numerous tensions in DP.

By failing to carry forward his earlier ideas, Foucault was unable to see how the religious body is shaped by, and shapes, belief in a non-binary social operation. If he had developed his earlier work, he would have

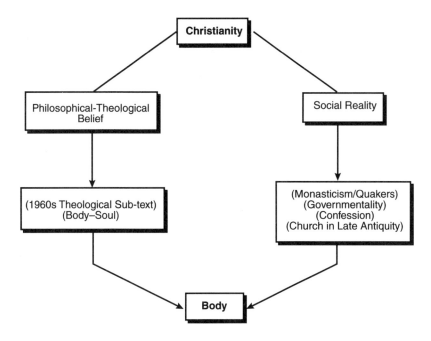

Figure 6.1 Coordinates of Foucault's discussion of religion

realised that by locating theological belief in the body the social organisation of religion becomes more directly a manifestation of theology;
theological ideas cover the surface of the body. Belief in such an understanding is not a separate and distinct process of the social positioning of
bodies; belief 'is' the social positioning. The body is the receptacle of
theology; bodies become theological organs. In a non-transcendent understanding of religion, theological beliefs are ways of mapping the body,
imaginative constructs socially organising the body. The lack of clarity in
Foucault's 'religious question' means that he obscures the relationship
between belief and the body.

The tension which I am outlining can be seen by, first, outlining the
methods of Foucault's genealogy, and, second, examining in greater detail
his work, DP. Foucault's DP is particularly significant because his examination of the religious organisation of monasticism and spiritual discipline are
separated from the belief structures through a genealogical analysis, while at
the same time, equally supported by the genealogical project, he argues that
the 'soul', a dislocated theological concept, shapes the body. The problems
within DP are also important to Foucault's later studies because they reveal
clearly the tension in holding together both the social and theological discussions of religious phenomena located in the body; they reveal the difficulties
of separating thought and practice. The central problem is the way the social

and the theological fold back onto each other when belief becomes embodied. By rethinking religion through the body, a whole series of binary oppositions collapse. However, by maintaining the binary opposition between body and belief in his later social and historical analysis of religion, the poverty of Foucault's underdeveloped 'religious question' is revealed.

Genealogy and the religious body

The assimilation of religion and the body in Foucault's later work arises from the development of his genealogical method of historical inquiry. The emergence of this conceptual framework resulted in the displacement of religion not only in terms of its associated concept of power but in terms of the creation of an apparatus (*dispositif*) of both discursive and non-discursive elements.[10] Genealogy was, as Owen recognises, 'an abandoning of the methodological commitment to the *autonomy* of discourse' as seen in the earlier archaeological inquiries.[11] This change in the relationship to discourse altered the relationship to religion. The 'spiritual' themes of language were superimposed with a consideration of the social dimensions of religion. Genealogy effectively changed the focus of how Foucault dealt with religion, but as the archaeological dimensions were still present in genealogy, so his earlier understanding of religion was awkwardly present in the later religious questions. There was a whole array of ideas combined together in these later religious questions which brought about the tensions between belief and practice.

The central features of genealogy, as Scott Lash's incisive study on genealogy and the body indicates, can be seen in three key methodological essays at the beginning of the 1970s: 'The Discourse on Language' (1970); 'Theatrum Philosophicum' (1970); and 'Nietzsche, Genealogy, History' (1971).[12] These three essays provide a number of important strands in the emergence of Foucault's later religious ideas, although they do not offer anything like the more coherent outline of archaeology in the AK, and fail to develop the later power–knowledge matrix.[13] However, by isolating a number of key features from these essays I want to demonstrate how genealogy continues to carry forward the earlier religious questions and show how these are subsequently adapted.

Silence and the body

In all three essays there is an emphasis given to the forgotten and excluded aspects in the history of Western thought, recalling earlier works such as MC and AK.[14] Foucault's genealogical period continues to reclaim the denied aspects of thought and to identify the systems of constraint. It attempts to work in a 'field of entangled and confused parchments' and explore the 'most unpromising places'.[15] The work is therefore a venture into the shadows of thought, into an alien and difficult territory. It is, according to Foucault, creating a 'counter-memory' to the dominant tradition.[16] The 'counter-memory' obviously continues the theme of silence in the genealogical project, but it is given an institutional rather than a linguistic dimension. Foucault's genealogical work also continues to rescue the body silenced by Western religious thinking. The genealogical exercise involves a process of 'descent' (*Herkunft*) which aligns and 'attaches' itself to the body.[17]

> Genealogy, as analysis of descent, is thus situated within the articulation of the body totally imprinted by history and the process of history's destruction of the body.[18]

Following Nietzsche, this genealogical work, what Foucault calls 'effective' history, focuses not on speculative and abstract notions but on the immediate reality of 'the body, the nervous system, nutrition, digestion, and energies'.[19] The body is an 'inscribed surface of events' formed and shaped by language and ideas in the historical process.[20]

This reordering of the historical process does not, as recent commentators have pointed out, simply reflect a Nietzschean understanding of the body. Foucault's genealogical appreciation of the body varies from a Nietzschean perspective.[21] Lash and Grosz, in particular, have critically appraised Foucault's understanding of the body by showing the relationship of different notions of the body, and demonstrating the difference between Nietzsche, Foucault and the French philosopher Gilles Deleuze.[22] Foucault's notion of the body differs from Nietzsche's more biological construction and lacks the more active forces of desire and phantasy in Deleuze.[23] What Foucault constructs is a body surface 'moulded' by history, a passive object interlaced by language, knowledge and power.[24] This historically constructed body is a clear indication of how religious knowledge (belief) informs and shapes the body. Although Foucault's theory of the body reveals distinct differences from that developed by Nietzsche or Deleuze, his work retains the metaphysical critique of religion. The genealogist questions the unity and ideality of the soul and relocates religion in the body.[25] Much of Foucault echoes Deleuze's own rendering of Nietzsche, in emphasising the affinities between the body and the spiritual. As Deleuze quotes Nietzsche in his own study of the German philosopher:

> Perhaps the body is the only factor in all spiritual development.[26]

Foucault's earlier work on religion, sexuality and the body in the 1960s is central to the evolution of these ideas. In many ways he continues to be informed by the avant-garde reading of Nietzsche.[27] Nietzsche's philosophy of religion once again forms the platform, with Deleuze, of Foucault's own theological agenda. Nietzsche's instinctual forces of the body combine with Deleuze's 'phantasms' (the incorporeal surface of bodies) to transform the soul into an embodied reality.[28] Deleuze's influence is very important to the way Foucault reconfigured the soul because Deleuze offered the creation of a 'new metaphysics' on the surface of bodies, a metaphysics 'freed from its original profundity'.[29] Foucault carries forward earlier ideas of a 'spiritual corporality' by developing aspects of a Deleuzian metaphysics in his work on the soul in the 1970s.

The body–soul relationship in Foucault's work is a complex formation which emerges in his study of the prison. Foucault, as we shall see, firmly locates the soul on the surface of bodies in a way similar to Deleuze, but without the psychoanalytical framework of phantasy. The body is shaped and controlled by the idea of the soul as a mechanism of power not phantasy. It is this correlation of religious ideas and the control of the body that extends into the later considerations of sexuality and the confession. The body is continually controlled and organised by religious discourse in the creation of religious technologies of the body. It is precisely the 'political investments of the body' made by religious discourse and institutions that animates the work of Foucault and forms the bedrock of his study of religion.[30] While Foucault, in close association with Nietzsche, suggests religion is fictitious, the contemplative life a regrettable invention and metaphysics an 'alien form', he still retains a more positive assimilation of bodies and souls in terms of Deleuzian metaphysics. He does not, following Deleuze, see metaphysics as necessarily an 'illusion'.[31] 'Illusion is a metaphysics', but 'metaphysics is not illusory'.[32] If metaphysics is embedded in the phantasms of body surfaces, if body and soul are, following Nietzsche, unified, the illusion is eradicated. Souls form bodies like a text; they mould the surface and shape its movements. The position of the body in the genealogical project repositions religious discourse as a formative construction and opens the way for a new examination of the Christian archive.[33] Given this outline of the body and soul, it is surprising that Foucault maintained such a strong separation of religious ideas and practice in his later work.

Critique of metaphysics

The division between religious ideas and practice appears to be partly constructed on a second genealogical strand. In line with Foucault's earlier archaeological project, genealogy is critical of the unities within the history of ideas.[34] In his outline of archaeology Foucault stipulates that 'genesis', 'continuity' and 'totalization' are 'the great themes of the history of ideas.'[35] These themes are presented with a renewed onslaught and attack in the later genealogical outlines, a point illustrating the consistency within Foucault's approach. However, in the later studies the attack against traditional history is situated within a sharper Nietzschean critique of metaphysics.

In AK Foucault was already aware of the dangers of reducing Nietzsche's genealogy to 'the level of a search for origins', and in the later study of Nietzsche's genealogy he develops the argument.[36] The clarification takes place by acknowledging a distinction between 'descent' (*Herkunft*) and 'emergence' (*Entstehung*) as opposed to 'origin' (*Ursprung*). The point is that Foucault wants to free thought from the tendency to explain things with reference to any preconceived unity or underlying origin. Traditional historical analysis ignores the 'ruptures' and 'discontinuities' within thought; it seeks to find a transcendent reference behind history which smooths over any irregularities.

> However, if the genealogist refuses to extend his [*sic*] faith in metaphysics, if he listens to history, he finds that there is 'something altogether different' behind things: not a timeless and essential secret, but the secret that they have no essence or that their essence was fabricated in a piecemeal fashion from alien forms.[37]

The genealogist attempts to identify the 'hazardous play of dominations' rather than locate everything at a point of singular origin and create a 'suprahistorical history'.[38] Genealogy, like archaeology, is interested in the 'haphazard conflicts' and the 'profusion of entangled events', in what ruptures and creates instability.[39] The stronger metaphysical critique, arising out of a close reading of Nietzsche, means that a certain number of religious issues are briefly flagged up in Foucault's genealogical critique. First, the 'soul' is questioned as a specific unity, the 'after-life' rejected as a mistake of 'effects for causes', and 'eternal truths' extinguished.[40] The Nietzschean critique of religion continues to come strongly through the text when Foucault emphasises the 'randomness of events' in opposition to the desire for transcendent truths.

> The inverse of the Christian world, spun entirely by a divine spider, and different from the world of the Greeks, divided between the realm of will and the great cosmic folly, the world of effective history knows only one kingdom, without providence or final cause, where there is only 'the iron hand of necessity shaking the dice-box of chance'.[41]

The genealogical method meant that Foucault, in opposition to metaphysics and religious ideology, avoided any detailed consideration of religious ideas in DP.

This avoidance of religious ideas prevented Foucault from exploring the full implications of his earlier ideas of embodied belief in terms of the social organisation of religion. In consequence he moves erratically in DP, incorporating the body into the religious space without realising the fundamental interdependency between belief and practice. He also fails to articulate the radical implications of a sexed-soul-body. In order to highlight the tensions and problems in Foucault's work between belief and the body, I will explore DP in greater detail.

Monasticism, discipline and embodied belief

Foucault's discussion of monasticism and Christian discipline arises in a discussion of educational and penal disciplinary control. His study is very much at this point a description of a social phenomenon. He is aware of a very complex interrelationship between military, religious and educational structures. He links together examples from these domains and shows there is a distinctive overlapping and borrowing in the historical development of the various disciplinary regimes. This is made clear in a footnote on spiritual exercises, where he explains that the Roman army unit, the 'decury', was transferred into Benedictine monasteries, taken over and adapted by other religious groups dedicated to education, eventually finding its way into the Jesuit 'scenography' of schools.[42] The various networks, divisions and ruptures form a series of sophisticated points of 'emergence' for disciplinary practice which, as Michael Donnelly indicates, 'comes ironically close to the perils of argument from the origins'.[43] Foucault had attempted to reject a single point of historical origin but uses monasticism precisely in this way.

Foucault's amalgamation of different institutional structures can be seen in the way his examination of religion and monasticism is often historically fused with a consideration of education, as in the case of the Jesuits, who feature strongly in his discussion.[44] The importance of the Jesuits in DP is due largely to Foucault's reliance on Gabriel Codina Mir's 1968 work *Aux sources de la pédagogie des Jesuites*.[45] He takes from Mir's study a number of examples from the Brothers of the Common Life, who he believed were strongly influenced by Ruysbroek and Rhenish mysticism. The Brothers of the Common Life took spiritual techniques and applied them to educational practice. This cross-over and interplay of ideas provides a fascinating historical web but ignores the central questions of theological ideas. Foucault, for example, takes no account of the Jesuit belief system in the history of educational practice, a belief system which provided the main source of inspiration behind this educational religious order.

The absence of theological ideas becomes even more apparent in the main section of DP when Foucault examines how disciplinary practices control docile bodies; 'discipline' being the direct relation between 'docility and utility'.[46] The docile body is 'subjected, used, transformed and improved'.[47] Monasticism is seen by Foucault to provide one of the earliest paradigm structures of this disciplinary regime.[48] According to his study, the monastic type of discipline was developed to obtain 'renunciations' and 'obedience' in terms of self-mastery over the body.[49] This understanding of monasticism closely follows his later consideration of 'obedience and contemplation' as the key principles of monastic spirituality.[50] While Foucault recognises that the mastery of the body is born out of Christian belief, he fails to make any significant connection in terms of his earlier 'spiritual corporality'. It is of course important to recognise that he had no intention of developing these concepts; but by carrying forward his earlier ideas on religion I wish to highlight the premature nature of his 'religious question'. When Foucault examines the social organisation of the body in Christian history, he distorts the interpretation of practices if the beliefs around which they are constituted are excluded from consideration.

Theological space and time

The tensions between belief and the body can be seen again in Foucault's treatment of the 'regulation' and 'monitoring' in monasticism according to space and time, a section which recalls his earlier 1967 study 'Of Other Spaces'.[51] The religious life provided him with a convenient baseline to demonstrate the complex networks of institutional power.

> For centuries, the religious orders had been masters of discipline: they were the specialists of time, the great technicians of rhythm and regular activity.[52]

In the attempt to establish broad links between different regimes of discipline Foucault failed to consider how monastic space and time were theologically determined, how belief organises space and orders time. He conveniently linked the detailed ordering of bodies in the Classical age with the established practice of 'theology and asceticism' in monastic life without appreciation of the fundamental religious belief behind such structures.[53] There is insufficient consideration in Foucault's work as to why theology orders the body in a disciplined structure, and little consideration of how theology has marked the body. His *dispositif* is strategically focused in such a way as to distort the 'heterogeneous ensemble' of discourses and practices which inform the birth of the monastery and religious institutions.[54] He never really considers the discourse of theological belief.

Foucault's strategic approach means that he reads monasticism in the restricted terms of architectural space, one of the identified strands of his *dispositif*, isolating in particular the 'cellular' organisation and the 'structural surveillance'. By linking the singular actions of the monk to the larger community, he saw this structure as 'the base for a micro-physics of what may be called a "cellular" power'.[55] This cellular power was subsequently seen by Foucault to be implanted into schools and prisons and formed the basis of the panoptic gaze, but the rationale of cellular power is fundamentally different in each case. If, as he appreciates, monastic discipline is different from the 'formulas of domination' in the seventeenth and eighteenth centuries, in so far as the former were not principally concerned with 'utility', then the theological ordering ought to be given a greater priority in his understanding of the religious architecture.[56]

In the monastic space the cell is seen by Foucault to represent the omnipotent gaze of God. On the walls of the cell, according to him, it says 'God sees you.'[57] God's surveillance is impossible to escape; it is the ideal apparatus, 'a perfect eye that nothing would escape and a centre towards which all gazes would be turned'.[58] While Foucault acknowledges that solitude was necessary to confront temptation, he again fails to develop fully the crucial link between these architectural powers and theological belief; it is not the 'stones' in isolation which 'make people docile and knowable'.[59] Unfortunately it was his priority to demonstrate how the structures of monasticism shape the body rather than question the 'body' which shapes the building (let alone its 'beliefs'). While architectural theory demonstrates that, once created, buildings shape bodies and influence ideas in an organic evolution, perhaps what is not considered is how bodies are inscribed by symbolic orders prior to and in the process of building. Buildings manifest the bodily inscriptions and fold them back onto the body. The Christian belief of renouncing the world created the isolation of monastic life which later reinforced an identity of bodily control in the construction of the monastic cell. There is always an indefinable and entangled evolution of ideas and practice.

Quaker technologies of control

The tension between belief and practice becomes particularly acute when we consider Foucault's discussion of the coercive techniques in Puritan spirituality. This occurs when he extends the religious technologies of domination beyond the monastic model to consider two American penal systems, one at Auburn ('work in common and absolute silence') and the other at Philadelphia ('absolute isolation').[60] As in his study of madness, Foucault examines the effect of Quaker spiritual ideals in the reformation of social institutions, in this case the Philadelphia system at Cherry Hill. In this discussion he indicates a series of technologies of control underlying the Whiggish mentality of Quaker social reformers. In the isolation of the cell, the individual conscience was seen in Puritan philosophy as the central tenet in the reformation of the inmate. According to Foucault, Quaker spirituality reinforces the physical mechanism of control through an 'internalisation' of the carceral architecture.[61]

There is a distinct strategic move within Quaker foundations to shift the locus of control from the external environment to the inner world. These Puritan models of spiritual orientation are then applied to the organisation of medical and penal institutions. The Quaker technique is to 'encourage the influence of religious principles over the mind' of the mad and the criminal individual.[62] In a moral therapy the mad are cured by the religious 'safeguards' of reason, and in the prison the inmate is reformed through the power of conscience.[63] In both situations 'segregation' and 'isolation' predominate. Solitude and silence become the coercive techniques of normalising minds.

In the Pennsylvanian prison, the only operations of correction were the conscience and the silent architecture that confronted it.[64]

There appears to be a kind of internal panoptic-consciousness in such a penal philosophy, which monitors and guides the soul. Foucault, in a poignant footnote, elucidates the mechanisms of control by referring to the theological ideas of the Quaker founder George Fox: 'Every man [*sic*] is illuminated by the divine light and I have seen it shine through every man.'[65] Quaker spiritual values are turned upside down when the idea of the 'divine light' ceases to be seen as a positive quality and is turned into a technology of control. This technique, according to Foucault, could be seen in many nineteenth-century religious groups, where the 'fear of God' was used as an effective way to police souls/individuals. The effectiveness of this strategy can be seen in the way it permeates into secular society as a form of social control.[66] The striking fact here is that, even without the architecture, theological ideas are seen to shape the body through a process of internalised self-examination and fear.

Foucault's work becomes confused when he assumes that the Quaker technologies of control were adopted by Catholicism.[67] Catholicism obviously had its own internal spiritual panopticon before George Fox. This confusion reflects the problematic positioning of Quakers as a distinct form of internalised spiritual control. In his later genealogy of the modern subject Foucault sees the formation of the self as related to a wider Christian tradition. For example, the corrective technique of 'biographical' knowledge within penitentiary operations can be linked to a wider tradition of self-examination in the Christian tradition.[68] The self is something to write about, a theme or object (subject) of writing activity. That is not a modern trait born of the Reformation or of Romanticism; it is one of the most ancient Western traditions. It was well established and deeply rooted when Augustine started his *Confessions*.[69]

Quaker spirituality was not an internalisation of the architectural structures but a reflection of the religious techniques of self-examination. The internal-panopticon, as Foucault's later work on John Cassian indicates, preceded the architectural forms. It was 'vigilance' through self-examination, the process of 'discrimination', which controlled the body, a theological imperative and not stone.[70] As Foucault stated in 1982 when considering monasticism from the perspective of the technology of self:

> The organisation of monasticism and the dimorphism that developed between monastic and secular life brought about important changes in the problem of sexual renunciation. They brought with them the development of very complex techniques of self-analysis.[71]

In Christianity the need for 'complex techniques of self-analysis' was born out of a theological worldview, a need to develop a closer relationship with

God, a need to overcome the flesh. The social realities reflect the theological order which idealised the ascetic life.

In his consideration of the 'analytic of finitude' in his 1966 OT, Foucault refers to the body as a 'fragment of ambiguous space', and in his later work we see how this body is shaped in a power–knowledge matrix.[72] The soldier in DP is a 'fragment of mobile space'. In this respect we may see the religious subject as a fragment of 'theological space'.[73] The body is shaped and ordered by theological belief. What Foucault failed to realise is that the surface of the body in the monastery (and subsequently in the prison) is shaped through the regulation of space and time according to 'theological' models of authority. The body is thus 'manipulated by authority', which in due course redefined the nature and understanding of the body.[74] Although Foucault never appreciates how theological ideas control the body, it is implicit in many of the examples he takes from monasticism. This can be seen in his brief reference to the spiritual 'exercise'; a 'technique by which one imposes on the body tasks that are both repetitive and different, but always graduated'.[75] The body was trained and mastered in the mystical and ascetic life in the hope of salvation and 'a beyond'.[76] These religious ideas are seen by Foucault to be 'illusory'.[77] But earlier we saw that when he followed a 'spiritual corporality' and a Deleuzian metaphysics, theological ideas were no longer 'illusory'. His later remarks about the illusion of religious ideas were created, therefore, by falling back into a traditional religious epistemology and failing to recognise how theological ideas were earlier grounded in the body. It is precisely at this point, when Foucault shifts the basis of his 'religious question', that the tensions between religious belief and religious practice become manifest.

Theological illusions: body and soul

Although Foucault attempted to document aspects of the social phenomena of religion in DP, he inadvertently introduced a secondary analysis of embodied religious belief in terms of the body and soul. The two discourses collide, confusing the social analysis with strands of his 'spiritual corporality'. However much Foucault may have wished to drop the radical understanding of his 'spiritual corporality', the force of these avant-garde ideas continued to take effect. It also becomes clear that the social understanding of religion is substantially illuminated when positioned in the context of embodied belief. The interconnection of belief and practice at the site of the body transforms the entire discussion of religion. Once the embodied understanding of religious ideas is accepted, the social location of religion is intrinsically the manifestation of the belief without transcendence. In order to understand the full force of this dynamic reorganisation of religious belief we need to take a closer look at Foucault's sub-text of the body and soul in DP.

When Foucault states that DP is a 'correlated history of the modern soul', he claims that this understanding of the 'soul' is a very specific construct related to the penal body and not to theology.[78] In a very short parenthesis he specifically differentiates between a theological soul and the modern (penal) soul. The theological soul is built on sin and (theological) punishment, unlike the modern soul of penal practice, which came about in a shift from corporal punishment, the physical spectacle of hanging, to specific methods of 'punishment, supervision and constraint'.[79] Foucault's use of the idea of soul in this context is taken from Mably's 1789 treatise *De la Législation*, which states: 'Punishment, if I may so put it, should strike the soul rather than the body.'[80] The 'soul' of the criminal becomes a central part of the juridical and penal system in the creation of a 'political anatomy'.[81]

There are, however, tensions in Foucault's attempt to separate the idea of the modern soul from the theological baggage, especially as the idea of his modern soul derives some theoretical leverage from the adaption of Ernst Kantorowicz's 1957 work on medieval political theology, *The King's Two Bodies*. This work examines the political and legal history of the idea of the 'two bodies' of the King: a natural body which faces death; and a timeless body politic, the 'immortal part of kingship'.[82] Kantorowicz shows the historical evolution of this idea from Christian liturgical practice, a borrowing and adaption of the *corpus mysticum*. The *corpus mysticum*, as opposed to the Pauline *corpus christi*, was an idea about the mystical body of Christ. This idea developed from the eleventh-century controversies surrounding Radbertus' and Ratramnus' beliefs about the consecrated host, an argument which would eventually result in the Dogma of Transubstantiation in 1215.[83] The implication of this 'remarkable analysis' is that Christian theological thought resides at the base of political and legal terminology.[84] Foucault seems unaware of this correlation and is unable to realise that his own 'modern soul' is also in part derived from a theological discourse.

Foucault believes that Mably's penal soul can be linked to the 'surplus power' of the King's body politic in Kantorowicz's study. This tendentious argument by Foucault is based on the supposition that the corresponding 'surplus power exercised on the subjected body' creates a soul. The idea is indeed interesting and imaginative, but has little foundation in Kantorowicz's own study. The 'body politic' of the King has evolved from the Christological identifications of regency; the only theological parallel for a 'modern soul' has to be the Christian soul, and no mention of this idea is made by Foucault. There is of course no reason why Foucault cannot rupture the traditional discourse of souls, but using theological structures to achieve this weakens his position. There is also no examination of the theological strands embedded in Mably's own notion of the soul. Many of the ideas of the soul in eighteenth-century penal reform, like those of Quakers, have a specific theological basis.

Foucault is, however, very careful to make it clear that the modern soul, unlike the Christian soul, is not to be seen as a substance. The modern soul is constructed from the effects of power and knowledge; it does not hold any metaphysical referent. The 'illusion of the theologians', according to Foucault, is that they 'substitute' the physical human person for the greater reality of the soul. The soul in a juridical and penal sense is 'the effect and instrument of a political anatomy', a regime of power–knowledge which manipulates and controls the body. The soul as a political anatomy 'inhabits' the body and brings it into existence; the body is thus shaped by power.[85] The body is 'subjugated' by turning it into an 'object of knowledge'.[86] This positioning of the 'soul' as a network of 'power–knowledge relations', which attempt to manipulate and control the body, supports Foucault's religious sub-text of embodied belief and follows Deleuze in understanding metaphysics as covering the body surface.

Foucault wants to hold in this outline of the body and soul a fundamental inseparability between the two notions. In the history of punishment, he argues, it is not possible to separate the discussion of the soul from the body. The impacts on the soul are fused with the impacts on the body.

> ... it is always the body that is at issue – the body and its forces, their utility and their docility, their distribution and their submission.[87]

The soul covers the surface of the body with a series of forces which in turn give it 'existence'.

As we noted earlier in the outline of aspects of genealogy, Foucault is unable to validate theological ideas and reorganise his understanding of body and belief because of the importance to him of Nietzsche's critique of metaphysics and Christianity. This is particularly true in relation to the interrelationship of body and soul. Nietzsche saw the soul as part of the lies and deceit of Christianity, an 'imaginary' and 'fictitious' form which diminished life.[88] In an attempt to counteract the Christian use of the term 'soul' Nietzsche sought to bring the concept back into a physiological understanding of theology.[89] He repeatedly repositions the soul on and in the body, seeing it as the 'internalisation' of instinctive forces, an idea similar to the 'surplus power' Foucault discusses in relation to Kantorowicz.[90] The power of Zarathustra's words conveys the weight of Nietzsche's disruption of Christian dualism:

> But the awakened, the enlightened man [sic] says: I am body entirely, and nothing beside; and soul is only a word for something in the body.[91]

There are many brief notes and allusions scattered through Nietzsche's writing which hold the same aim of dismantling the Christian and metaphysical idea of the soul. Foucault, who is very much aware of the Christian contempt for the body, can be seen to be following a comparable mission in reorganising the history of punishment in terms of the 'history of bodies'.[92]

The fusion of the concepts of body and soul by Nietzsche, and later by Foucault, reveals an underlying necessity to retain the idea of soul. This may appear confusing, but the deployment of the term 'soul' is a provocative gesture in a campaign to revitalise historically influential terminology. As Nietzsche writes in relation to the soul:

> Between ourselves, it is not at all necessary by that same act to get rid of 'the soul' itself and thus forgo one of the oldest and most venerable of hypotheses; as is often the way with clumsy naturalists, who can hardly touch 'the soul' without losing it. But the road to new forms and refinements of the soul-hypothesis stands open ... .[93]

The fact that Nietzsche and Foucault do not reject vocabulary of the soul for an exclusive reading of the body provides some fundamental insights into the epistemological understanding of the body. One of the few writers to appreciate this is Judith Butler in a brief interpolation found in her essay on Irigaray and the body, 'Bodies that Matter'.[94] In this essay Butler questions the *a priori* assumptions in the discussion of body/matter. She seeks to 'displace' the 'irreducible specificity' of matter in contemporary discourse and experiments with a 'contemporary redeployment of Aristotelian terminology' in relation to Foucault's work on the soul in DP.[95] Butler sees the soul in Aristotle's *De Anima* as a kind of 'schema' which 'constitutes' body/matter, in the sense that 'materiality and intelligibility' are inseparable. She goes on to see Foucault's work on the soul as an 'implicit reworking of the Aristotelian formulation'. In discussion of DP Butler states:

> There the soul is taken as an instrument of power through which the body is cultivated and formed. In a sense it acts as a power-laden schema that produces and actualizes the body itself.[96]

What Butler enables us to see through her comparative study of Aristotle and Foucault is the way that the materiality of the body is not separable from the 'schema' of power relations that form it. The body in DP, as distinct from the discussion in HS1, does not have an *a priori* materiality and form.[97]

The 'displacement' of the body and soul as interconnecting surfaces not only reorientates the understanding of the body, but reconstitutes the understanding of spirituality as well. Foucault's understanding of the soul opens the possibility of an embodied religion, a religious discourse which animates the body materiality. Spirituality is transformed into a process of shaping matter, of making bodies matter. The idea of the soul is the recognition that a conceptual world shapes life. In this sense, the soul is not, as Foucault makes clear in DP, an 'illusion'. However, this contradicts his conception of 'theological illusions' about the soul.[98] This tension reflects the extent to which his understanding of religious 'illusion' depends on the integration of his earlier 'spiritual corporality'. Theological ideas are perceived by him as 'illusions' only when they are detached from a body materiality. Once again we see how his inability to integrate and clarify his earlier foundations of a 'spiritual corporality' causes misunderstanding and contradiction in his later work.

Foucault's lack of interest in developing his discussion of religious ideas in DP leaves his 'religious question' floating at the boundaries of his work. However, if we follow the Deleuzian model of metaphysics in the light of the discussion of the soul-body and bring together body and belief, then the strands of Foucault's earlier 'spiritual corporality' are strengthened. We might also consider that if the operations of the soul in penal practice apply 'in a more general way' and the basis of discipline is created from monastic structures, then the 'soul' of Christianity must have been created on the same power–knowledge forces as Foucault's modern soul. If this were not the case, then the structures of monasticism would cease to be a valid paradigm. In fact the only distinctions Foucault makes between the Christian soul and the modern soul relate to the differing forces (i.e. sin and theological punishment) and the question of substance (a metaphysical entity). If we take the (theological) soul out of the illusory metaphysics, which postulates a 'beyond', then his understanding of the (penal) soul could apply equally to Christianity. He could then be seen to be working out a post-Nietzschean conception of the soul. Christianity could be seen to have a value as a non-illusory metaphysical event. This would then follow Foucault's 'spiritual corporality' in locating belief in and on the body.

Foucault, as we have seen, makes it clear that not all metaphysics is illusion. By following the idea of a non-illusory metaphysics, we can liberate the religious discourse of the soul from its 'fictitious' constraints.[99] This creates a whole new possibility for understanding and interpreting religion. Religious ideas become ways of expressing the body which can be both a technology of domination and a more positive technology of self, a religious aesthetic which animates matter. If the soul is 'around', 'within' and 'on' the body, then the implications of a religion on the surface of the body create a completely new understanding of religious discourse. The body is valorised and theological dualism is eliminated in the creation of a 'spiritual corporality'. The spirit becomes 'a question of the body'.[100]

Gendered religious-bodies

The discussion so far has attempted to bring together body, belief and practice and reignite Foucault's 'spiritual corporality' in a wider Deleuzian metaphysics. However, the interrelation between belief and practice becomes even more apparent when we return to the feminist critique of Foucault briefly unfolded in chapter 4. The social mapping of the religious position of women depicts the theological doctrines and stories which have controlled, distorted and manipulated women's bodies. If (male) theology is read in an embodied mode, as soul-body, the doctrine (the symbolic) can be seen to socially organise male and female bodies. We may also, following the fascinating archaeological work of Roberta Gilchrist, draw links between monastic architectural structures and gendered belief. Religious belief becomes a 'sexed-discourse' manifest in space.[101] Theological ideas are sexed most notably, as Grosz strikingly documents, in religious violations of the body and in the notions of cleanliness and bodily fluids.

> The formation of stigmata, perforations, cuts, bleeding, even the production of a quite literal alphabetic script across the body can be induced or produced through the adherence to certain beliefs (about religious piety, worship, a sense of worthlessness or supreme value, the notion of the body as a vessel for divine intervention or satanic interference, etc.).[102]

These more overt religious practices are also supported by more subtle notions of theology and religious belief which organise male and female bodies, such as confession, religious language and doctrine.

A number of feminist writers, as we have seen in chapter 4, have done much to identify the 'gender-blind' constructions in Foucault's work. If we follow this hermeneutical lens, and if the soul is seen as the 'schema' of bodies, then the religious and theological question is no longer just a 'matter' of 'sexed-bodies' but also of 'sexed-souls', of 'sexed-doctrine'. The soul-body creates a gendered spirituality because the 'schema' which materialises the body is sexed. We can also speculate that if gendered forces cover the body surface and animate the body, then sexuality easily becomes a religious 'phantasm'. The male God becomes a 'phantasm' which controls and manipulates the surface of male and female soul-bodies, and the discovery of new images of God is simultaneously a new understanding of soul-bodies. The soul, and spirituality in general, are intrinsically bound up in the understanding of the sexed-body. This radical displacement of religion shows the importance of locating Foucault's 'spiritual corporality' in a gendered context. Perhaps Nietzsche's words, in the light of this discussion, should read: 'the entire evolution of the spirit is a question of the *sexed-body*'.

The question of sexed-souls may seem a long way from the genealogical procedures of *Entstehung* and *Herkunft* and the embodied theology of the 1960s, but it reveals the wider implications of Foucault's strategy of positioning religion in the body. Once the body is the central site of religious thinking its sexed and gendered nature becomes crucial. Religion and theology are transformed and transfigured into sexually embodied processes, doctrines become religious disciplines of the body, rituals and religious architecture are reconfigured as constraints and venerations of sexed-bodies in space and time. Belief and practice fold back upon each other in an 'imaginative somatology'.[103]

Foucault's later study of sexuality and Christianity failed to develop these insights, preferring instead awkwardly to separate issues of belief and embodiment through the indices of sexuality and the technology of self. The philosophical-theological ideas of embodiment eventually gave way in his work to a more restricted analysis of confession and Christian practice. Despite this shift in emphasis, his work continued to promote an embodied understanding of Christian thought by establishing the fundamental relation between the question of Western sexuality and Christianity. His final studies attempt to show how Christianity from its earliest times was preoccupied with the body. But why was Christianity so preoccupied with the body? Did it simply reflect a need to control the body in order to reach towards a God in a higher spiritual realm, or was there a deeper political technology of the body involved? Perhaps Foucault answered this question not only by showing how bodies 'were' theological organs in a 'spiritual corporality' but also by later revealing the technology of domination in confessional practice, by developing a 'political spirituality'. Theology, according to this reading of his work, was an imaginative process through which human beings politically organ-ised their bodies.

7   Towards a political spirituality

> But experience has taught me that the history of various forms of rationality
> is sometimes more effective in unsettling our certitudes and dogmatism than
> is abstract criticism. For centuries, religion couldn't bear having its history
> told.
>
> Foucault (1979c) 'Omnes et Singulatim', p. 83

Foucault's work on religious themes, from the early sub-textual fragments to
the later unpublished volume on Christianity, constitutes a diverse series of
interventions, disruptions and questions. There is no systematic treatment of
religion. What we find is a critical suspension of religious discourse in the
wider trajectory of his work. The 'religious question' was a restricted and
inconsistent project, but Foucault's analysis was radical enough and his
interest sufficient to raise profound questions about religion and bring
Christianity from a marginal excess to a central strategic theme of his later
work. He questions the hegemony of religious discourse and reveals its
excluded Other; he identifies the hidden currents of confessional practice
and uncovers the silenced body. Religion in Foucault's work was no longer
allowed to exist in a neutral space; it emerged and evolved in a power
dynamic of the said and the unsaid. Religion was seen inseparably to exist in
the social, cultural and political exclusions which attempt to control human
experience through the values and ideals of religious belief. In unravelling
these aspects of religious discourse Foucault contested the 'spiritual' in
terms of the politics of experience, in terms of a corporality which challenges the very fabric of theological dualism.

Foucault's 'religious question' was not simply content to recover the silent
body of religion and play with the avant-garde flirtations. With the emergence
of Christianity as a key theme in his later work he revealed a broader understanding of religion. Alongside the unsaid, he identified the powers which
silenced. He began to demarcate the structures which enmeshed the religious
subject. There was a bridging of the unsaid with an analysis of the said,
reflecting a profound inseparability and interconnection between these conceptual maps. The idea of a 'spiritual corporality' was thus later veiled in terms of a
second feature of Foucault's 'religious question', a 'political spirituality'.[1]

Together they formed a twofold critique of religion, a rescuing of the body silenced by religion and an analysis of the technology of pastoral power. The later work exposed the way individuals were made into religious 'subjects'. By identifying the constraints of the religious 'subject', Foucault's later work supported the earlier avant-garde attempts to break free from such religious control. As a whole his work on religion was a project which attempted to locate religion, and more specifically Christianity, in the context of a different order of events. His 'religious question' was in effect a 'problematisation' of religion. It jolted the safe paradigms of religious understanding by questioning the very constitution of the 'religious space'. In this final chapter I will show how Foucault's work on religion can be read as a 'problematisation', and how the emphasis of his work moved from a 'spiritual corporality' towards a 'political spirituality' in his late work.

The problematisation of religion

The notion of 'problematisation' emerges in Foucault's work during his later studies of sexuality. It is a key concept in the historical construction of 'sexuality'. The idea of 'problematisation' forms a way of identifying how and why issues are positioned in a particular matrix of concern in different historical periods.[2] The idea originally gained force in 1976 as part of HS1, but it only assumed prominence from 1983 in an article in *Le Débat* explaining the direction of his current project on sexuality, a section subsequently incorporated into the second volume of his *History of Sexuality*.[3] Towards the end of his life Foucault regarded the notion of 'problematisation' as applicable to all his work since the *Histoire de la folie*, although he admits he 'never isolated this notion sufficiently'.[4] This wider applicability of the notion provides added weight for understanding his 'religious question' in these terms. It confirms how religious ideas were introduced and suspended in a series of 'problematic' contexts. Foucault did not deal with the issues of religion consistently; rather they were thrown up in a variety of spasmodic episodes during his literary and historical work.

As with many of the ideas that Foucault unfolds, he provides no systematic elaboration of the idea of 'problematisation', but it can be seen to be situated, first, within the ethical domain of sexual morality as a question of 'how, why, and in what forms' sexuality is 'constituted as a moral domain'; and, second, through various interviews and retrospective reflections on his work, as related to a question of 'discursive and non-discursive practices that introduces something into play of true and false and constitutes it as an object for thought'.[5] Foucault's question is: 'How is a particular body of knowledge able to be constituted?' What he was attempting to identify was an area within the history of thought (distinct from the history of ideas and mentalities) which dealt with the 'element of problems' or 'problematisations'.[6] The history of thought attempts to discover how certain objects of thought are set up and to plot the 'development of acts, practices, and thoughts' that present certain problems.[7] In discussing the idea of 'problematisation', Foucault highlights the practices, political structures and ethical forces which 'constitute' an issue. This procedure allows him eventually to see his work as evolving into a 'genealogy of problems, of "problématiques" '.[8]

Foucault sees his *History of Sexuality* (HS) as mapping the conditions of a 'problem'; he regards the work not as a history of the patterns of sexual behaviour, morals or acts, but as a 'history of the *way* in which pleasures, desires, and sexual behaviour were problematized'.[9] As we noted earlier, he is concerned with historical practices, deployments and strategies which form and shape the idea of sexuality. According to this methodology, the later volumes of Foucault's HS emphasise the 'arts of existence' or 'technologies of self' which frame issues of (male) 'sexuality' in terms of health, marriage, social position and relations with boys.[10] Sexuality is thus problematised in terms of technologies of self, or, more broadly, 'governmentality'. In a similar fashion Foucault's earlier 'religious question' problematises the 'spiritual' in terms of the body; it introduces a denied or tangential aspect into the equation to create a problem. His work is in this sense creative not so much for issues he raises but through the *way* he introduces divergent contexts to explore the issues.

In Foucault's work from 1976 the 'spiritual' is problematised in terms of the political ordering of knowledge or in terms of the question of governmentality. Foucault isolated the various techniques and strategies which made Christianity a major force in the 'constitution' of sexual discourse in the West. He attempted to present the underlying historical structures of the Christian technology of the self. There were, however, as we have seen in connection with confessional practice, a number of tensions with this 'problematisation' of religion in the way it deals with historical material.[11] These tensions have been examined in more detail by Castel, who demonstrates how a 'problematisation', while relying on historical data, does not follow the same strict criteria of 'historical methodology'.[12] While the construction of 'historical facts' is itself a complex issue, the method of 'problematisation', as Castel indicates, 'can be refuted if it contradicts historical knowledge'.[13] Foucault's discussion of Christianity is therefore often hindered by a lack of historical rigour, a point made by Elizabeth Clark in her examination of Foucault and the Church Fathers.

> Foucault's treatment of Christian materials requires a more energetic 'leap of faith' than the historian would desire, for only scattered references to specific Christian writers and their theories can be found in his work published to date.[14]

As I have already suggested in chapter 2, it is easy to challenge the historical material, but the force of Foucault's writing is lost if the historical lacunae overshadow the 'problematisation' which he is framing in his work. I am not wishing to underestimate the important (and extensive) debates around Foucault and the writing of history, such as the question of 'fictional histories' or 'the history of the present'. Rather I am attempting to ascertain for the purposes of this discussion Foucault's own 'tactic' in introducing religion and theology into his 'history of thought'.[15] I am suggesting that it may be possible to read his work on Christianity and religion as a 'problematisation' in its own right. How and why, we may ask, are Christianity and religion constituted in his work?

In order to understand the nature of this 'problematisation', which I am folding back on Foucault's work, it is necessary to return to a key feature of Foucault's procedure we touched on in the last chapter. Foucault acknowledged in a discussion at Stanford University in October 1979 that it is both a tactic and a methodological choice to start with the 'practice' rather than the 'ideology'. In this discussion he went on to show that his interest in 'confession' rested on examining the 'techniques' rather than exploring the theory or ideology behind such developments. When asked how he was to overcome his own preconceptual ideology, he responded by stating that he had to understand *not* his own ideology but rather what he was *doing* when trying to understand what others are *doing*.[16] Despite the implicit confusion of separating ideology and practice, the question of what Foucault is *doing* (in terms of both ideas and practice) is crucial to understanding the 'problematisation' of religion.

What Foucault appears to be *doing* in his discussion of religion and theology is positioning certain historical developments of Christianity within a series of 'relations of force, strategic developments, and tactics'.[17] His work reveals the battles, struggles and strategies of religious ideas in terms of ordering the body, the sexual, the organisation of states, the individual relationship to self and the religious construction of subjects, each representing a series of religious or theological 'fragments put to work in a historical field of problems'.[18] It is therefore possible to see the various evolutions of Foucault's religious ideas – the death of God, the embodiment of theology, the confessional practice, the modalities of pastoral power and Christian ethics – as holding a certain 'problematisation' of religion in terms of the historical problems of 'corporality' and 'politics'. What Foucault is *doing* is questioning religion from his own ideological value of the body and his politicisation of knowledge.

Foucault and Christianity

The emergence of the second 'problematisation' of religion in Foucault's work arises out of his multi-volume HS, but it was not restricted to this enterprise. The HS was a complex project which splintered into many directions, creating tensions and problematics which Foucault had never envisioned before he embarked on the exercise. The conglomeration of issues that arose out of the problematic of sexuality can be seen in the way

Mitchell Dean captures the period of Foucault's work from 1976 under the latter's dynamic title of 'governmentality'.[19] According to Dean, Foucault's work developed a 'novel thought-space' cutting across ethics and politics, the practices of self and practices of government.

As Dean suggests, Foucault's general notion of 'governmentality' brings together many disparate themes of the last eight years of his life. His course outline for 1979–80 captures the eclectic field of subjects under examination:

> This year's course drew upon analyses made in preceding years bearing on the notion of 'government': this notion being understood in the wider sense of techniques and procedures designed to direct the behaviour of men [*sic*]. Government of children, government of souls or consciences, government of a household, of the State or of oneself.[20]

In meandering across this broad territory of 'governmentality', Foucault's concern with Christianity moves from a preoccupation with confessional practice into a wider collection of issues related to questions of state power and the Christian pastoral. The focus on Christianity thus shifts from a parasitic theme of psychoanalysis in a confessional-discursive order (HS1) to a distinctive strategy of government in terms of a 'pastoral modality of power' and an evolving technology of self determined by 'renunciation', 'obedience and contemplation'.[21] This development of ideas eventually leads in the late 1970s to a more extensive examination of the ethico-political nature of Christianity. What I want to demonstrate is that Foucault's later work on Christianity represents a new 'problematisation' of his earlier 'religious question'; that it is technologies and power, a 'political spirituality', which determines his later work. The early strategy of 'problematising' religion in terms of a 'spiritual corporality' gives way to a wider 'political' understanding of religion. However, as I will show, the ideas of a 'spiritual corporality' and a 'political spirituality' have an important relationship in Foucault's wider critique of Christianity.

Christianity and the economy of austerity

While a small number of works have outlined Foucault's later discussion of Christianity, there have been few works which have explored the specific 'role' and 'function' of Christianity during the later period. However, one notable exception stands out. In a rare attempt to understand the position of Christianity in Foucault's HS, Bevis, Cohen and Kendall, through a critique of the genealogical procedure in the three published volumes, seek to examine the role of Christianity in what they regard as an 'economy of austerity' operating through the works. They argue that in Foucault's HS there is a propensity towards homogenisation and monolithic constructions in dealing with the Greek, Roman and Christian documents, and that he 'works on the principle of "eliding" the complexity of sexuality in the ancient world'.[22] There is, they believe, a lack of rigorous examination and a selective use of source material which seeks to 'adjust the emphasis'.[23] The 'moderation' of the Greeks is merged with the 'austerity' of Christian asceticism to unify material and create 'an over-arching continuity' based on austerity.[24] What Bevis, Cohen and Kendall attempt to show is that Foucault's characterisation of Christianity as a monolithic austere regime, supported by his wider work on the developments in the Greco-Roman world, provided him with the necessary order for understanding psychoanalysis as a 'descendant of the Christian confessional', an argument originally unfolded in HS1.[25] Referring to Foucault's work they state:

> His project became enmeshed in a concern with austerity to the extent that it was this theme which came to be the managing principle, the economy, for Foucault's story of antiquity and Christianity.[26]

There is much evidence to support Bevis, Cohen and Kendall's argument. They are correct to highlight the problems of Foucault's reading of antiquity and Christianity and the selective use of sources, a critique which had been previously made by Lloyd and has been elaborated more recently by Goldhill.[27] There is also much support for the 'elision' of the complexity of sexuality in the ancient world and the developing of an economy of austerity. Foucault acknowledges in 1983 the common austerity between the Greco-Roman and Christian worlds. 'We are not talking', he emphasises, 'about a moral rupture between tolerant antiquity and austere Christianity.'[28] This point is reinforced later in the same discussion:

> Consequently, between paganism and Christianity, the opposition is not between tolerance and austerity, but between a form of austerity which is linked to an aesthetics of existence and other forms of austerity which are linked to the necessity of renouncing the self and deciphering its truth.[29]

However, the argument put forward by Bevis, Cohen and Kendall too easily reduces the problems of Foucault's reading of antiquity and Christianity to a prioritisation of psychoanalysis in the overall construction of the HS. They see psychoanalysis as determining the conceptualisation of Christianity (a monolithic ascetic and confessional religion), which in turn shapes the other material. Christianity is the '"silent presence", the omnipresent spectre which constrains his conceptual categories, governs his choice of sources, and dictates the form that this developing work will take'.[30] But such an argument relies too heavily on positioning HS1 as the 'key orienting' document and ignores the evolution of Foucault's thought since 1976 when the original direction of the 'introductory' essay had been suspended. Foucault makes it clear, following criticism for the delays in publication, how he had moved 'far from my original project' and how he had to 'reorganize' his study around the ideas of the hermeneutics of the self.[31] He may well remain 'committed' to the conceptualisation of Christianity in HS1, but the role and function of Christianity in his work ceases to be linked to the problematic of sexuality and psychoanalysis when it becomes part of a problematic of state power and the government of self after 1976. It is insufficient to argue that the notion of Christianity is consistent through the HS and therefore dependent on psychoanalytical directives, particularly when, as Bevis, Cohen and Kendall indicate, Foucault is obviously influenced by the legacy of an ascetic Christianity in Nietzsche and Weber.[32]

There are in fact a number of shifts or dislocations in Foucault's discussion of Christianity which remove it from the domain of the archaeology of psychoanalysis. First, the psychoanalytical explanation for the positioning of Christianity may gain support from the fact that the second volume on sexuality to be written (though not published) was on Christianity. It may also be noted that the volume on Christianity was only suspended because of Foucault's desire to correct the introductory 'clichés' he had made about the Greco-Roman world in the early sections of this second volume. However, it remains the case that the psychoanalytical orientation from HS1 was not the final determining factor which shaped Foucault's understanding of Christianity.[33] There was a significant reorganisation of material on Christianity from 1976. We can, for example, deduce from circumstantial evidence that Foucault only embarked on his reading of Cassian from around 1977, and that the interest in the Christian pastoral was partly restimulated from his work on state power and 'governmentality'.[34] We know from other taped discussions in the Foucault archive that Foucault was studying the work on confession in late 1979.[35] There is also much support from his discussion with Dreyfus and Rabinow in the early 1980s to show that what he referred to as 'the Christian book' (the fourth volume of the HS) was constantly put back in order of publication because of his primary interest in the technologies of self. The shift is reinforced in his lectures on Christianity in 1980 and 1982, where a more complicated picture of 'confessional' practice emerges from the later material on the Christian technologies of self.[36] Foucault was reshaping his understanding of Christianity and introduced new conceptual frameworks in his assessment of religion far from those pursued in HS1. (Perhaps the final word of the debate can only be answered if and when the infamous fourth volume of his HS is published, but the shifts in his orientation are manifest even without the unpublished volume.)

Foucault may have simplistically emphasised the continuities in sexual ethics between the Greco-Roman period and Christianity, and developed an economy of austerity, but the key issue for him in his final studies is a desire not to support his introductory thesis but to show how Christianity offered a new technique of self, a new relation of power. He stresses this point in 1982:

It has often been said that Christianity brought into being a code of ethics fundamentally different from that of the ancient world. Less emphasis is usually placed on the fact that it proposed and spread new power relations throughout the ancient world.[37]

Foucault's interest in the 'new relations of power' was part of his overall strategy to place religion within the framework of 'governmentality'. Whether or not his account of Christianity is accurate, his overall aim was to highlight how these regimes of power and the 'techniques of self' were a fundamental part of religious discourse. His work was an attempt to show the inescapable 'political' techniques of religion.

Political spirituality

One of the central features of Foucault's later 'religious question' is how religion, and Christianity in particular, creates 'forms of subjection' by developing 'new power relations'.[38] The 'spiritual', as Foucault elaborated in his 1982 lecture series at the Collège de France, involves a transformation of the subject. It is, as he tentatively stated in a later interview, 'a subject acceding to a certain mode of being'.[39] The 'spiritual', in this sense, refers to the construction of the subject through a series of power relations which shape life, the body and the self. Religious beliefs, ceremonies and rituals enact those relations of power and maintain a system of control through the mechanism of pastoral authority. Religion is constituted as a political force which brings people under a certain system of control. In Foucault's work the 'spiritual', like the 'sexual', does not exist apart from the 'political structures, requirements, laws, and regulations that have a primary importance for it'.[40]

Foucault transforms religious understanding by examining ideas/practice in terms of their 'political' efficacy, in terms of their 'mode of subjectification'. This strategic approach to religious ideas/practice 'problematises' religion and theology in terms of the 'political' which disrupts and places the 'spiritual' in quotes. Foucault had attempted to suspend the 'spiritual' by prioritising the 'relations of power' against the 'relations of meaning', but, as we have seen, this failed to establish the interconnection between the two.[41] The Reformation, therefore, was seen by him not in terms of the struggles of theological belief and doctrine but in terms of 'religious and moral power' and a 'crisis of the Western experience of subjectivity'.[42] Despite this confusion, his focus on the enactments of power was part of his wider strategy to 'inscribe the figures of spirituality on the earth of politics'.[43]

Although Foucault's principal discussion of religion in the early 1980s concerned Christianity (confession, pastoral power, techniques of self, ethical practice), this later 'problematisation' of religion in terms of the politics of subjectification received greater stimulus during one of the most controversial periods in his life, his journalist reportages of the Iranian Revolution in 1978.[44] While it would be wrong to suppose, as Georg Stauth's excellent paper on the subject indicates, that Foucault's interest in Iran arose only from a fascination with the 'spiritual transformation of subjectivity', it did bring the question of 'political spirituality' to the centre of his work.[45] As Stauth points out, despite the fact that the concept of 'spirituality' in Foucault's academic writing was not central, in his texts on Iran 'the constitution of a spiritual subject and the study of related practices' was a 'major concern in Foucault's thinking'.[46] The Iranian Revolution, in its attempt to overthrow the Shah, revealed to Foucault the full force of religious phenomena in holding the 'collective will', 'spirituality' forming the key factor in the people's challenge to institutional power.[47] The Shi'ite religion in Iran, according to Foucault, brought to the Iranian people 'the promise and guarantee of finding something that would radically change their subjectivity'.[48] Foucault was particularly intrigued by the new revolutionary phenomenon found in religion and the way the 'spiritual' (a 'highly prized additional level of meaning') 'mobilises a "political will"'.[49]

The controversy surrounding Foucault's reportages and his silence on the matter from May 1979 make it difficult to appreciate the relationship between his ideas of a 'political spirituality' in the reports on Iran and his work on Christianity and pastoral power; besides the biographical documentation, only a few writers, such as Jambet and Stauth, and to some extent O'Farrell, pick up the issue in any detail.[50] There are however significant connections between the interest in Iran and Foucault's work on Christianity. The bridging of these worlds can be seen when Foucault in his October 1978 article for *Le Nouvel Observateur* saw the West as having forgotten a 'political spirituality' since the Renaissance and 'the great crisis of Christianity' (the Reformation).[51] The concept of 'political spirituality' had also occurred earlier in a round table discussion in May 1978, where Foucault relates it to the wider question of 'government' and 'truth'.

> How can one analyze the connection between ways of distinguishing true and false and ways of governing oneself and others? The search for a new foundation for each of these practices, in itself and relative to the other, the will to discover a different way of governing oneself through a different way of dividing up true and false – this is what I would call 'political *spiritualité*'.[52]

Foucault had previously raised these issues of spiritual 'government' in relation to the Reformation and Counter-Reformation in his Collège de France lectures in February 1978, demonstrating his interest in this question some time before his work on the Iranian Revolution.[53] The Iranian question was therefore part of a whole series of issues related to the 'problematic of government' and 'spirituality' which gripped him in 1978 and which would eventually lead him to explore early Christianity. Although his idea of a 'political spirituality' is a marginal concept, it is, I would like to argue, applicable to the wider scope of his later work, precisely because it first gained its currency within the context of the 'novel thought space' of 'governmentality'.[54] As we noted earlier, the dynamic of 'governmentality' explored 'how to govern oneself', 'how to be governed' and 'how to govern others', each of these held together by what Allen refers to as 'the government of truth'.[55] Although 'truth' is a complex notion in Foucault's work, for our purposes the force of its position within 'governmentality' is linked to how it operates through the discourses and regimes of power in a particular culture or society where 'truth' is produced through 'multiple forms of constraint'.[56] 'Government' and 'truth' are therefore bound together in a single process. It was inside this 'problematic of government' that the political, ethical and spiritual were originally interwoven; they formed the 'mechanisms', 'techniques and procedures' in the production of 'truth'.[57]

This fusion of terminology in the matrix of 'governmentality' is one of the most complex and creative parts of Foucault's work, for it destabilises intellectual boundaries by reframing religion and theology within a wider 'problematic'. The understanding of Foucault's 'political spirituality' can easily become confused if it is taken out of the framework of 'governmentality'. When Bernauer and Mahon, for example, talk of a 'Foucaultian spirituality', they are specifically documenting, through a critical ethics, a 'force of resistance, of revolt against modern power–knowledge–subjectivity relations'.[58] There is here an overlapping and merging of ethics, politics and spirituality as each pertains to a 'mode of self-formation' or a 'mode of being'.[59] The interrelationship of terms is captured by Bernauer and Mahon in their examination of a 'political ethic', but the force of Foucault's work is perhaps more accurately held in Connolly's representation of his ethical sensibility as an 'ethico-political spirituality'.[60]

Foucault appears to collapse the 'spiritual', the 'ethical' and 'political' into a single trajectory of 'truth', 'subjectivity' and 'power', a strategy which can only be appreciated by locating it within the original 1978 framework of 'governmentality'. The notion of 'governmentality' holds together the 'ethical', 'spiritual' and 'political' inside a single framework, outside of which the terms become dislocated and redundant by being fused together. Foucault's 'political spirituality' is therefore part of a 'problematisation of government', developed in terms of a politics of 'subjectivity', which in its turn revolves on the dual meaning of the word 'subject' as both 'subject to someone else by control and dependence' and an 'identity by a conscience or self-knowledge'.[61] This play on the 'subject', as Jambet notes in relation to spirituality, represents a fundamental union of the governance of self and the governance of others which in the process challenges the dualism at the heart of theology.

Hence the ceaselessly repeated question of the link between religion and politics, between mysticism and power, between the spiritual and the material world disappears.[62]

The fusion of the political and spiritual – the conjunction being removed in the notion of 'political spirituality' – was given extra weight by the Iranian question because it provided Foucault with a contemporary manifestation of religion as an overt political force. It is also important to realise, as Jambet and Stauth make clear, that his emerging ideas on Iran follow a particular reading of Islam developed from the work of French Orientalists Louis Massignon and Henri Corbin, which supported his overall problematic of religion in terms of the political.[63] Corbin's work *Spiritual Body and Celestial Earth* examined a series of Islamic texts concerned with the 'world of Hūrqalyā', which, although difficult to represent in rational terms, is, as Corbin explains, 'the place where spirit and body are one, the place where spirit, taking on a body, becomes the "caro spiritualis", "spiritual corporeity"'.[64] What Corbin reveals in his study of Sufi and Shi'ite spirituality, as Jambet indicates, is how in certain forms of Islam 'this world is the threshold of the spiritual universe'.[65] The notion of 'spiritual corpor*eity*' in Corbin's study of Islam, although fundamentally different, recalls Foucault's earlier work of a 'spiritual corporality'. The location of the spiritual in the body, whether maintaining a dualism or not, brought the 'spiritual' back in relation to the material and the body politic.

The appeal of Corbin's work is to be found in the way it brushes against the language of Bataille, Klossowski and Blanchot in pointing towards a thought 'outside of dialectics'.[66] In 1964 Foucault admired Klossowski's attempt to overcome the Same and Other through the play of the 'simulacrum', and years later the challenge to a fundamental religious dualism is ignited in Foucault by the intersection of the 'spiritual' and 'political' subject in the Iranian Revolution. The essentialist language of 'transcendence' is broken by his incorporation of the body and the political technology of self into religious discourse.[67] His work is distinct from Corbin's interpretation of Islam in so far as Foucault ceases to operate on the idea of a 'spiritual' hierarchy where an 'intersection' or, as Jambet states, a 'threshold' between worlds is conceptualised.[68] Foucault's 'spiritual corporality' and 'political spirituality' is a fusion of terms, a 'messing up' of the binary categories of the 'spiritual' and the material, and, more specifically for Foucault, of the Christian order of things. Such a reordering transforms the entire field of religion into an immanent process of 'governmentality'. It challenges the entire understanding of religion. Foucault 'problematises' religious language and experience in such a way as to make the body and the politics of the subject unavoidable issues in religious discourse.

What emerges from Foucault's reportages, whether or not he correctly understood Islam and the Iranian situation, was an attempt, as Jambet indicates, 'to escape from the opposition between materiality and mystical phenonmena'.[69] There were clearly huge miscalculations of Iran and Islam in Foucault's journalistic work, but the force of his interest in the power of religious subjectivity in the shaping of human life is clear. As his description of the Iranian revolutionary movement in the Milan daily newspaper *Corriere della Sera* illustrates, religion for him was very much an immanent power.

> A movement that rejects being dissolved in political decision-making, a movement that has the imprint of a religion which speaks less of Beyond than of the transformations in this world.[70]

There are, as Stauth's more detailed study of the Iranian question illustrates, many 'ambiguities', 'contradictions' and complications in trying to understand Foucault's interpretations of Iran and Islamic spirituality; many of his earlier critiques of 'transcendent' categories and 'deeper meaning' are unsettled in the respect and value he attributes to these phenomena.[71] Foucault appears to acknowledge religious and spiritual belief, the 'additional level of meaning', the ideas of salvation and the Book, but interprets all these as struggles for a particular subjectification in the power of government, both of the self and others; they hold no interest as tenets of theological 'truth'.[72] It is surprising given the enormous political force of these theological ideas that Foucault, as we saw in the last chapter, can continually separate religious belief and practice. The precarious avoidance of the veracity of religious beliefs is perhaps partly explained by the return in one of his later interviews on Iran to the Marxist interpretation of religion, not as the opium of the people, but as 'the spirit of a world without spirit'.[73] This acknowledgement of the force of religion while disregarding its metaphysical claims provides a key indication of Foucault's evaluation of religion. Yet his 'religious question' is not simply a reworking of Marxist theory.

In the process of developing ideas of a 'political spirituality' and a 'spiritual corporality', Foucault is presenting a central challenge to the entire dualism of the theological apparatus and challenging the organisation of such categories as body and spirit, the material and the spiritual, and the religious and the secular. He is, from his earliest essays on Klossowski to his late works on Christian technologies of the self, effectively remapping the territory of religious discourse. What he is exposing is the 'technology of power' held within religious discourse. He is strategically bringing to light the way religion attempts to create a monopoly on experience through its ordering, categorising and subjectifying of human life.

Foucault's work on religion is a study, as he suggests in 1979, of the relations between experience, knowledge and power.[74] His tactic is to show how the 'spiritual' (religious and theological) can be suspended in the 'political' and the 'material', where the 'spiritual' is 'political' and the 'political' is 'spiritual', where these terms dissolve into the same network of power relationships, fighting for space in a 'strange game whose elements are life, death, truth, obedience, individuals, self-identity'.[75] The 'spiritual' becomes a form of discursive power in the attempt to win territory in the governance of human life.

Western Christian experience

The discussion of Foucault's 'political spirituality' enables us to see how he had started to link his discussion of religion and 'governmentality' to a non-Western context. Before embarking on his Iranian adventure he had returned to Japan in April 1978 and followed up a personal interest in the 'practice' of Zen, which, in a short interview, he had attempted to compare to Christian mysticism.[76] These short excursions into the Eastern traditions of Iran and Japan border a new set of frontiers in Foucault studies which have explored both an Orientalist 'sub-text' (Liebmann Schaub) and more recently a very illuminating 'sub-text' of race and bio-power (Stoler).[77] These studies have rescued the 'subjugated knowledges' within Foucault's own writing and provided useful critical registers to demonstrate how he is principally working in a white Western cultural context and how he lacked 'analytical concern' for wider colonial and racial issues within his discussion of religion.[78] This cultural bias enables us to see the problems in the slippage in Foucault's work between concepts of religion and concepts of Christianity, or more specifically Christianity in the Western context. His 'problematisation' of religion, outside his discussion of Iran, is more accurately a 'problematisation' of 'Christianity' in its dominant institutional formation – it is a critique of a Western 'religious' phenomenon. Foucault's underlying aim was principally to critique the binary oppositions at the heart of Christian doctrine – to bring the body and politics back into Western religious discourse.

Conclusion
Religion after Foucault

> Where religions once demanded the sacrifice of bodies, knowledge now calls for experimentation on ourselves, calls us to the sacrifice of the subject of knowledge.
>
> Foucault (1971a) 'Nietzsche, Geneaology, History', p. 163

In this work I have tried to draw out the strands of Foucault's examination of religion and attempted to show how he transforms the map of religious thinking. I have shown throughout how the critiques of a 'spiritual corporality' and a 'political spirituality' offer a radical re-evaluation of religion, and Christianity in particular, in terms of developing religion as an immanent political experience which attempts to govern human life. My aim has been to show that prior to Foucault's discussion of Christianity in his late work there was a significant religious sub-text which developed a critical religious perspective. His late studies of Christianity were not therefore some sudden turn to religion but part of his wider critical reading of Christianity.

In order to understand Foucault's style of critique towards Christianity we must remember that his approach is selective and strategic. (There would be just as many dangers in creating a theologian or church historian out of him as there are in making him a mystic!) His work effectively unfolds a series of tactical interventions in his 'problematisation' of Christianity. The central tenets of this 'problematisation' were the dynamics of speech (the said) and silence (the unsaid). Together the silence and speech of Christianity formed a single entity. Foucault's critique is similarly held together on these two fronts. His earlier avant-garde work subverts theology from within, by integrating the silent Other of religion in an embodied reorientation or 'spiritual corporality'; while his later studies of 'governmentality' disrupt the power structures which silenced, by documenting the 'subjectifying' forces of Christianity in the creation of a 'political spirituality'. 'Spiritual corporality' and 'political spirituality' in this sense were mirror images of a single critique. This twofold critical analysis of Christianity was an attempt by Foucault 'to refuse what we are' by empowering others through a 'political spirituality' and offering, in however limited a way, 'new forms of [religious] subjectivity' in a 'spiritual corporality'.[1]

What I have been suggesting throughout this work is that Foucault's early studies developing avant-garde religious ideas on embodiment can be read through the lens of the later studies. The creative tension of the silence within the discursive practice of Christianity can be seen when Foucault's 1963 essay on Bataille, 'A Preface to Transgression', is read alongside his 1982 study of John Cassian, 'The Battle for Chastity'.[2] There is perhaps some consistency in Foucault's critique of Christianity when we consider how his description of the 'technique for analyzing and diagnosing thought' in Cassian is part of his wider 'shattering of the philosophical subject'.[3] The direction of Foucault's 'religious question' throughout his life is best captured if we read 'philosophical' as 'Christian' in the following declaration from 1963:

> The breakdown of philosophical subjectivity and its dispersion in a language that dispossesses it while multiplying it within the space created by its absence is probably one of the fundamental structures of contemporary thought.[4]

Foucault's earlier avant-garde explorations were strategic repulsions of the Christian techniques of self, reorderings of Cassian's inductions and rejections of the confessional practice by empowering bodies in a new discursive regime. Such a strategy shows how Foucault, in line with Sade, the Surrealists and Bataille before him, effectively unpicks the threads of the Christian technology of the self in a 'refusal' of the 'religious' subject. He opens up ways to 'think differently' about religion as the 'spiritual' and 'religious' are collapsed, or 'dispersed', into a new set of force relations. This new set of force relations brings the body and sexuality into a new space of government, both of the self and of others, where new relationships and new modes of being can be established.

The foundations of Foucault's critique of religion

Although I have argued that Foucault's work on religion can be located under the categories of a 'spiritual corporality' and a 'political spirituality', these broad categories function to gather up the fragments of his work on religion – they are ways of framing the sub-text of his writing. These categories are, however, constituted by a series of underlying theoretical moves that shape his critique of traditional Western conceptions of religion. In summary, it is possible to see Foucault's work on religion as operating on the basis of five interrelated factors from his wider work: an analysis of cultural facts (the integration of religion and culture); the historical and social location of discourse (religious immanence not transcendence); the prioritisation of the body and sexuality (the embodiment of belief); an analysis of the mechanisms of power (the micro-politics of religious utterances and silence); and the development of a technology of the self (the religious government of the self). These areas are not surprisingly reflections of Foucault's archaeological and genealogical methods. Aspects of these methodologies have already been taken up and integrated by scholars in an analysis of religion and theology; they form the basis of formulating an understanding of religion after Foucault. In conclusion, I want to take each of these factors in turn and briefly highlight a few studies in religion and theology that have taken up Foucault's challenge. I want to show how his work has provided rich resources for rethinking religious studies and theology. My discussion is not intended to be exhaustive but aims simply to mark out the contours of religion after Foucault.

An analysis of cultural facts (the integration of religion and culture)

In Foucault's work religion is an inseparable dimension of the 'history of the present'; it always informs an understanding of the contemporary cultural context. It is not possible to examine the Western history of madness, medicine, prisons and sexuality without appreciating the cultural roots of these discourses and practices in Christianity. Foucault's genealogy has, with other intellectual projects of the late twentieth century, provided a significant shift in reshaping not only the understanding of religion but also the study of religion itself. It has been through the linking of religion and culture that the fields of religious studies and theology have been challenged to rethink not only the place of religion and theology within a specific culture but also the politics of defining 'religion' as a specific practice within culture. This position has been most recently taken up by Richard King, who, informed by a Foucauldian critical perspective, states:

> 'Religion' ... is a theoretical construction useful for the purposes of examining one particular aspect of the human experience but should not be reified, as if it could exist apart from that context. Increasing academic specialization, appeals to the sui generis and privileged status of religion, and the legitimation and preservation of the institutional 'expert on religion' in the secular Academy, have all led to a tendency to treat 'religion' as if it were more than an explanatory construct with a particular cultural and ideological genealogy of its own.[5]

King's analysis also draws attention, following Said's critique of Foucault, to the need for a cross-cultural analysis of religion in order to reveal the hegemonic structures of Western cultural practices in the formation and understanding of religion. Foucault's brief excursion into the religious traditions of Islam and Buddhism also shows the importance of appreciating the growing complexity of cultural exchange and the interconnections of different religious beliefs and practices. In this regard it is important, as Ann Laura Stoler has indicated, to be aware of what Foucault 'categorically chose not to explore'.[6] If religion is a central part of cultural analysis, then it is not possible in a global context to limit this analysis to Christianity or to the traditions and philosophies of the so-called 'Western' world. After Foucault, religion is inescapably bound up with cultural practices, and if we take the implications of this position seriously, we have to recognise the limits of his project – after Foucault we have to go beyond Foucault. But we also have to recognise that an analysis of culture cannot ignore questions of religion.

The historical and social location of discourse (religious immanence not transcendence)

Foucault's work has always been concerned with the historical conditions through which an object of study has been constituted – the ground from which a particular discourse emerges. Religious discourse for him is part of the 'complex' and 'restrictive' exchange and communication in a particular system or culture. It forms part of a 'ritual that determines the individual properties and agreed roles of the speaker'.[7] Foucault's work provides a way of exploring the operations of religious discourse as a part of the ritual and practice of 'limitation' and 'exclusion' within a culture – it marks out the boundaries of life and death, the possible and impossible, the acceptable and unacceptable. Religious doctrine, like political and philosophical doctrine, shapes the 'utterances' and 'subjectivity' of an individual – it 'subjectifies' an individual.[8]

> We must conceive discourse as a violence that we do to things, or, at all events, as a practice we impose upon them; it is in this practice that the events of discourse find the principle of their regularity.[9]

This 'archaeology of knowledge' locates religious discourse in the practices of human life; it is concerned not with a 'transcendent' order outside the historical conditions of our being but with the very limits of human existence.

Although Foucault never explored the nature of religious and theological ideas in any specific depth, it is possible to see from his brief excursions into religious discourse how his critique of the discourse of sexuality is equally applicable to religious concepts. In his discussion of sexuality he wants to mark out the 'apparatus of knowledge' that constitutes a certain idea, such as sexuality; he wants to explore the deployment of the concept. In this analysis he puts forward the 'rule of immanence'.

> One must not suppose that there exists a certain sphere of sexuality that would be the legitimate concern of a free and disinterested scientific inquiry were it not the object of mechanisms of prohibition brought to bear by the economic or ideological requirements of power.[10]

146   *Conclusion*

In a similar way, theological doctrine, for example, cannot be explored in some 'free and disinterested' realm; it is always caught in wider 'ideological requirements'. We gain further insight into Foucault's analysis of religious discourse if we replace the word 'sexuality' with 'theology' in the following expansion of the 'rule of immanence'.

> If sexuality was constituted as an area of investigation, this was only because relations of power had established it as a possible object. ... Between techniques of knowledge and strategies of power, there is no exteriority, even if they have specific roles and are linked together on the basis of difference.[11]

Foucault's work does not necessarily deny the possibility of religious experience; rather, it locates this experience in the politics and strategic relations of human struggles. Religious discourse is not some privileged arena free from human prejudice and bias, but is rather constructed in and through the ambiguities of human living. Discourses about the limits of existence and the mystery of being are always framed and positioned in and through the human process of power/knowledge. In this sense 'transcendence' is only a useful concept if it is grounded in the transformations that occur within the immanent processes of life.

This shift in religious understanding brings the embodied practices of religion into sharper focus, and because of this scholars of religion have often coupled discussion of religious immanence with the discussion of the body and sexuality. I will therefore provide some examples of the engagement of religious studies and theology with the idea of immanence in the next section. What remains, however, is that after Foucault religious discourse functions not as some statement of a reality 'outside' of this life but as the organisation and ordering of this life – it is about the politics of human living at the limits of knowing and the limits of life itself.

The prioritisation of the body and sexuality (the embodiment of belief)

Foucault's early engagement with the avant-garde and his later genealogical method brought the body and sexuality to a central pivot of analysis. The body, for Foucault, was marked by history and was in effect a point from which the historical process could itself be marked out as a 'counter-memory' – those parts of history which were concealed and denied. The discourses of the body and sexuality were therefore parts of the 'counter-memory' of religion. After Foucault, religion and theology are seen as inseparable from questions about the body and sexuality. Religion is always about the body and sexual orientation, in so far as the body maps or anchors discourses about religious practice and belief. This can be seen from the fact that religious discourses are always concerned with what individuals are doing with their bodies, with whom and where they are doing it.[12] Foucault, of course, is not the only writer to draw attention to this correlation between the body, sexuality and religion: feminist writers have in some ways provided a more extensive examination of the body politics of religion.[13] However, despite the limitations of Foucault's work, Bruce Knauft is correct in identifying how '[g]ender and feminism have moved to a post-Foucauldian era'.[14] Contemporary theories of the body and sexuality are indebted to the strategic frameworks Foucault has provided for breaking up the oppressive hegemonic structures of patriarchy and homophobia.

Despite Foucault's lacuna of gender, his social constructivist model of the body and sexuality has also provided a major resource for rethinking the nature of religious and theological studies. There are now a whole new series of studies on the body and religion, from the investigations of the body in the sociology of religion to more radical studies that bring the erotic and sexual desire into the heart of theology.[15] 'In contrast to the fading postmodernism,' as Knauft indicates, 'the critical deconstruction of gender and sexuality continues with gusto across a multidisciplinary front.'[16] These critical studies have opened up the fields of religion and theology to recognise that 'beliefs' are not simply articulations of some abstract knowledge but statements about embodied practice. Religious discourses 'inscribe' the surface of the (sexed) body, even if those discourses are dominated by male heteronormative paradigms and attempt to detach themselves from the body. The emergence of 'body theology' and debates between theology and sexuality echo much that is found in Foucault's writing, even if such work has only picked up fragments of his 'spiritual corporality'.

Foucault's work, alongside other feminist and post-structuralist thinkers, has challenged the binary oppositions of body and spirit. In this space we begin to see the emergence of new imaginative theologies and the development of what Grace Jantzen sees as a 'divine horizon for human becoming' where 'sexuality cannot be left out'.[17] In such a new climate of opinion, we find, alongside Foucault's 'spiritual corporality', other flourishing non-dualistic ideas such as a 'transcendental somatics' and a 'sensible transcendental'.[18] The gods and goddesses, it would seem, are being brought back to flesh, not in some binary incarnational theology, but as an embodied and lived reality where spirit is body and body spirit. After Foucault and feminism, religion and theology become questions of the sexed-body.

An analysis of the mechanisms of power (the micro-politics of religious utterances and silence)

While the concept of power has not been an explicit theme in this work, it is, however, very much implicit in the operations of 'silence' and 'speech', in the mechanisms of the 'said and unsaid'. The power of religion sets up the point of resistance in a 'spiritual corporality' and is demarcated in a 'political spirituality'.

It is important to recognise in this respect that power for Foucault is always a 'multiplicity of force relations' in any given context; it is everywhere and comes from everywhere. It is not simply some institutional hierarchy of relations.

> Power is not something that is acquired, seized, or shared, something that one holds on to or allows to slip away; power is exercised from innumerable points, in the interplay of nonegalitarian and mobile relations.[19]

Religion is a sphere of force relations in the wider cultural network – it inescapably exists as a manifestation of power.

Foucault's analysis of power/knowledge has been the most developed aspect of his work in the dialogue with religious studies and theology. There have been a wide range of responses from biblical hermeneutics to comparative religion which have utilised his work to provide a new critical analysis. Elizabeth Castelli, for example, developed his thinking on power (with 'a feminist gloss') to explore the 'repressed knowledges and discourses' in the New Testament works of Paul. As Castelli points out:

> Foucault's understandng of power is important to a reading of Paul because it refocuses the analysis: if power is seen as something which circulates within a system, something inhering in relationships rather than as a possession of a person or group, then one can rethink what is going on in the texts this way; rather than looking for Paul's 'opponents' one can look for his conversation partners.[20]

In a different feminist analysis, Grace Jantzen has utilised Foucault's work on power relations to develop a genealogy of gender in Christian mysticism. His methodology allowed her to show how any history of Christian mysticism is a history of power, and, recognising his limitations, she goes on to indicate how this history is always a 'gendered power'. As she states: 'Those who are in control are the ones who define what shall count as genuine and what shall count as deviant.'[21]

Richard King, working in the area of the comparative study of religion, has also developed Foucault's idea of power as a useful lens for examining truth/knowledge claims in religious studies. What King wants to demonstrate is how

> ... the central normative concepts of the discipline of 'religious studies' – terms such as 'religion' and 'mysticism', as well as constructs such as 'Hinduism' and 'Buddhism' – have a discursive history that is bound up with the power struggles and theological issues of Western Christianity.[22]

He argues for a recognition of the 'mutual imbrication of religion, culture and power', where religion and culture are understood as 'the field in which power relations operate'.[23] In a very different manner Kyle Pasewark has used Foucault's work to develop a more adequate theology of power outside the traditional models of domination. 'Power', in Pasewark's work, 'is affirmed as ubiquitous and unavoidable, the fundamental description of being-itself.'[24]

What becomes clear from these studies is that religion after Foucault always exists as a system of power, meaning that it orders life through a set of force relations; not through a violence which forces people to do things but through the shaping of individual subjects to voluntarily carry out a particular way of life. This does not mean, as King, following Steven Parrish, has indicated, that everything is reduced to power, but rather it means appreciating power as one of the many 'strategies' Foucault employed in a wider genealogical framework.[25] This point becomes much clearer when we appreciate that Foucault in 1983 acknowledged that his later work moved from a hermeneutics of domination to a hermeneutics of the subject.[26] In this sense, it is important to recognise that 'religious practices', and the study of religion, are not necessarily negative manifestations of power but points of resistance and tension for the shaping of a particular way of living and understanding of life. As Giddens indicates, power is a 'mobilising phenomenon, not just one that sets limits'; through power we create ways of living.[27] There is no ideal or neutral pattern of living, only different forms of living set against each other – however, the ethical question remains as to which of these are more or less oppressive.

The development of a technology of the self (the religious government of the self)

Finally, Foucault's later work on Christianity showed that religion forms part of a technology of the self as a 'truth' game. As he indicated: 'The truth obligations of faith and the self are linked together.'[28] The fascinating feature of Christianity was how the self was formed and shaped through the paradoxical act of renouncing the self – there was a mutual act of disclosure and renunciation in the practice of confession. What Foucault's later work demonstrated is that religious discourses 'govern' the self, both at the macro level of institutional order and at the micro level of individual subjectification. What Foucault revealed about religious practice was a series of

> ... techniques which permit individuals to effect, by their own means, a certain number of operations on their bodies, on their souls, on their own thoughts, on their own conduct, and this in a manner so as to transform themselves, modify themselves, and to attain a certain state of perfection, of happiness, of purity, of supernatural power, and so on.[29]

The religious self is always part of an historical technology which produces and maintains the self. After Foucault, religion is, amongst other things, a politics of self.

Religion after Foucault is involved in the shaping of individual subjects; it creates what we are by revealing the 'truth' of what we are in the practices we perform. The practices of a religion create the 'truth' of ourselves, which in turn, as Asad and others have pointed out, questions the prioritisation of 'belief' over 'practice' in the Western conception of religion.[30] In Foucault, as I have indicated, 'belief' is a form of 'practice'. Religious beliefs order and regulate the embodied subject. Religion as a power–knowledge matrix forms a technology of self, not necessarily in a negative way, but as a force among others shaping life. There is no neutral free-floating life, only certain technologies and operations that mark out a life.

The engagement of theology and religious studies with Foucault's technologies of the self in Christianity has so far been limited and to some extent merges with the (extensive) literature on his ethics of the self, which is beyond the scope of this work and cannot adequately be addressed in these concluding reflections.[31] One of the reasons for the lack of engagement of religious studies and theology with Foucault's work on the self is the fact that the fourth volume of his *History of Sexuality* on Christianity remains unpublished.[32] The discussion of the self has thus become submerged with details about the historical accuracy of his work on the Greco-Roman period. Those like Pierre Hadot, for example, have been critical of Foucault's interpretation of the Greco-Roman world and have questioned his work for putting forward 'a culture of self which is *too* aesthetic'.[33] It is, however, recognised that Foucault to a large extent was engaging in a 'history of the present'.

Foucault's analysis of the practices of the self, as Hadot indicates, 'is not merely an historical study, but rather a tacit attempt to offer contemporary mankind [*sic*] a model of life, which Foucault calls "an aesthetics of existence"'.[34] According to Herman Nilson, this aesthetic was motivated by Foucault's Nietzschean project and his own personal attempt to explore, through such ideas as 'friendship', the nature of a ' "gay" stylistics of existence' outside notions of sexual identity and modern conceptions of homosexuality. Nilson, quoting Foucault, even goes as far as to suggest that Foucault's later work on the self offered opportunities to explore critically the entire nature of (Western) ethical thinking.

> For today, at the end of the twentieth century, and after two thousand years of Christian ethics, the problem of homosexuality can no longer be reduced to a bigoted tolerance towards him who feels differently, but should be considered as an aesthetic experiment. Here lies the challenge and the open horizon of a culture of self which is being revealed in gay lifestyle – at the end of an era in which 'the idea of morality as obedience to a code of rules is now disappearing, has already disappeared. To

this absence of a morality, one responds, or must respond, with an investigation which is that of an aesthetics of existence.'[35]

The construction of ethics as an 'aesthetics of existence' rather than as a code of behaviour has been developed in Don Cupitt's popular rethinking of Christian ethics as 'solar ethics' – a morality 'aestheticized as lifestyle'.[36] While there are many problems with Cupitt's ethical model and his lack of detailed discussion of Foucault, it does reflect yet another example of how the tropes of Foucault's work are being creatively carried forward into contemporary religious thinking. It reflects how after Foucault the boundaries of traditional religious thinking are continually been contested.

Foucault's analysis of religion

As we can see, religious studies and theology have started to open up some engagement with Foucault's work by developing aspects of the five underlying factors of his analysis of religion; a situation which reflects the impact of his archaeological and genealogical methods on Western intellectual debate. It also becomes clear when looking at the five underlying factors that they overlap and cannot be separated; they form interlocking parts of Foucault's wider critical work. In the process of developing these critical perspectives Foucault applied them (often at a sub-textual and marginal level) to religion and they have in turn been applied to religion by later scholars (who have often neglected or not been concerned with Foucault's own religious questions). What I have attempted to show in this book is that by integrating the fragments of Foucault's work on religion it is possible to formulate broader categories which reflect his own religious question. It is for this reason that I refer to a 'spiritual corporality' and a 'political spirituality'. These categories hold together the various strands of Foucault's work and offer a sense of his own understanding of religion.

The emergence of 'religion' in its disappearance

The idea that there is a single 'religious question' arising from Foucault's work has principally been a hermeneutical tool to explore the variegated religious content of his writing. In the realm of the 'specific intellectual' a single direction to Foucault's religious thought is difficult to substantiate.[37] There may or may not be a wider desire to reorientate theology; there may or may not be an unconscious Catholic agenda in his work. Whatever the ideological intention, the strategic significance of Foucault's critique of Christianity is clear: what he is *doing* is breaking down the 'spiritual' into a new politics of human experience. While most of my argument operates on a 'sub-text', it none the less serves to bring together aspects of Foucault's thinking which would otherwise remain marginal and hidden. His attempt to think differently about religion not only reveals the richness of his work;

it also provides us with a clearer understanding of religion. When religion is situated in the Foucauldian model of critical analysis it assumes a far greater cultural significance than has otherwise been acknowledged in academic studies. Religion needs to be rediscovered outside the superstitions, misconceptions and illusions through which 'secular' academics have so far dismissed the subject. We need to find religion in the very fabric of the 'secular' – in the absence.

Foucault's 'religious question' finally rests on an 'absence', not only the 'absence' of his voice and the 'absence' of the fourth volume of *The History of Sexuality*, but the 'absence' of a transcendent and normative religious ideal. In this 'absence' we are left with questions of how to create new forms of embodied subjectivity through a 'spiritual corporality' and a 'political spirituality'. From this 'absence' a new 'religious space' will emerge in its disappearance – it will perhaps no longer be recognisable – 'like a face drawn in sand at the edge of the sea'.[38]

Notes

Preface

1 Davidson (1997), p. 1.
2 See, for example, Dreyfus and Rabinow (1982); Gutting (1989); Bernauer (1990); E.A. Clark (1988); Milbank (1990).
3 Landry and Maclean (1996), p. 158.
4 Asad (1993), p. 29; R. King (1999), p. 210.
5 Bruns (1997), p. 20.
6 Private review. The placing of the word 'analytical' in part parenthesis is an attempt to draw attention to the tight control within certain forms of logic and analysis and the desire within binary thought to dismiss certain areas of experience as valid parts of theological reflection (i.e. the rejection of bodily fluids as 'tasteless'). The highlighting of the prefix 'anal' in this instance is a technical reference to Freud's 1908 essay 'Character and Anal Eroticism' (Freud [1908] 1959). Anal, according to Freud, refers to such character traits as 'orderliness, parsimony and obstinacy' (p. 171). For a critical assessment of binary logic within certain forms of analytical philosophy, see Jantzen (1998).
7 Foucault (1969a), p. 210.

Introduction: Approaching Foucault's work on religion

1 Works in the sociology of religion include Turner (1991, 1996). Cf. Shilling (1993). Foucault's work has also been explored from a number of other perspectives within religious studies and theology: see Welch (1985); Chidester (1986); Ray (1987); Lalonde (1993); Moore (1992); Castelli (1992); Behr (1993); Milbank (1990); Davis (1994). See also the conclusion of this work for further discussion of the ways Foucault's methodology has been applied to religion and theology.
2 The idea of the a 'history of the present' is taken from Foucault (1975a), p. 31. See Castel (1994) for a discussion of this idea and Foucault's historical method.
3 Levinson (1981), p. vii.
4 Macey (1993), pp. 192, 415. I am grateful to Lois McNay for indicating how this work may appear 'fetishistic' if the 'religious question' is not contextualised and substantiated by linking the question to Foucault's main texts.
5 Foucault (1967c), p. 605.
6 Foucault (1975c), pp. 53–4. Cf. Cousins and Hussain [1984] (1990), p. 265.
7 Levinson (1981), p. vii.
8 See E.A. Clark (1988).
9 Deleuze [1986] (1988), pp. 96ff. Foucault (1966a), p. 340. Deleuze also suggests with a slightly different emphasis that the fourth volume of *The History of Sexuality* 'concerns the whole problem of the "fold" (incarnation) when it

stresses the Christian origins of flesh from the viewpoint of the history of sexuality'. Deleuze [1986] (1988) p. 149 n. 36. This illustrates how creative the idea of the 'fold' can be to different readings of Foucault's work on religion. I am, however, using the idea of the 'fold' to play different parts of Foucault work against each other and also to play with the idea of an 'inside' and an 'outside' in Foucault's thinking. I am suggesting Foucault's 'religious question' exists within this fold.

10 See E.A. Clark (1988); Brown (1988). The question of historical accuracy has also been addressed in relation to Foucault's work on the Greco-Roman period: see Cameron (1986) and Goldhill (1995).

11 It is certainly possible, for example, to establish links between 'spiritual corporality' and Foucault's late work on the ethics of the self. I, however, make a distinction between the early and late work according to a 'spiritual corporality' and a 'political spirituality' because the 'emphasis' in Foucault's writing is different in each period. While I am accepting, as Lois McNay suggests, that the work on ethics 'recalls' the earlier work on transgression, I maintain a difference between the early and late reflections on religion because Foucault is tactically drawing out a different 'emphasis' from a single critique. There are, for example, no references to the early death of God discourse in Foucault's late discussion of the Christian technologies of self, although one could make interesting and valid links. See McNay (1994), p. 145. I am grateful for Lois McNay's comments on this aspect of my work which enable me to make this clarification.

12 This definition and usage of 'corporal' and 'corporeal' is taken from the *Universal Dictionary* (London: Reader's Digest Association Ltd, 1993), p. 354. Although it may not assume a common acceptance, it none the less provides a valuable framework for my discussion of Foucault's work.

13 For a valuable discussion of the increasingly popular term 'spirituality', see A.S. King (1996). It is King who suggests the term 'spirituality' is used to avoid the use of the term 'religion', which is associated with more traditional and oppressive ideas. Following King's examination of the word 'spirituality' it can be seen how Foucault's critique of religion adopts a non-religious use of the term 'spiritual' to signify 'an escape from the unnecessary confines of religion into the more inclusive realm of our common humanity, rendering any necessary reference to the transcendent obsolete' (A.S. King, 1996, p. 343).

14 Foucault (1964b), p. 338. The debate organised by *Tel Quel* took place in September 1963.

1 Outline of Foucault's work and the question of religion

1 Foucault (1981d), p. 314. I have used the phrase the 'mythology of the postmodern' because of the difficulties inherent within this term and its current proliferation. The phrase is also used to draw attention to the fact that Foucault did not regard himself as a 'postmodern' or 'post-structuralist' thinker (Foucault, 1983e, p. 34). He is perhaps best disassociated from the ambiguous word 'postmodern' (he still operates on Modernist and Enlightenment paradigms) and understood more in the context of 'post-structuralism', particularly as he argues for constructed positions of knowledge and history, and challenges any underlying or given structure of knowledge. For a discussion of the complexity of the term 'postmodern', see Jameson (1991), pp. ixff. and Wakefield (1990), pp. 20ff.

2 See Halperin (1995) and Seigel (1990), for whom a gay politic is inseparable from Foucault's life and work. However, others, such as Eribon, while not ignoring Foucault's homosexuality, believe it can be overplayed in understanding his work.

Obviously, one cannot pretend that Foucault's entire work is explained by his homosexuality, as certain American academics do, imagining, moreover, that this would be enough to discredit it. Sartre's answer to vulgar Marxism might be useful here: of course Paul Valéry is a 'petit-bourgeois', but not all 'petits-bourgeois' are Paul Valéry.

(Eribon, 1992, p. 28)

Eribon, in the attempt to present a balanced and uncontroversial picture of Foucault to his French audience, seems to ignore the possibility of a positive interpretation of Foucault's work through his homosexuality and fails to consider the wider questions of a gay political life so convincingly demonstrated by David Halperin. There have been few works exploring the interface of Foucault, religion and gay identity, but for a useful introduction to these issues see Vernon (1996).

3 Foucault's disruptive style is captured in a 1975 interview: 'I would like my books to be sorts of scalpels, Molotov cocktails or minefields and that they would explode after use like fireworks' (Foucault, 1975b, p. 14). Translation taken from O'Farrell (1989), p. 93.

4 Certeau (1986), pp. 193–8. Foucault can be seen to deliberately play with an 'enigmatic gesture'. See Foucault (1981d), p. 314. Lemert and Gillan believe that Foucault's style is central to understanding his work. 'If Foucault creates the impression of obscurity, it is for a reason. ... Actually Foucault's literary style is a direct consequence of his intellectual, especially historical, method' (Lemert and Gillan, 1982, p. ix).

5 Bove (1988), p. xix. Cf. Bove (1986).

6 See Cousins and Hussain [1984] (1990), p. 253.

7 Foucault (1978g), p. 27.

8 Foucault (1977i), p. 197.

9 Foucault (1970a), pp. 224ff.

10 For a detailed discussion of the influence of Bachelard and Canguilhem, see Gutting (1989), pp. 9–54. The influences of phenomenology on Foucault's work have been documented by Dreyfus and Rabinow, who describe Foucault's work as a 'phenomenology to end all phenomenologies'. See Dreyfus and Rabinow (1982), pp. 44ff. Cf. Deleuze [1986] (1988), pp. 108ff.

11 Foucault (1978g), p. 26; Foucault (1976g), p. 115; Foucault (1984d), p. 257.

12 Hoy (1986), p. 2.

13 Foucault (1954a), p. 32.

14 Foucault (1954b), p. 1.

15 Dreyfus (1987), p. viii.

16 See Bernauer (1990), p. 45 and n. 113.

17 Foucault (1966a), p. xi; Foucault (1969a), p. 60.

18 Foucault (1969a), p. 107.

19 Ibid., p. 80.

20 Ibid., p. 87.

21 Dreyfus and Rabinow (1982), pp. 44ff.

22 Foucault (1969a), p. 100.

23 Ibid., pp. 103–4.

24 Ibid., p. 117.

25 Ibid., p. 121.

26 Ibid., p. 127.

27 Ibid., p. 170.

28 Ibid., p. 131.

29 There have been a number of works which are critical of Foucault's writing of the history of madness. See in particular Midelfort [1980] (1988) and Porter (1987), pp. 6–9. Cf. Goldstein (1994) for a wider discussion of issues related to Foucault and history.
30 Foucault (1961b), p. 73. Foucault suggests that madness is constructed and maintained through a series of cultural 'images' or 'iconographic powers'. See ibid., pp. 206ff.
31 Foucault (1961b), pp. 26, 95.
32 Foucault (1961b), p. 205; Porter (1987), p. 5.
33 Foucault (1961b), pp. 212, 278.
34 Ibid., p. 241.
35 Foucault (1963a), p. xix.
36 Ibid., p. 197.
37 Ibid., p. 196.
38 Ibid., p. 196.
39 Ibid., p. 196.
40 See, for example, Jantzen (1995), who examines Christian mysticism from a Foucauldian and gender perspective.
41 Foucault (1963a), p. xvi.
42 Foucault (1961b), p. 244. Foucault also explored, through the idea of the 'system of the transgressive', the relationship between religious deviation of the demonic and the medicalisation of this parareligious experience. See Foucault (1962/1968).
43 See Foucault (1962a); Foucault (1963b, 1963c, 1963d, 1964a). Many of these literary studies hold key religious ideas and I will examine them in detail in chapters 3–5.
44 Foucault (1969a), p. 191.
45 Foucault (1966a), pp. xx, xxii.
46 Ibid., p. 39.
47 Ibid., pp. 59, 72–3.
48 Ibid., pp. 59, 75.
49 Ibid., p. 74.
50 Ibid., p. 203.
51 Ibid., p. 51.
52 Shumway (1989), pp. 75–6.
53 Foucault (1966a), p. 207.
54 Ibid., p. 251.
55 Ibid., pp. 221–36.
56 Ibid., p. 296.
57 Ibid., p. 298.
58 Ibid., pp. xxiii, 307–8.
59 Ibid., pp. 318, 336.
60 Ibid., p. 318.
61 Ibid., p. 322.
62 Ibid., p. 329.
63 Ibid., pp. 329–30, 335.
64 Ibid., pp. 383–4.
65 Ibid., p. 386.
66 Foucault (1970a), p. 224.
67 Ibid., p. 232.
68 Foucault (1983q).
69 Foucault (1971a, 1969a).
70 Foucault (1971a), p. 160.

71 The relationship between genealogy and archaeology has been adequately explored by other writers, particularly in the early 1980s when it formed a central area of discussion in the attempts to find conceptual and methodological clarification in Foucault's work. See Sheridan (1980); Dreyfus and Rabinow (1982); Donnelly (1982); Cousins and Hussain [1984] (1990); Minson (1985); Gane (1986). It is now generally accepted that genealogy is an 'enlargement' of archaeology. See Kusch (1991), p. 115; Foucault (1969a), p. 162; Foucault (1976b), p. 85. Smart (1985), pp. 54–5. Donnelly sees the 'similarities' between archaeology and genealogy as 'unmistakable and worrying' (Donnelly, 1982, p. 26). The 'similarities' can be seen as presenting problems of coherence between archaeology and genealogy. As Donnelly indicates: 'There is doubtless need for more discussion still before Foucault's work becomes generally accessible' (Donnelly, 1982, p. 15).The question of power is certainly a new dimension in genealogy. See Sheridan (1980), pp. 115ff. Cf. Smart (1985), pp. 71ff. This angle on genealogy and power is adopted strongly by Kusch (1991), pp. 115ff. Kusch isolates power as the key strand of genealogy and makes a valuable comparison with other models of power. For a more critical perspective of Foucault's work on 'power' see Cousins and Hussain [1984] (1990), pp. 201, 225ff. and O'Farrell (1989), p. 102. In Foucault's genealogical studies the concept of power is added to widen the focus of archaeology, a fact not least brought to the forefront by the events of May 1968 in Paris. Foucault acknowledges that his earlier studies can be understood in terms of the later concept of power, which was, due to the political situation, a conceptual 'field of analyses' previously unavailable (Foucault, 1976g, p. 115; Sheridan, 1980, pp. 112–15). Foucault's later work is not so much a break or a change, as a refinement, where discourse is built into a new understanding of power–knowledge. The beginnings of this reworking can be seen in his 1970 inaugural lecture, where the discursive structures are built onto a larger social framework (Foucault, 1970a, pp. 231–3). The notion of '*dispositif*' is also seen as important to the development of genealogy. See Bernauer (1990), pp. 145ff.; Macey (1993), p. 355.
72 Foucault (1975a), pp. 26–8.
73 Ibid., p. 93.
74 Ibid., p. 95.
75 Ibid., p. 105.
76 Ibid., p. 30.
77 Ibid., p. 136.
78 Ibid., pp. 138, 193.
79 Ibid., p. 194.
80 Ibid., p. 251.
81 Ibid., pp. 226, 251.
82 Foucault (1983r).
83 Eribon (1992), pp. 317ff.; Macey (1993), pp. 354, 466.
84 With the recent publication of Foucault's lectures at the Collège de France the strict adherence to such an interpretation of Foucault's request has been broken and in this light it is possible to see that eventually the fourth volume will be published. For a discussion of the fourth volume see Carrette (1999b).
85 Foucault (1976a), p. 151.
86 Ibid., pp. 105–6.
87 Ibid., pp. 5, 130.
88 Ibid., p. 71.
89 Ibid., p. 92.
90 Ibid., p. 127.
91 Ibid., pp. 154–9.

 92 Foucault (1984a), p. 6.
 93 Foucault (1980c), p. 203. Cf. Foucault (1982i).
 94 Foucault (1984a), p. 10.
 95 Foucault (1984b), p. 41.
 96 Ibid., pp. 43–5.
 97 Ibid., p. 58.
 98 Ibid., p. 103.
 99 Ibid., p. 239.
100 Foucault (1984b), p. 240; Foucault (1980c), pp. 221–2.

2 Silence and confession

 1 Foucault (1977h), p. 194.
 2 The areas of study listed here constitute the 'apparatus' (*dispositif*) of Foucault's genealogical inquiry. See Foucault (1977h), pp. 194ff. and chapter 6 in this work.
 3 Foucault (1982g), pp. 3–4; Foucault (1982i), p. 32.
 4 Foucault (1982g), p. 4.
 5 Foucault (1982i), p. 40; Foucault (1980c), p. 211; Foucault (1980b), p. 5; Foucault (1980d).
 6 Foucault (1982i), p. 40.
 7 Ibid., p. 41. It is worth noting that in Foucault's discussion of confession there are few references to God and no mention of Christ or Christology. Foucault is not interested in theology or religious belief. See chapter 6, 'Body and Belief', for a discussion of the inherent problems in such a stance.
 8 Foucault (1980c), p. 211.
 9 Foucault (1970a), p. 232; Bernauer (1990), p. 161.
10 Foucault (1976a), p. 27.
11 Ibid. It is important to note that Foucault's language in HS1 confuses the distinction between speech/silence and discourse/silence. This shift is a result of Foucault referring to the particular speech act (confession), which is at one level a verbal act and part of a wider discursive framework (i.e. a network of statements both said and unsaid). In his 1969 study AK Foucault was aware of the difficulties in his term 'discourse' and outlined the various ways he had used the term, acknowledging the interchangeable nature of speech and discourse: 'We can now understand the reason for the equivocal meaning of the term "discourse", which I have used and abused in many different senses: in the most general, and vaguest way, it denoted a group of verbal performances....' He goes on to outline other broader conceptions of discourse as, for example, 'the group of statements that belong to a single system of formation', like psychiatric discourse (Foucault, 1969a, pp. 107–8). I will return to this issue of silence and speech later in the chapter.
12 Foucault (1961b), p. xii.
13 Ibid., p. xiii.
14 Derrida [1967] (1978), p. 35.
15 Jaworski (1993), p. 36.
16 Derrida [1967] (1978), p. 35.
17 Jaworski (1993), pp. 32ff.
18 See Derrida [1972] (1982). The idea that madness or the silence of madness represents the marginal is supported in Foucault's 1978 interview with Duccio Trombadori, where he asks: '[D]idn't madness and the mentally ill represent something that was located at the margins of society?' (Foucault, 1978g, p. 77).

19 Peterson (1982). The mad, as Peterson's work documents, often write accounts of their experience; they are not outside of reason, but 'silenced', persecuted and invalidated by a dominant regime. See Foucault (1961b).
20 Foucault (1976a), p. 4.
21 See Boyne (1990) for a wider analysis of the Derrida–Foucault debate. Cf. Jaworski (1993), p. 36.
22 Foucault (1976a), p. 27.
23 Jaworski (1993), p. 167. Cf. pp. 1ff and 98ff.
24 Ibid., pp. 29–32, 81–4.
25 Foucault (1976a), p. 27. Cf. Jaworski (1993), pp. 44, 98.
26 Foucault (1976a), pp. 17ff.
27 Foucault (1976b), p. 101.
28 Foucault (1970a), pp. 215ff. Cf. Foucault (1971b).
29 Eribon (1992), pp. 27–9, 133. Cf. Miller (1993a), pp. 55–6; Macey (1993), pp. 30, 40; Seigel (1990).
30 Foucault (1971b), p. 193.
31 Foucault (1975a), p. 293. Cf. p. 23.
32 Foucault (1961b), p. 244.
33 Foucault (1954b), p. 65.
34 Foucault (1975a), pp. 149, 150, 161.
35 Ibid., p. 239. Cf. pp. 60, 128, 243, 294, 295; and Foucault (1979e), p. xiv; Foucault (1976a), pp. 37, 41.
36 Foucault (1970a), p. 216.
37 Ibid., pp. 217, 219. Truth, according to Foucault, 'relies on institutional support' (Foucault, 1970a, p. 219, cf. p. 225), and in this sense the confession is 'institutionalized as a discursive truth-game' (Foucault, 1980c, p. 227 n. 50).
38 Brummett (1980), p. 290, quoted in Jaworski (1993), p. 106.
39 Jaworski (1993), pp. 124–5, cf. p. 118.
40 Jaworski notes the work of Mendez (1980), although the literature in this area is extensive. See Jaworski (1993), p. 121. For a wider discussion of women and silence see Hedges and Fishkin (1994), and as an example of the poignancy of the concept to feminist writing see Erickson (1993).
41 See Marks and de Courtivron (1981). I will return to the theme of women's language in chapter 4.
42 Foucault (1976b), p. 98.
43 Foucault (1976a), p. 92.
44 Ibid., p. 39.
45 Foucault (1961b), p. 14. Cf. Foucault (1977d), pp. 78, 82; Foucault (1979e) and Foucault (1973a).
46 Foucault (1977d), p. 77.
47 Ibid., pp. 78–9.
48 Ibid., pp. 79–80, 82.
49 Ibid., pp. 83–4.
50 See Foucault (1982g).
51 Foucault (1963c), p. 30. Cf. Foucault (1961b), pp. 287ff.
52 Mrosovosky (1980), p. 31.
53 For a discussion of the confusion between 'discursive' and 'transcendent' silence see chapter 5.
54 Foucault (1976a), p. 101.
55 Ibid., p. 121.
56 Foucault (1977d), pp. 83–4.
57 Foucault (1961b), p. 244.

58 Jaworski (1993), p. 44. Jaworski at this point relies on Tyler's *The Said and Unsaid* (1978).

59 The distinction of a technology of domination and a technology of self is made by Foucault in a self-critique devised from the work of Habermas. Following Habermas, Foucault identifies a series of methodological techniques for examining human society. In addition to techniques of production, signification and domination, he adds a fourth area of techniques of self. See Foucault (1980c), p. 203.

60 Foucault (1976a), p. 21. Cf. pp. 20, 113–19, 158.

61 Ibid., pp. 3–13. When Foucault discusses the argument that 'sex is not repressed' he indicates the risk of 'falling into sterile paradox' and points out the difficulties of following such a position. These tensions are created because of the inability to hold silence and discourse (speech) together. The cutting edge of Foucault's challenge to the 'repressive hypothesis' is based on the ability to hold these two dynamics together (ibid., p. 8). Unfortunately, as I have stated, Foucault does not sufficiently work out this argument to carry the ideas into his study of confession.

62 Bevis *et al.* (1989), pp. 203, 206. The work of Bevis *et al.* is very important for understanding Foucault's work on religion and I will discuss it in more detail in chapter 7. For a discussion of reconciliation and justification in confessional theology, see Osborne (1990).

63 Osborne (1990), p. 53.

64 Foucault's discussion of Tertullian is fragmentary and lacks scope. See Foucault (1982i), pp. 41–2; Foucault (1980c), p. 214; Foucault (1977h), p. 211. Cf. Foucault (1980d). The complexities involved with Tertullian and the definitions of '*exomologesis*' have been noted by Dallen [1986] (1991), pp. 30ff. Dallen also draws attention to the range of interpretations surrounding '*exomologesis*' by noting Lampe's lexicon of Greek terms. See Dallen [1986] (1991), p. 53 n. 4; Lampe (1961) pp. 449–500.

65 See, for example, Foucault (1976a), p. 58; Foucault (1977h), p. 215.

66 See Foucault (1976a), pp. 18–19, 63, 116. Cf. Osborne (1990), chapters 7 and 8.

67 Foucault (1977h), p. 217; Foucault (1976a), p. 21 n. 4.

68 Foucault (1977h), p. 216.

69 Ibid.

70 Ibid., p. 215. The French word '*aveu*' is translated 'confession' but can mean more generally admission/avowal. The word can also incorporate '*l'examen de conscience*', which precedes the actual act of confession. See, for example, DE III, p. 257. I am grateful to Richard Townsend for highlighting the issues surrounding the translation of '*aveu*'.

71 'Avowal': Foucault (1976a), p. 58; 'ritual of avowal': Foucault (1977d), p. 84; 'direction of conscience': Foucault (1977h), p. 214; Foucault (1977f), p. 111.

72 See Foucault (1982i), p. 14; Foucault (1975a), p. 37.

73 Foucault (1980c), p. 201. In Foucault's 1980 Howison lecture at Berkeley he acknowledged that his interest in confession was dictated by his interest in the genealogy of the modern subject. He states:

> I have tried to explain why I was interested in the practice of self-examination and confession. Those two practices seem to me to be good witnesses for a major problem, which is the genealogy of the modern self. This genealogy has been my obsession for years because it is one of the possible ways to get rid of a traditional philosophy of the subject.
>
> (Foucault, 1980c, p. 225 n. 26)

74 Ibid., pp. 215–17.
75 Foucault (1976a), pp. 61–2.
76 Foucault (1977h), p. 217.
77 Foucault (1976a), pp. 58–9.
78 Tambling (1990), p. 2.
79 Cousins and Hussain [1984] (1990), p. 3.
80 Foucault (1978g), p. 37.
81 Foucault (1982c), p. 208.
82 I have introduced the ideas of 'truth' and 'power' without extensive discussion because these concepts have been explored in greater depth elsewhere. For a discussion of 'truth' see Prado (1995), pp. 119ff. and Allen (1993), pp. 149ff; and for a discussion of 'power' see Kusch (1991), pp. 115ff and Cousins and Hussain [1984] (1990), pp. 201, 225ff. For the purposes of this discussion we can see 'truth' as created as a form of 'institutional support' and 'power' as a non-hierarchical set of 'force relations'. There is, of course, a fundamental relationship between these two ideas. As Foucault states: 'Truth is a thing of this world: it is produced only by virtue of multiple forms of constraint. And it induces regular effects of power' (Foucault, 1976g, p. 131).
83 Foucault (1982c), p. 212.
84 The nature of 'subject' as discipline can be developed out of Foucault's inaugural lecture at the Collège de France. See Foucault (1970a).
85 Foucault (1982f), p. 238.
86 Foucault (1982i), p. 46.
87 Ibid., pp. 46–7; Foucault (1980c), pp. 217–18; Foucault (1982f), p. 238.
88 Foucault (1982f), p. 239.
89 Ibid., p. 240; Foucault (1977h), p. 216.
90 Foucault (1977f), p. 111. On the issues of sex and religious 'truth' see Foucault (1976a), pp. 56ff., 61, 77, 113; Foucault (1977f), pp. 111, 121.
91 Foucault (1982i), p. 47; Foucault (1980c), p. 220.
92 Foucault (1980c), p. 219.
93 Foucault (1982i), p. 47; Foucault (1980c), p. 220. Foucault (1982i), pp. 41, 44. It is worth noting in passing that the process of '*exomologesis*' involved a silent, non-verbal act, which demonstrates the oscillations of power in the development of silence and speech. Foucault (1982i), p. 43.
94 Foucault (1980c), p. 221. Cf. Foucault (1982i), p. 48; Foucault (1982f), p. 235.
95 Foucault (1984c), p. 5. Cf. Foucault (1980c), p. 222. Foucault is able to acknowledge that this understanding of self could be seen as a 'great richness' of the Christian technology of self rather than a 'contradiction', but this could only be appreciated with an outline of Christian theology, which was not forthcoming in his work.
96 Foucault (1980c), pp. 222–3.

3 Surrealism and the religious imagination

1 Foucault (1984g), p. 243; Porter (1988), p. 13.
2 Foucault (1961c), p. 8. Cf. Macey (1993), pp. 72–8, 80; Eribon (1992), pp. 75, 78.
3 ffrench (1995), pp. 1ff. ffrench's study provided an excellent and much needed analysis of *Tel Quel* and I have been indebted to its detailed and careful documentation in locating Foucault in the movement. For further treatment of the *Tel Quel* see ffrench and Lack (1998); Kauppi (1994), esp. pp. 65–6, 144–5. Cf. Macey (1993), pp. 148–51.
4 See Foucault (1962b, 1963e, 1963f, 1964e). For a useful overview of these texts see During (1992), pp. 68–91.

5 Foucault (1964b), p. 338. Translation taken from *Religion and Culture* (RC), p. 72
6 ffrench (1995), p. 62.
7 See ibid., p. 62; Miller (1993a), pp. 129–30.
8 ffrench (1995), p. 63.
9 Ibid., pp. 16, 28–30, 78.
10 Ibid., pp. 28–9.
11 Ibid., p. 78.
12 Ibid.
13 Foucault (1964b), p. 338; Foucault (1984c), p. 14.
14 Foucault (1967c), pp. 614–15.
15 See Carrette (1999b).
16 The terms 'avant-garde' and 'surrealism' are rarely defined with any precision. According to Shattuck, the term 'avant-garde', which was 'first used in journalistic writing in the expression "les artistes de l'avant-garde"', emerged in the 1890s after outgrowing its military metaphor (Shattuck, 1958, p. 24). In a useful study of the term 'avant-garde art' by Renato Poggioli it becomes clear that in the 1870s the term held both an artistic and a socio-political meaning. It was also found in a personal notebook of Baudelaire from 1862 to 1864 as a military metaphor (Poggioli, 1968, p. 10). Despite the disparate strands of its evolution the idea of the 'avant-garde' in common usage indicates art or writing which is ahead of its time; it signifies the advance of the new. There are tensions in such an idea, for as Poggioli points out, 'in the case of avant-garde art, the hypothesis that it existed previous to the era which coined its name is an anachronism twice over: it judges the past in terms of the present *and* the future' (Poggioli, 1968, p. 15). Although surrealism can be situated within the broad scope of 'avant-garde' thinking, I am using the term 'surrealism' as a distinct group of ideas which emerged in the inter-war period and became associated with André Breton and therefore distinct from the broader literary and artistic activity in France at the time. The situation is complicated by a range of divisions which attempt to sort out the diverse manifestations of the inter-war years. Wills, for example, uses Surrealism with a capital 'S' to refer to Breton and his Manifestoes, as distinct from 'surrealism', which is used to refer to the broader experiment of thought of the time (Wills, 1985, p. 25). We also find in Suzi Gablik's work distinctions between 'organic' surrealism (spontaneous expressions) and 'biomorphic' surrealism (calculated statements) (Gablik, 1985, p. 71). The divisions are to some extent motivated by affiliations and a certain political ordering of knowledge connected with Breton.
17 O'Farrell (1989), pp. 21–2.
18 For a discussion of the challenge to the Cartesian '*cogito*' see Braidotti (1991), pp. 16–45.
19 Balakian (1947), p. 1. Lewis also notes in passing the borrowing of ideas from Eastern mysticism. See Lewis (1990), p. x.
20 Cardinal (1986), p. 31. For a more detailed introduction to surrealism and the occult see Choucha (1991).
21 Shamdasani (1993), pp. 100ff.
22 Breton (1972), p. 26. See Breton and Soupault [1920] (1985) for a classic example of 'automatic writing' and Cocteau (1958) for an example of writing under the influence of opium. Cf. Nadeau (1973), p. 89.
23 Gablik (1985), p. 69. For useful histories of surrealism and Dada ideas see Nadeau (1973); Freeman and Welchman (1989); Tzara (1992).
24 Nadeau (1973), p. 86 n. 2.
25 Breton (1936), p. 66; Fowlie (1953), p. 106; Nadeau (1973), p. 174.
26 Nadeau (1973), pp. 105–6.

27 Breton (1972), p. 9.
28 O'Farrell (1989), p. 31. Cf. Wolin (1992), pp. 170–93.
29 Foucault, 'La Pensée du dehors', *Critique*, 1966, p. 528, quoted in O'Farrell (1989), p. 32. See Foucault (1966c).
30 Pefanis (1991), p. 16.
31 Wills (1985), p. 18.
32 Foucault (1984a), pp. 8–9.
33 Foucault (1966e), p. 10. Cf. Macey (1993), p. 173.
34 Foucault (1966a), p. 384. Cf. Foucault (1966c), pp. 17–19.
35 ffrench (1995), p. 2.
36 Hayman (1977), p. 159; Artaud (1988), pp. 483ff.
37 Foucault (1961b), p. 287. Cf. Simon (1963), p. 87.
38 Goodall (1994), pp. 1ff.
39 Artaud (1988), pp. 413–14, 555–71. Cf. Goodall (1994), pp. 200–8.
40 Hayman (1977) p. 159; S. Sontag, 'Introduction' in Artaud (1988), p. 591; Barber (1993), p. 141.
41 Artaud (1988), p. 105.
42 Ibid., p. 106.
43 See, for example, Artaud, 'The Nerve Meter'; 'The Theatre of Cruelty First Manifesto'; 'Heliogabalus, or the Anarchist Crowned', in Artaud (1988), pp. 79ff., 242ff., 317ff.
44 Foucault (1966a), p. 383.
45 Greene (1967), p. 194.
46 Artaud (1968), p. 180. Cf. Barber (1993), pp. 24–5.
47 See Foucault (1975a), pp. 23ff. Cf. Grosz (1994), pp. 145ff.
48 Bataille [1954] (1988), p. 147.
49 J. Harkness, 'Introduction' in Foucault (1968a), p. 2.
50 Magritte, *Écrits complets*, ed. A. Blavier, p. 379, quoted in Freeman and Welchman (1989), p. 81.
51 Foucault (1968a), p. 20.
52 Ibid., p. 44.
53 See Jay (1986), p. 201 n. 61.
54 Foucault (1966a), p. 47.
55 Foucault (1968a), p. 46.
56 Foucault (1966a), pp. xvii–xviii, quoted in J. Harkness, 'Introduction' in Foucault (1968a), p. 4.
57 Foucault (1968a), pp. 49, 20.
58 Ibid., pp. 37–8.
59 Ibid., p. 37.
60 Foucault (1966a), p. 383.
61 Ibid., p. 383.
62 Foucault (1962c), pp. 205ff.
63 Foucault (1963b), p. 3.
64 Ibid., p. 167.
65 Ibid., pp. 165–6.
66 Foucault (1983i), p. 185; Almansi (1982), p. 306.
67 Foucault (1984a), p. 3.
68 Visker (1995), p. 2.
69 Ibid., pp. 2, 109.
70 Ibid., p. 7.
71 Foucault (1964b), p. 340. Translation taken from RC, p. 74.
72 The idea of the 'spiritual' without spirit is taken from Foucault's discussion of a 'political spirituality' in Iran, where he refers to Marx's idea of religion as 'the

spirit of a world without spirit', Foucault (1979a), p. 218. I will discuss these issues in more depth in chapter 7.

73 Jay (1986); Flynn (1993); Certeau (1986), pp. 192, 196.
74 Quoted in Choucha (1991), p. 45.
75 See, for example, Sade [1785] (1990). It is important to note that Foucault would have been aware of the work of Alfred Jarry and his religious subversions. See Macey (1993), p. 123.

4 Male theology in the bedroom

1 Foucault (1970d),. p. xii.
2 Huppert (1974), p. 55.
3 The work on Foucault and feminism forms a growing body of literature, and the perspective and quality of the work vary enormously. Some interesting metaphors have been employed in this literature to describe the relationship between feminism and Foucault, including 'flirting' (Morris, 1979, p. 26), 'loving' (Fraser, 1989, p. 65) and 'dancing' (McNeil, 1993), reflecting the initial excitement in what became a love–hate relationship. For the best overall study see McNay (1992). See also a valuable collection of essays in Diamond and Quinby (1988) and Ramazanoglu (1993). In relation to Foucault and power see Hartsock (1987). A useful summary of the literature and issues can be found in chapter 2 of Bell (1993), pp. 14–56. For other studies see Flax (1990); Fraser (1989); Brodribb (1993); Braidotti (1991); Sawicki (1991). See also my brief discussion of this material in relation to Foucault studies in Carrette (1999b).
4 McNay (1992), pp. 32–3.
5 Foucault's own work on the history of sexuality has played a major part in the understanding of the social construction of sexuality. As Edward Stein indicates in relation to Foucault's HS1: 'This book has become, for many social constructionists, the *locus classicus* of their program' (Stein, 1992, p. 6). See Foucault (1976, 1984a, 1984b). Cf. Butler (1990), pp. 17–18, 91–106; Halperin (1995), esp. pp. 33–48; Caplan (1987), esp. pp. 82–112. Although Foucault has been extremely influential, we must also acknowledge that theories of sexuality have arisen from an interrelationship between the academy and activist movements. As Jonathan Ned Katz indicates, while acknowledging his indebtedness to Foucault:

> [S]ince younger scholars now often write as if Foucault initiated sexual history research from his chair on high in the French academy, I note that homosexual history research owes its main impetus to the gay, lesbian, and feminist movements, not to this one great man.
>
> (J.N. Katz, 1995, p. 10)

6 The literature on masculinity is expanding rapidly. For a useful overview of the issues see Hearn and Morgan (1990); Seidler (1992); Clatterbaugh (1997); Messner (1997).
7 Foucault (1961b), p. 210. Cf. C.J. Dean (1992), p. 164.
8 Foucault (1961b), p. 210.
9 Foucault (1972d), p. 101. In 1975 Foucault rejected the 'deification' of Sade, whose eroticism he regarded as 'disciplinary' and 'hierarchical'. Foucault rejected Sade and such strategies by stating:

> It's time to leave all that behind, and Sade's eroticism with it. We must invent with the body, with its elements, surfaces, volumes, and thickness, a

non-disciplinary eroticism: that of a body in a volatile and diffused state, with its chance encounters and unplanned pleasures.

(Foucault, 1975j, p. 189)

10 Miller (1993a), pp. 244, 291.
11 Foucault (1976a), p. 149.
12 Ibid., p. 150.
13 Miller's reports of Foucault's sadomasochistic experience remain 'speculative' because his work contains no direct accounts. See Miller (1993a), pp. 245ff. See also my account of Miller in Carrette (1999b).
14 See Miller (1993a), pp. 45, 243. I am grateful to David Macey for his comments on this issue.
15 Gallop (1981).
16 Quoted in Cohen and Dascal (1989), p. 311.
17 Blanchot (1949), p. 37.
18 Said (1972), p. 42.
19 Bataille [1957] (1987), p. 179.
20 See the 'Chronology' in Sade (1991), p. 93.
21 Sade [1785] (1990), p. 253.
22 Dworkin (1984), pp. 70, 80.
23 Ibid., p. 81; Gallop (1988), p. 2.
24 Beauvoir (1951).
25 Carter (1979); Dworkin (1984), p. 84; Gallop (1988), p. 54; Irigaray (1977).
26 C.J. Dean (1992). I am indebted to Carolyn Dean's brief historical analysis of Sadeian scholarship.
27 Ibid., p. 198.
28 Ellenberger (1970), pp. 297ff.
29 See C.J. Dean (1992), pp. 132–4.
30 Ibid., p. 159.
31 Ibid., pp. 164, 167.
32 Ibid., p. 159. Cf. p. 168.
33 Gallop (1981), pp. 115–16.
34 C.J. Dean (1992), p. 170.
35 Macey (1993), p. 155.
36 Macey points out how Foucault saw Klossowski's work as equal to that of Bataille and Blanchot. Ibid., p. 157.
37 Klossowski [1967] (1992), pp. 7, 100ff., 127.
38 Ibid., p. 127.
39 Ibid., pp. 117, 120.
40 C.J. Dean (1992), p. 176.
41 Gallop (1981), pp. 67ff.
42 Klossowski [1967] (1992), p. 36. For a valuable psychoanalytical discussion of anality and sadism and its relation to God, see Chasseguet-Smirgel (1983). I am grateful to Sandra Brown for drawing my attention to this material.
43 Klossowski [1967] (1992), p. 36.
44 Klossowski's ideas of bodies and language were developed further by the French philosopher Gilles Deleuze. Deleuze extends Klossowski's relation of bodies and language to create a new metaphysics based on the psychoanalytical category of 'phantasy' (the incorporeal surface of bodies) and Klossowski's 'simulcara' (the unfixed point of representation). See Deleuze [1969] (1990), pp. 280–301. Foucault responded briefly to Deleuze's new metaphysics in his 1970 work 'Theatrum Philosophicum'. Many of Deleuze's ideas influenced Foucault's religious question in the1970s, especially the idea that the 'soul' is a surface event

covering bodies. It is in this sense that metaphysics is 'freed from its original profundity' (Foucault, 1970c, p. 171). I will explore some of these issues in the next chapter.

45 Gallop (1981), p. 11. Gallop showed how the idea of 'sovereignty' in Bataille's Sade was to form the dominant strand of interpretation in French thinking, albeit misguided and incorrect. The idea of 'sovereignty' was an attempt to respond to Hegel's master–slave dialectic by developing an unrestricted life without dependency on another. This idea about Sade was, according to Gallop, a 'conspiracy' of 'monumental brilliance scattered through history', and one which she argues is adopted by post-war writers such as Barthes, Derrida, Foucault and Lacan (Gallop, 1981, pp. 10, 115). Gallop shows how the characters of Sade's work were caught up by laws and systems which control and regulate the expression of desire. The libertines are governed by a series of relationships and carefully organised patterns of behaviour. There was no random or mindless orgy, rather a calculated series of activities. The work of Sade is in this sense a rationalisation of desire. As Gallop states: 'Sovereignty is not to be found in Sade nor in Sade's heroes. Nonetheless, Sade somehow provides Bataille with the possibility for a dissertation on sovereignty, on the impossible' (Gallop, 1981, p. 26; cf. Richardson, 1994a, p. 118). Gallop to some extent misplaces the extent to which the sovereign subject is implanted into Foucault's work. While Foucault integrates Bataille's reading of Sade, it is not all-pervasive. Foucault recognises the importance of laws governing the libertine's life and in 1976 questions the whole idea of sovereignty. See Foucault (1966a), p. 109; Foucault (1976a), pp. 148–9; Foucault (1961a), p. 210. Cf. Foucault (1971f), pp. 199–204.

46 Richman (1982), p. 1.
47 Richardson (1994), p. 56. Cf. Hollier (1988).
48 Bataille [1957] (1987), p. 36. Cf. Bataille [1954] (1988).
49 Bataille [1957] (1987), p. 15.
50 Ibid., p. 170.
51 Ibid., p. 17.
52 Ibid., p. 16. Cf. Dworkin (1988).
53 Bataille [1957] (1987), pp. 29, 273.
54 Ibid., p. 22.
55 See Bataille [1957] (1987), pp. 18, 23.
56 Foucault (1963c), p. 33; Bataille [1957] (1987), p. 269. This phrase recalls Sade, who in his *Philosophy in the Bedroom* stated: 'as man doth "fuck", so he hath willed that his Lord "fucketh" too' (Sade, 1795, p. 212). In Sade there appears to be an anger towards the 'Other' which links the idea of God and women together.
57 Richardson (1994a), p. 6.
58 Le Brun (1990), p. xvi.
59 C.J. Dean (1992), p. 182.
60 Brodribb (1993), p. 131.
61 Ibid., p. 50.
62 Cixous (1976), p. 247 n. 1, quoted in Bartkowski (1988), p. 52. Cf. Gallop (1989), p. 1046.
63 I am, of course, arguing that the concern with death results from male social experience rather than assuming it is an inherent concern of men as opposed to women. See Flax (1983); Grimshaw (1986), pp. 36–74, esp. p. 59. Grace Jantzen has picked up this theme in her exploration of the tension between a philosophical discourse of natality and necrophilia in her feminist critique of Western philosophy (see Jantzen, 1998, pp. 128ff.).
64 Foucault (1963c), p. 31.

65 The concept of anxiety is here taken from psychoanalytical discourse. Anxiety, as Rycroft states, can be seen 'as the response to some as yet unrecognised factor, either in the environment or in the self', and the specific anxiety I have in mind in this chapter is what Freud called 'primary anxiety': 'the emotion which accompanies dissolution of the self' (Rycroft, 1977, p. 8). I am grateful to Hugh Pyper for his helpful comments on this idea.

66 For a definition of 'episteme' see Foucault (1969a), p. 191. The importance of the idea of God in Foucault's work remains unexplored. The influence of his Catholic background and writers like Nietzsche, Bataille and Klossowski have obviously informed his work.

67 Kearney (1986), p. 287.

68 Foucault (1966a), p. 33.

69 Ibid., p. 36.

70 Ibid., p. 59. Cf. p. 78.

71 Ibid., pp. 209–10.

72 Ibid., p. 211.

73 Ibid., p. 304.

74 Ibid., pp. 305, 382. This conception of language pervades the wider literature of the period. See Blanchot [1969] (1993); Deleuze [1969] (1990).

75 Foucault (1966c), pp. 17, 27. Cf. Bouchard [1970] (1992), pp. 17–19.

76 T. Clark (1992), pp. 67, 64. Cf. Greene (1975). For a discussion of the wider influence of Blanchot on Foucault's discursive practices and the idea of power/knowledge see Gregg (1994), pp. 188ff.

77 Bouchard [1970] (1992), p. 19.

78 See Sade (1795), p. 212.

79 See Foucault (1963c).

80 Gallop (1988), p. 7.

81 Nelson (1992a), pp. 92–6. Cf. Nelson (1992b). Many of the works in contemporary body theology lack a strong grounding in the roots of French continental philosophy and literature. More recent studies by Prosser MacDonald (1995) and Raschke (1996) have started to take account of Foucault and postmodern thinking, but their work still remains restricted to an idea of 'corporeality' rather than appreciating the radical disjunction of a 'spiritual corporality'.

82 Descombes (1980), p. 31.

83 Ibid., p. 29.

84 Foucault (1968b), p. 53.

85 Descombes (1980), p. 31.

86 Foucault (1966a), p. 385.

87 For an extremely useful discussion of Foucault and Nietzsche see Schrift (1988), pp. 278ff and Mahon (1992). Foucault took part in a major international colloquium on Nietzsche at Royaumont in 1964. See Foucault (1964d). As the title of the journal *Tel Quel* suggests, there was a resurgence of interest in Nietzsche in the 1960s. For a discussion of the journal *Tel Quel* see ffrench (1995); ffrench and Lack (1998); Kauppi (1994); Suleiman (1989). The writers who influenced *Tel Quel* provided a way for Foucault to 'exit from philosophy'. See Foucault (1975e), p. 153. Cf. Foucault (1978g), pp. 29–30.

88 Foucault (1966d), p. 553.

89 Schrift (1988), p. 282; Foucault (1966a), p. 385.

90 Foucault (1966a), p. 385.

91 David Macey locates Malraux as one source of Foucault's notion of the death of man/God. See Macey (1993), p. 90; Malraux [1926] (1974), pp. 97–8. For Nietzsche's discussion of the death of God, see Nietzsche [1887] (1974), p. 167 and fn. 1.

92 Foucault (1966a), pp. 318–19.
93 Ibid., p. 312. I have retained the exclusive language in the text as a strategic device to draw attention to issues of male sexuality.
94 Schrift (1988), p. 281. Cf. Foucault (1966a), p. 385.
95 Schrift (1988), p. 281.
96 Bernauer (1987a), p. 376.
97 Irigaray (1993), pp. 57–72. 'God', as Irigaray points out, 'has been created out of man's gender' (p. 61). Irigaray argues that women need a god figure to affirm and validate their own subjectivity (p. 64).
98 See Pyper (1993).
99 Foucault (1969b), p. 105.
100 'A Preface to Transgression' (Foucault, 1963c).
101 Ibid., pp. 34–6. For further development of the idea of 'contestation' see ibid., p. 36 n. 13 and Foucault (1966c), p. 22.
102 Foucault (1963c), p. 35.
103 Foucault (1963d), p. 62.
104 Foucault (1963c), p. 32.
105 Ibid.
106 Ibid., p. 30.
107 Ibid.
108 Ibid., p. 31.
109 Ibid., p. 51.
110 See Foucault's idea of the 'analytic of finitude'. Foucault (1966a), pp. 312–18.
111 Gallop (1981), p. 3.
112 The division of body and mind is one of a whole series of characteristics identified as forming male social experience. See Flax (1983); Grimshaw (1986), p. 59.
113 Foucault (1966a), p. 314. For a discussion of Foucault and the body, see Lash (1984); McNay (1992), pp. 11–47. It is important to note that these works tend to concentrate on the idea of 'docile' bodies in Foucault's study of the prison (Foucault, 1975a). Such a standpoint means the earlier literature on Sade and Klossowski tends to be overlooked when considering the development of Foucault's conception of the body.
114 Gallop (1988), pp. 3–4.
115 Ibid., p. 47.

5 Mystical archaeology

1 Foucault (1966c), p. 16. Foucault returned to the idea of negative theology in his lecture at the Collège de France on 30 January 1980. He also made the suggestion that his thought was a negative theology in a private meeting with James Bernauer SJ on 12 March 1980. I am extremely grateful to James Bernauer for this material and his wider support of my research work.
2 Blanchot (1986), p. 74.
3 James Miller's 'narrative account' of Foucault's life makes a number of links within Foucault's work to a kind of mystical discourse. See Miller (1993a), pp. 30, 42, 88–9, 154, 279, 306–7, 314, 376. Miller also refers to whole range of related terms such as 'hermetic' (pp. 7, 33, 124, 281, 284, 319, 335); 'esoteric' (pp. 7, 88, 321); 'visionary' (pp. 8, 399 n. 59, 445 n. 122); and 'ascetic' (pp. 334, 342, 344). Miller reads Foucault's work in terms of a limited Jamesian understanding of mystical experience and confuses the nature of Foucault's understanding of religion. For a more detailed discussion of the work of William James and the nature of mystical discourse see Jantzen (1989, 1995). The assumptions that Foucault's work held a mystical discourse is very different from

the attempts by James Bernauer to develop a negative theology from Foucault's work on the death of man. See Bernauer (1987a). Bernauer's work is a secondary elaboration of Foucault's work inside the tradition of theology. The essay on negative theology by Bernauer does not presume Foucault was a mystic of any sort. Bernauer's later work does suggest Foucault's work holds 'a worldly mysticism' and that his thinking is 'ecstatic', but these ideas can be read in terms of a 'spiritual corporality' and do not necessarily intimate a religious transcendence. See Bernauer (1990), p. 178. For my own critical discussion of James Miller's mystical iconography see Carrette (1999b).

4 See Caputo (1989, 1993a); Hart (1991); Taylor (1984).

5 George Steiner, who shows a deep appreciation of the intricacies of Heidegger's language, points out that 'a Heideggerian text is often strange and impenetrable beyond that of even the most difficult of preceding metaphysicians and mystics'. He later, commenting on Heidegger's creation of a new space of meaning, refers to 'a sort of mystical bullying' which makes understanding difficult (Steiner, 1992, pp. 9, 12). Although Steiner's allusions are merely passing references to elucidate the complexities of Heidegger's language, they reflect, however technically misplaced, the persuasive popular relation between enigmatic and mystical languages.

6 Although Foucault adopted a number of critical perspectives from surrealism, he did not develop any of the religious fascinations of surrealist writers with mysticism or the occult. See chapter 3.

7 See Foucault (1969a), p. 203 and Foucault (1972d), p. 99. The term 'transcendence' is, however, very complex and can easily be confused in a slippage between a religious 'transcendence' and a sense of personal (immanent) transcendence of the self.

8 Sheridan (1980), p. 90; Kusch (1991), p. 1. Cf. Macey (1993), p. 199.

9 See Kusch (1991), pp. 1–3 for a useful introductory overview of the literature. While Kusch acknowledges the value of previous introductory studies of Foucault, he correctly sees that 'these received perspectives have tended to leave central areas and aspects of Foucault's work somewhat underexposed' (p. xi). Kusch's study is one of the first to give a detailed assessment of AK from an appreciation of the conceptual issues of the history of science, and my debt to this work is clearly seen throughout my own study. While this work provides an important reading of AK from the corrective position of the history of science, it holds its own constraints. Kusch acknowledges the specific 'motivation' behind his own work (p. 3). In my own brief overview of the same literature on AK I attempt to acknowledge Kusch's work within the wider Foucauldian literature. It is important to note that Kusch's study only deals with the Foucauldian literature up to its date of publication in 1991, and by its own specific remit does not refer to wider philosophical literature, such as Megill (1985).

10 See Dreyfus and Rabinow (1982), pp. 44–100; Deleuze [1986] (1988), pp. 1–22; Megill (1985), pp. 220–56; Eribon (1992), pp. 187ff.; Macey (1993), pp. 198ff.; Miller (1993a), pp. 159ff.; Bernauer (1990), pp. 90–120; Major-Poetzl (1983), pp. 3–30. On the theme of breaking from the restriction of thought see Foucault (1970a, 1971a).

11 Megill (1985), pp. 227–8.

12 Ibid., p. 227.

13 Lemert and Gillan (1982), pp. xi–x.

14 Sheridan (1980), p. 90. Cf. Macey (1993), p. 199.

15 Foucault (1969a), p. 113.

16 Ibid., pp. 17, 113.

17 Ibid., p. 208.

18 Ibid., pp. 210, 30.
19 Ibid., p. 114.
20 Ibid., pp. 115, 116, 145, 159, 192.
21 Macey (1993), p. 198.
22 Foucault (1969a), p. 135.
23 Foucault on a number of occasions refers to the paradoxical nature of his enter-
    prise (ibid., pp. 71, 109, 121). These references do not, however, undermine his
    project as a whole, but rather illustrate the precarious nature of his thought at
    the limits of theoretical reflection.
24 Ray (1987), p. 45. See Miller (1993a), p. 161; cf. Foucault (1970a). Foucault is not
    a structuralist in the 'strict' sense of the term, but can be, and has been, located
    in this camp (see Megill, 1985, pp. 183–219; Sturrock, 1979, pp. 1ff.).
25 Foucault (1969a), p. 17; Foucault (1966c).
26 Foucault (1966c), pp. 25–6.
27 Macey (1993), p. 200. There is an interchange between the ideas of 'language'
    and 'discourse' in AK. The idea of discourse eventually assumes priority when it
    undergoes a political metamorphosis in Foucault's 1970 lecture 'The Discourse
    on Language'. See Foucault (1970a).
28 Foucault (1969a), p. 17; Foucault (1966c), p. 26. Cf. Seigel (1990), pp. 273ff.;
    Foucault (1963b).
29 Kusch (1991), p. 41.
30 Ibid., p. 58.
31 Macey (1993), p. 201. The idea of the 'Other' is an important dimension of
    Foucault's work which will be explored in subsequent chapters. See O'Farrell
    (1989); Seigel (1990).
32 Foucault (1969a), p. 5. This series of ideas are taken principally from the work of
    Bachelard and Canguilhem. For a good overview of these thinkers in relation to
    Foucault, see Gutting (1989), pp. 9–54. Cf. Kusch (1991), pp. 27ff.
33 Foucault (1969a), p. 210.
34 Ibid., p. 21.
35 Bernauer (1990), pp. 90ff.; Foucault (1969a), p. 14. The reference is to Kant, who
    awoke from a dogmatic sleep (see Dreyfus and Rabinow, 1982, p. 44).
36 Bernauer (1990), p. 178 and n. 82.
37 Deleuze [1986] (1988), p. 14.
38 Foucault (1966c), p. 16.
39 Ibid. In his discussion with James Bernauer on 12 March 1980 Foucault
    suggested his work could be compared to negative theology, but as applied to the
    human sciences *not* the divine sciences. Recalling this conversation Bernauer later
    wrote: 'Foucault's negative theology is a critique not of the conceptualisation
    employed for God but of that modern figure of finite man whose identity was
    put forward as capturing the essence of human being' (Bernauer, 1990, p. 178).
    Cf. Bernauer (1987a), pp. 375ff.
40 Foucault (1966c), p. 21.
41 Blanchot (1986), p. 74.
42 See note 3 above. Miller correctly describes his study of Foucault as a 'narrative
    account' because it tends to read Foucault's life in a Nietzschean mould and is
    therefore not following a strict biographical account. By following the idea of
    'limit-experience' Miller falls into a limited modern understanding of mysticism.
    Miller (1993a), pp. 5, 154.
43 Rorem (1993), p. 183. I am indebted to Rorem's authoritative work on the
    Dionysian corpus in constructing this comparison with Foucault.
44 Foucault (1969a), pp. 102–3, 88, 103.
45 Ibid., p. 103. Cf. pp. 103–5.

46 Ibid., p. 103.
47 Ibid., p. 105.
48 See Jantzen (1995).
49 Foucault (1969a), pp. 15, 21.
50 'Uncover' – ibid., p. 15; 'suspend' – ibid., p. 23; 'question' – ibid., p. 22; 'disconnect' and 'renounce' – ibid., p. 25; 'define', 'interrogate', break-up' and 'replace' – ibid., p. 26.
51 'Attacking' – ibid., p. 108; 'unravelling' – ibid., p. 125; 'invert arrangements and usual values' – ibid., pp. 171, 174; 'practise a quite different history' – ibid., p. 138.
52 Ibid., p. 22.
53 Ibid., p. 76.
54 Ibid., pp. 109, 170. Cf. pp. 118, 144, 168.
55 Descombes (1980); Dreyfus and Rabinow (1982). Although Foucault is partly influenced by Heidegger, it is important to realise that he is also moving beyond Heideggerian thought. As Dreyfus and Rabinow correctly point out, Foucault is 'explicitly rejecting both Husserlian phenomenology and Heideggerian hermeneutics when he opposes to the exegetical account the exteriority of the archaeological attitude' (Dreyfus and Rabinow, 1982, p. 57). Cf. Dreyfus (1992).
56 Heidegger (1927) [1993], p. 44. Cf. Kant [1793] (1960).
57 Foucault (1969a), p. 25.
58 Ibid., p. 131.
59 'Groupings' – ibid., p. 27; 'relations' – ibid., p. 29; 'rules' – ibid., pp. 25, 30.
60 Ibid., p. 25.
61 Ibid., pp. 30, 168.
62 See ibid., pp. 38, 74, 91, 172–3, 209, 211.
63 'Mapping' – ibid., pp. 189, 203; 'surveying' – ibid., p. 206.
64 'Regularities' – ibid., p. 37; 'multiple relations' – ibid., p. 76; 'relations of resemblance, proximity, distance, difference, transformation' – ibid., p. 44; 'discontinuities, ruptures, gaps', 'redistributions' – ibid., p. 169.
65 Ibid., p. 169. For 'non-discursive practices' see ibid., pp. 45, 157, 162.
66 Ibid., pp. 25, 28, 119.
67 Ibid., p. 203.
68 Ibid., p. 205.
69 Bernauer (1990), p. 91; Foucault (1969a), pp. 131, 204–6. Cf. Ibid., pp. 170–5, 135, 200.
70 Louth (1989), pp. 20–31.
71 Ibid., p. 78.
72 Louth (1981), p. 37.
73 Ibid., p. 40; Rorem (1993), p. 51.
74 Plotinus *The Enneads* (VI.9.11), quoted by Louth (1981), p. 51. Cf. p. 50.
75 Rorem (1993), p. 136.
76 Pseudo-Dionysius (1987), p. 50.
77 The texts *The Theological Representations* and *The Symbolic Theology* are thought to be fictional works introduced by Dionysius to support his overall work; at least no copies of the works have been found. See ibid., pp. 138–9. nn. 13 and 16.
78 Rorem (1993), p. 192.
79 Pseudo-Dionysius (1987), p. 53. Cf. Rorem (1993), p. 136.
80 Anderson (1989), p. 26.
81 Foucault (1966c), p. 22.
82 Ibid.

83 Plenary session 'Locating Foucault' at the *Signs ofthe Times* 'Foucault: The 10th Anniversary Conference', 25 June 1994, London.
84 Bouyer (1981), p. 43.
85 Pseudo-Dionysius (1987), p. 135 n. 2.
86 Rorem (1993), p. 184.
87 Jantzen (1989).
88 Jantzen (1995).
89 Pseudo-Dionysius (1987), p. 135. Cf. p. 139.
90 Foucault refers to both '*le silence*' and '*le mutisme*' and in translation these are both rendered as 'silence'. This appears to be justified by the interchangable way they are employed in Foucault's text. See *La Pensée du dehors* (Paris: Éditions Fata Morgana, 1986), pp. 22, 23 and 28 and *L'Archéologie du savoir* (Paris: Gallimard, 1969), pp. 15, 36, 65 and 100.
91 See Foucault (1963b, 1968a). Miller uses the concept of the 'limit' to read Foucault's life in terms of a Nietzschean quest. See Miller (1993a), p. 29 n. 49.
92 Pseudo-Dionysius (1987), p. 141.
93 Rorem (1993), p. 213.
94 Pseudo-Dionysius (1987), p. 138. Emphasis my own. In the translated text the phrase 'clearing aside' is supported by a footnote which explains the term is a translation of '*aphairesis*', which is also rendered as 'denial' (ibid., p. 138 n. 11).
95 Ibid., p. 135.
96 Foucault (1969a), p. 149.
97 Ibid., p. 25.
98 Ibid., p. 28. The idea of the 'manifest', which has a distinct Freudian association, is used a number of times. See ibid., pp. 25, 75, 67. Cf. p. 62 and Bernauer (1990), p. 109.
99 Pseudo-Dionysius (1987), p. 138.
100 Foucault (1969a), p. 15 n. 2.; Bernauer (1990), pp. 109, 216 n. 118. Cf. Foucault (1963a).
101 Bernauer (1990), p. 109.
102 Foucault (1969a), pp. 109, 110.
103 Ibid., p. 111.
104 Ibid.
105 Ibid., p. 109.
106 Ibid., p. 7.
107 Ibid., p. 47.
108 Ibid., p. 47 (my emphasis). Cf. pp. 32, 49.
109 Foucault (1966a), p. xi; Bernauer (1990), p. 109.
110 Foucault (1966c), p. 22. Foucault was also fascinated with this sense that words 'come from elsewhere' in the work of the surrealists (see Foucault, 1968a, p. 37; Foucault, 1963b).
111 Emphasis my own. Foucault (1969a), p. 76. Cf. 'prediscursive' and 'preconceptual' (ibid., pp. 47; 60, 62, 63). Foucault picked up on the silence from which words arise in his essay on Magritte when he wrote: '[I]t is in dream that men [*sic*], at least reduced to silence, commune with the signification of things and allow themselves to be touched by enigmatic, insistent words that come from elsewhere' (Foucault, 1968a, p. 37).
112 Ibid., p. 76. The tension is perhaps resolved by recognising a non-binary opposition between speech and silence which Foucault develops in 1976 and which I explored in chapter 2. See Foucault (1976a), p. 27.
113 Pseudo-Dionysius (1987), p. 52.
114 Foucault (1967a), p. 23.
115 Foucault (1969a), p. 162.

116 Ibid., p. 47.
117 Foucault explains that he is not trying to develop a 'history of the referent', but attempts to allow discourse to emerge on its own. His aim is therefore to pre-empt fixed assumptions about what would constitute something like the idea 'God' or the 'mystical'. He makes this point in relation to madness, explaining, somewhat in correction of his earlier work, that there is no fixed object 'madness', but a multitude of statements which continuously construct some form. There may in fact be little correspondence between these objects. In this sense Foucault questions the 'unity of the discourse'. He interestingly makes the same point in relation to 'mysticism' (see ibid., pp. 47, 32). Grace Jantzen demonstrates the problematic of the 'unity of discourse' in relation to mysticism through a Foucauldian critical history of Christian mystical thinking. She persuasively illustrates how it is the 'space of emergence', to use Foucault's term, in institutional structures that determines the object. As Foucault's work developed, the issue of 'power' is introduced into the historical equation. Grace Jantzen's work explores this dimension of mysticism and overcomes Foucault's gender-blind analysis by showing how this relates to the position of women mystics. See Jantzen (1995). Such a view of 'mysticism' exposes the problems of associating, mainly male, continental philosophers with 'mysticism'.
118 See, for example, Pseudo-Dionysius (1987), pp. 136–7.
119 Foucault (1969a), pp. 79, 39, 113, 121, 189, 202–5.
120 Sells (1994), p. 4.
121 Ibid., p. 220.
122 Ibid., pp. 7, 207.
123 The use of metaphor in theology is very complex. For an extremely valuable study of the subject see Soskice (1985).
124 Derrida [1967] (1978), p. 27; Megill (1985), pp. 216–17.
125 Rorem (1993), p. 185; Pseudo-Dionysius (1987), p. 135.
126 Pseudo-Dionysius (1987), pp. 135, 138.
127 See reflections on the 'gaze' by Certeau (1986), pp. 192, 196; Jay (1986); Flynn (1993).
128 Foucault (1967a), p. 22. Foucault states: 'The present epoch will perhaps be above all the epoch of space.' He continues in the same work:

> We are in the epoch of simultaneity: we are in the epoch of juxtaposition, the epoch of near and far, of the side-by-side, of the dispersed. We are at a moment, I believe, when our experience of the world is less that of a long life developing through time than that of a network that connects points and intersects with its own skein.
>
> (Foucault, 1967a, pp. 22ff.)

In this passage we can see the close connection between Foucault's 1967 work and the metaphors in AK, although it is important to realise that he does not regard the ideas of 'space' as unique to our time but historically evolved.
129 Ibid., p. 23.
130 Foucault (1969a), p. 32.
131 'Surfaces' – ibid., pp. 7, 26, 41, 47, 48, 109, 119, 128, 184–5; 'networks' – ibid., pp. 23, 55, 98, 120, 168; 'domains' – ibid., pp. 59, 75, 91, 96, 100, 121, 122, 128, 135, 148; 'regions' – ibid., p. 130. Closely associated with this is the idea of 'borders' and 'boundaries' – ibid., pp. 130, 137, 179; 'distribution' – ibid., pp. 46, 99, 119, 169; 'proximity' – ibid., p. 46; 'nexus' – ibid., p. 48; 'web' – ibid., pp. 98, 126, 146; 'map' – ibid., pp. 155, 161, 169, 179, 189, 203, 208; 'sites' –

ibid., pp. 51, 52, 55; 'grid' – ibid., p. 52; 'constellations' – ibid., p. 103; 'positions' – ibid., p. 200; 'configurations' – ibid., pp. 57, 158.

132 Cupitt (1987). Author's note.
133 The reference to a 'horizontal' analysis is complicated by the fact that on one occasion Foucault utilises a 'vertical' analogy (Foucault, 1969a, p. 109).
134 Rorem (1993), p. 163.
135 Pseudo-Dionysius (1987), pp. 58ff., 116.
136 Ibid., p. 129.
137 Foucault (1969a), pp. 205–6.
138 Pseudo-Dionysius (1987), p. 94.
139 Ibid.
140 Ibid., p. 116; Foucault (1966a), pp. 339ff.
141 See Descombes (1980). Cf. Allen (1993), pp. 149ff.; Prado (1995).
142 Foucault (1969a), p. 152.
143 Foucault (1967a), p. 24.
144 Ibid., p. 27. Cf. Harkness 'Introduction' in Foucault (1968a), pp. 4–5.
145 Foucault (1969a), p. 55.
146 Ibid., p. 12. Cf. Major-Poetzl (1983), p. 44.
147 Foucault (1969a), p. 13; Foucault (1966a), pp. 379ff. The idea of the 'death of Man' (*sic*) arises in the work of Malraux in 1926. This must have been formative on Foucault, who read Malraux avidly. See Tannery (1991), p. 20; Macey (1993), pp. 33–4.
148 Foucault (1969a), p. 211.
149 Ibid., p. 106.

6 Body and belief

1 See Turner (1991, 1996); Shilling (1993).
2 The idea of 'philosophical theology' is briefly developed by Paula Cooey from Kant's *Religion within the Limits of Reason Alone* to define her own work. It refers to a 'critical, constructive, and theoretical' study separate from doctrinal, ecclesial or biblical authority. See Cooey (1994), pp. vii–x.
3 Foucault (1975d), p. 58; Turner (1991), pp. 2, 7–10, 131.
4 Turner (1991), pp. 130, 1.
5 Foucault (1982i), p. 17. Cf. Foucault (1980c), pp. 211–12 where Foucault refers to the 'relative autonomy' between the 'truth obligation' of belief and the 'truth obligation' to know oneself, although he also acknowledges they are 'linked'. See earlier comments in chapter 2.
6 Fraser (1989), p. 18. The priority of religious practices over and against religious beliefs was also put forward by Talal Asad. See Asad (1993), pp. 27–54.
7 Foucault (1982i), p. 40. Foucault does at times suggest ideology (belief) is important. See his comments on Tunisia in Eribon (1992), p. 195.
8 See Marks and Courtivron (1981). For an introduction to a number of French feminist writers see Sarup (1993), pp. 109–28; Grosz (1989).
9 Cooey (1994), p. 9.
10 Owen (1994), p. 147; Macey (1993), p. 355. Cf. Foucault (1977h), p. 194.
11 Owen (1994), p. 146. (Emphasis my own.)
12 Lash (1984), p. 18.
13 See Kusch (1991), p. 116. As Kusch writes:

… Foucault's genealogy is a highly complex bundle of ideas, difficult to present coherently, and hard to assess. This is due partly to the fact that Foucault has not given us for genealogy what he has provided us with for archaeology, i.e. a book-size elaboration of its main concepts, theses and methodological assumptions.

(Kusch, 1991, p. 116)

14 Foucault (1970c), p. 172; Foucault (1970a), pp. 215ff.; Foucault (1971a), pp. 140–1, 156. Cf. Foucault (1969a), pp. 40, 42, 73; Foucault (1961b), pp. xiff.
15 Foucault (1971a), p. 139.
16 Ibid., p. 160; Foucault (1970c), p. 172.
17 Foucault (1971a), pp. 156, 158. Cf. pp. 147, 148.
18 Ibid., p. 148.
19 Ibid., p. 155. Cf. p. 153.
20 Ibid., pp. 148, 153.
21 See Lash (1984); Grosz (1993a). Cf. Turner (1992, 1996); Shortland (1986); Grosz (1991).
22 See Lash (1984); Grosz (1993a, 1993b). Gilles Deleuze (1925–95) collaborated with Foucault on a number of projects, although they became more distant in the 1970s. (See Eribon, 1992, pp. 258ff.) As Lecercle indicates, Deleuze 'occupies a rather special position on the French philosophical scene'. He originally worked as a traditional historian of philosophy, with works on Hume, Kant and Spinoza, and then shifted to critical philosophy with works such as *Difference and Repetition* and *The Logic of Sense* in 1969. Foucault reviewed Deleuze's 1969 works in his 1970 piece for *Critique*. (See Lecercle, 1985, p. 90; Foucault, 1970c.)
23 Lash (1984), pp. 20, 24. Cf. Deleuze and Guattari [1972] (1984).
24 Foucault (1971a), p. 153.
25 Ibid., p. 145. See the discussion of Foucault, Nietzsche and the soul later in this chapter.
26 Deleuze [1962] (1983), p. 39.
27 See Allison (1985).
28 Deleuze [1969] (1990), pp. 280–301; Foucault (1970c), p. 170. Deleuze uses a kind of Kleinian notion of 'phantasy' based on early childhood development, where every perception is constructed by a series of unconscious fantasies. The child's external perception is thus inescapably interwoven with unconscious emotional states. (See Rycroft, 1977, p. 118; Segal, 1992, pp. 28ff.)
29 Foucault (1970c), p. 171.
30 Foucault (1975a), p. 31.
31 Foucault (1971a), pp. 142, 147; Foucault (1970c), p. 170.
32 Foucault (1970c), p. 170.
33 See Foucault (1984a).
34 See Foucault (1969a), pp. 25ff., 135ff. Foucault is critical of the metaphysical notions operating in the history of ideas.
35 Ibid., p. 138.
36 Ibid., p. 13; Foucault (1971a).
37 Foucault (1971a), p. 142.
38 Ibid., pp. 148, 160.
39 Ibid., pp. 154–5. Cf. Foucault (1969a), p. 169.
40 Foucault (1971a), pp. 145, 147, 156, 159–60.
41 Ibid., p. 155.
42 Foucault (1975a), p. 315 n. 8.
43 Donnelly (1982), p. 25.
44 Macey (1993), pp. 8–10. Cf. Foucault (1975a), p. 141.
45 Foucault (1975a), p. 331. It should be noted that Foucault has often been criticized by historians for poor and inaccurate source references. See, for example, Midelfort [1980] (1988). For a review of DP see Geertz (1978).

46 Foucault (1975a), p. 137. Cf. Donnelly (1982), pp. 20–1.
47 Foucault (1975a), p. 136.
48 The emphasis at this point is clearly in terms of the 'technique of domination', but later Foucault's views of monasticism and confession are modified in terms of his 'technologies of the self', where power gives way to a greater appreciation of the aesthetics of the body. See, for example, Foucault (1980c).
49 Foucault (1975a), p. 137.
50 Foucault (1982i), p. 44.
51 Foucault (1967a), p. 27.
52 Foucault (1975a), p. 150.
53 Ibid., pp. 139–40.
54 Foucault (1977h), p. 194.
55 Foucault (1975a), p. 149. Cf. p. 123.
56 Ibid., p. 137.
57 Ibid., p. 294.
58 Ibid., p. 173.
59 Ibid., pp. 172, 143.
60 Ibid., pp. 237, 239, 318 n. 6; Foucault (1961b), pp. 243ff.
61 Foucault (1975a), p. 239. Cf. Foucault (1967a), p. 27, where Foucault has previously referred to Puritan spirituality. Foucault's work shows a consistent interest in Puritan and Quaker spirituality, perhaps reflecting the influence in France of Voltaire's essay *Letters Concerning the English Nation*. Voltaire [1733] (1994).
62 Foucault (1961b), p. 244.
63 Ibid., p. 244; Foucault (1975a), p. 238.
64 Foucault (1975a), p. 239.
65 Ibid., p. 318 n. 7.
66 Ibid., pp. 212–13.
67 Ibid., p. 239.
68 Ibid., p. 252. Cf. Foucault (1982k, 1983j).
69 Foucault (1982i), p. 27.
70 Foucault (1982f), p. 238.
71 Ibid., p. 239.
72 Foucault (1966a), p. 314.
73 Foucault (1975a), p. 164.
74 Ibid., p. 155.
75 Ibid., p. 161.
76 Ibid., p. 162.
77 Ibid., p. 30.
78 Ibid., p. 23. Foucault had previously referred to the nineteenth-century view of the 'soul' and 'body' in his 1969 AK. In this work he defines the nineteenth-century view of the 'soul', 'as a group of hierarchized, related, and more or less interpenetrable faculties'; and the 'body', 'as a three-dimensional volume of organs linked together by networks of dependence and communication' (Foucault, 1969a, p. 42).
79 Foucault (1975a), p. 29.
80 Ibid., p. 16. Cf. p. 29.
81 Ibid., p. 28.
82 Kantorowicz (1957), p. 13.
83 Ibid., pp. 194ff.
84 Ibid., p. 506.
85 Foucault (1975a), p. 30.
86 Ibid., p. 28.
87 Ibid., p. 25.

88 Nietzsche [1883–8] (1968), p. 266; Nietzsche [1888] (1968), p. 125. Nietzsche rejected ideas of the soul as a distinct metaphysical entity, seeing the idea as part of a life built on what he calls, using the French term, '*ressentiment*'. See Nietzsche [1887] (1967), pp. 5ff., 38–9; Nietzsche [1888] (1968), p. 156.

89 Nietzsche [1883–8] (1968), p. 78.

90 Nietzsche [1887] (1967), p. 84; Foucault (1975a), p. 29.

91 Nietzsche [1883–5] (1969), p. 61.

92 Foucault (1975a), p. 25. Cf. p. 54.

93 Nietzsche [1886] (1973), p. 25.

94 Butler (1994), pp. 141–73. For a discussion of Plato's conception of the soul and its relation to Aristotle, see Hatab (1990), pp. 210–16, 259–71.

95 Butler (1994), pp. 142, 146.

96 Ibid., p. 147.

97 Ibid.

98 Foucault (1975a), p. 29. The idea of 'theological illusion' in 1975 appears to be in conflict with Foucault's earlier statements in relation to Deleuze. Foucault (1970c), p. 170.

99 Foucault (1970c), p. 170. Foucault (1982i), p. 16. Foucault sees certain 'desires' as holding 'illusory forms'.

100 Nietzsche [1883–8] (1968), p. 358.

101 See Grosz (1993b), p. 188; Gilchrist (1994).

102 Grosz (1994), p. 190.

103 See Raschke (1996); Prosser MacDonald (1995). These works have opened up a new scope of theological thinking, although in the attempt to build a vision for a radical reworking of theology through the constructs of the body and imagination they at times suspend a more critical and detailed reading of the primary texts. However, they remain key landmarks in the grappling with a new theological agenda. Cf. chapter 4 n. 81.

7 Towards a political spirituality

1 The idea of a 'political spirituality' first arises in relation to a discussion of 'governmentality' in 1978, Foucault (1978d), p. 82. It is important to realise that Foucault develops a critical politics through his work on 'governmentality' and 'ethics', redefining politics, as Dumm states, 'as an activity of self-constitution'. See Dumm (1996), p. 3. We will explore these issues later in the chapter. At this stage the term 'political' is introduced to show the redirection of the 'spiritual'. For an illuminating discussion of Foucault's critique of political thought see Simons (1995), esp. pp. 55ff.

2 Foucault (1976a), pp. 105–6, 117. Foucault (1976c), p. 167; Foucault (1982m), p. 368. The concept of 'deployment' is perhaps connected to the development of the idea of 'problematisation' in so far as both set up, through the 'mobile, polymorphous, and contingent techniques of power', a specific series of concerns. Foucault (1976a), p. 106.

3 Foucault (1984a), pp. 15–32. The original version of this section, 'Usage des plaisirs et techniques de soi', appeared in *Le Débat* no. 27, November 1983, pp. 46–72. See DE IV, pp. 539–61.

4 Foucault (1984d), p. 257. This lack of specification of the notion of 'problematisation' reflects the way Foucault's thinking evolves through a series of elaborations and clarifications. The concept of 'power' was introduced on a similar basis, a recognition and clarification of something beneath the surface of his earlier work. See Foucault (1976g), p. 115.

5 Foucault (1984a), p. 10; Foucault (1984d), p. 257. Cf. Foucault (1984a), p. 12.

6 Foucault (1984f), p. 388.
7 Ibid., pp. 384, 388–9; Foucault (1983p), pp. 420ff.
8 Foucault (1983g), p. 343.
9 Foucault (1984d), p. 256. Emphasis my own.
10 Foucault (1984a), p. 10. Cf. Foucault (1984b).
11 See chapter 3.
12 Castel (1994), pp. 242, 248.
13 Ibid., p. 252.
14 E.A. Clark (1988), p. 625.
15 The subject of Foucault and history is a huge area of work, particularly as it formed one of the first frontiers of Foucault scholarship, which has expanded along a number of different routes. See in particular: White (1973) and (1987), ch. 5; Megill (1979, 1987); Roth (1981); Goldstein (1984); Midelfort [1980] (1988); Goldstein (1994). In relation to Christian history see E.A. Clark (1988). No doubt these debates will continue to run alongside new developments in Foucault studies.
16 Foucault (1979g).
17 Foucault (1976g), p. 114.
18 Foucault (1978d), p. 74.
19 M. Dean (1994), p. 174.
20 Foucault (1980d), p. 154.
21 Foucault (1979c), p. 60; Foucault (1982f), pp. 239–40; Foucault (1982i), pp. 44, 48; Foucault (1984c), p. 9.
22 Bevis *et al.* (1989), pp. 197–8.
23 Ibid., p. 201.
24 Ibid., pp. 200–1.
25 Ibid., p. 205.
26 Ibid., p. 208.
27 Lloyd (1986); Goldhill (1995). Cf. Porter (1988), pp. 13ff.; Hadot (1995), pp. 206ff.
28 Foucault (1983g), p. 361.
29 Ibid., p. 366.
30 Bevis *et al.* (1989), p. 206.
31 Foucault (1984a), p. 6; Bevis *et al.* (1989), p. 204.
32 Bevis *et al.* (1989), p. 206.
33 Foucault (1983g), pp. 341–2. It is interesting to note the subtle shift from a 'technology of "flesh"' in HS1 to a 'technology of self' in the work of the early 1980s. Compare Foucault (1976a), pp. 113, 116 to Foucault (1982i), pp. 44–5.
34 Foucault (1980f); Foucault (1979c), p. 83; Foucault (1978b), pp. 87, 104.
35 Foucault (1979g).
36 Foucault (1983l); Foucault (1983g), p. 342; Foucault (1980b); Foucault (1982i). Foucault does acknowledge changes, shifts and differences between the Greco-Roman world and Christianity while maintaining other continuities, although there is no doubt these are limited. See Foucault (1984a), pp. 20–1; Foucault (1984d), p. 256; Foucault (1979c), p. 70. The principal feature of Foucault's argument is to show a transition within 'ethics' as 'the self's relation to itself', and the 'problematics' therein, as opposed to changes in an external moral code. See Foucault (1984b), pp. 238–40; Foucault (1983g), pp. 351ff.; Davidson (1986), p. 228. For a very useful introduction to Foucault's wider ethical theory see Davidson (1986, 1994). Cf. Bernauer and Mahon (1994); Connolly (1993).
37 Foucault (1982c), p. 214. Cf. Foucault (1984b), pp. 238–9; Foucault (1983g), p. 355; Davidson (1986), pp. 230–1.
38 Foucault (1982c), pp. 213–14.

39 Foucault (1984c), p. 14; O'Farrell (1989), p. 73. It was this direction of thinking that led Foucault to study the 'ethical' practice of the Greco-Roman world. Foucault (1984a, 1984b). As we shall see, 'ethics' and 'spirituality' merge in Foucault's thought according to his definition of 'ethics' as *'rapport à soi'* (the relationship to oneself). See Foucault (1983g), p. 352.

40 Foucault (1984f), p. 384.

41 Foucault (1976g), p. 114.

42 Foucault (1982c), p. 213.

43 Foucault (1979b), p. 7.

44 Macey (1993), pp. 406ff.; Eribon (1992), pp. 281ff.; Miller (1993a), pp. 306ff.

45 Stauth (1991), p. 389.

46 Ibid.

47 Ibid., p. 385.

48 Foucault (1979a), p. 218.

49 Ibid., p. 223; Stauth (1991), pp. 389, 395.

50 Jambet (1989); Stauth (1991); O'Farrell (1989), pp. 72–4. Bernauer and Mahon only pick up the issue in passing. See Bernauer and Mahon (1994), p. 144. Cf. Bernauer (1990), pp. 175–6. O'Farrell's work, although not principally concerned with theology and spirituality, provides some very useful perspectives on these questions, not only in highlighting issues from the reports on Iran, but in discussing questions of the 'limit' and the 'Same' and the 'Other'. Along with Bernauer's work, I am indebted to O'Farrell's work for originally directing my attention to the question of Foucault and religion. O'Farrell obviously makes reference to Jambet's pioneering work on Foucault and Islamic 'spirituality', an indispensable work, along with Stauth, for considering Foucault's Iranian question. The biographical material is extremely varied on the question of Foucault and Iran. See note 44 above.

51 Foucault (1978o), p. 694; Macey (1993), p. 410.

52 Foucault (1978d), p. 82. Cf. O'Farrell (1989), p. 107.

53 Foucault (1978b), pp. 87–8.

54 M. Dean (1994), p. 174. Dean's work clearly demonstrates the central importance of 'governmentality' to Foucault's later work. See ibid., pp. 174ff.

55 Foucault (1978b), pp. 87–8; Allen (1993), p. 155.

56 Foucault (1976g), p. 131.

57 Ibid., p. 131, quoted in Allen (1993), p. 170. Allen (1993), pp. 149–76 provides a valuable discussion of the issues of 'politics' and 'truth'. The question of 'truth' plays an important part in shaping the direction of Foucault's work and not surprisingly it forms the theme of some of his final lectures in an examination of the Greek notion of *parrhēsia*. See Foucault (1978d), p. 82; Foucault (1983n); Flynn (1991). For an excellent summary of the use of the notion of 'truth' in Foucault's work see Prado (1995), pp. 119–50. Prado unfolds five notions of 'truth': the Relativist, the Constructivist, the Perspectivist, the Experiential and the Semi-Objectivist, showing the diversity of Foucault's style and writing. Cf. Rajchmann (1991), pp. 121ff. The question of 'truth' continues to emerge as a central theme in philosophical studies of Foucault's work. See McCarthy's discussion of Rorty and Foucault: McCarthy (1991), pp. 11–42.

58 Bernauer and Mahon (1994), p. 153.

59 Bernauer and Mahon refer to Foucault's 'ethics' as 'a stylization, a mode of self-formation', focusing their essay on Foucault's assertion of a 'politics of ourselves' and 'politics as an ethics' (ibid., pp. 154, 147). The definition of 'ethics' parallels with Foucault's definition of 'spirituality' in 1984, as a 'mode of being' (Foucault, 1984c, p. 14). This relationship between 'ethics' and 'spirituality' rests on the redefinition of 'ethics' as *'rapport à soi'* (Foucault, 1983g, pp. 352ff.).

Foucault uncritically merges 'politics' into 'ethics', and 'ethics' into 'spirituality', and thus successfully expunges any metaphysical referent from 'spirituality', arguably leaving his work open to the criticism of reducing 'religion' to a political ethics. Foucault's later work begins with the premise of non-belief and challenges Christianity by exposing its political constructions of the self; his work shows no interest in the structures of belief.

60 Connolly (1993), pp. 378ff. Cf. pp. 365, 368.
61 Foucault (1982c), p. 212.
62 Jambet (1989), p. 241.
63 Stauth (1991), p. 394.
64 Corbin (1977), p. xiii.
65 Jambet (1989), p. 235.
66 Foucault (1964a), p. xxv. Foucault is critical of any transcendent categories of thought. See Foucault (1969a).
67 Jambet (1989) p. 239.
68 Ibid., p. 235; Corbin (1977), pp. xii–xiii.
69 Jambet (1989), p. 247.
70 Foucault (1978p), p. 716. Translation taken from Stauth (1991), p. 391.
71 Foucault (1979a), p. 223; Stauth (1991), p. 396.
72 Foucault (1979a), p. 223; Foucault (1982c), p. 213. Foucault stressed in relation to the Iranian Revolution that he was interested not in the 'ideological cloak' of religion but in the 'live revolts'. Foucault (1979b), p. 6. However from the discussion in chapter 6 we can see how such a separation is deeply flawed.
73 Foucault (1979a), p. 218; Stauth (1991), p. 398.
74 Foucault (1979c), p. 71.
75 Ibid.
76 Macey (1993), pp. 399ff.; Foucault (1978i).
77 Liebmann Schaub (1989); Stoler (1995). Cf. Said. (1978).
78 Liebmann Schaub (1989), p. 307; Stoler (1995), p. 28. Cf. Foucault (1976b), p. 81. While Stoler uncovers the racism and colonialism within discourses of sexuality, there is still a lot of work needed to open up the relationship between racism and religious technologies of power. See Carrette and Keller (1999).

Conclusion: Religion after Foucault

1 Foucault (1982c), p. 216. Cf. Bernauer and Mahon (1994), p. 147.
2 Foucault (1963c, 1982f).
3 Foucault (1963c), p. 43.
4 Ibid., p. 42.
5 R. King (1999), p. 210.
6 Stoler (1995), p. 209. Cf. Foucault (1978i) p.113 for cross-cultural debate.
7 Foucault (1970a), p. 225.
8 Ibid., p. 226.
9 Ibid., p. 229
10 Foucault (1976a), p. 98.
11 Ibid.
12 The body is a threshold or boundary of the sacred. See Carrette and Keller (1999).
13 See, for example, Daly (1973); Ruether (1983); and Fiorenza (1983); and, more recently, excellent studies by Cooey (1994) and Jantzen (1998).
14 Knauft (1996), p. 239. I am grateful to my colleague Richard King for drawing my attention to this incisive work.

15 See, for example, Turner (1991); Coakley (1997); Jordan (1997); Krondorfer (1996); Eilberg-Schwartz (1994); Jantzen (1995, 1998); Mellor and Shilling (1997); Raschke (1996); Prosser MacDonald (1995). For a critical review of some of this material on the body and religion see Carrette and King (1998).

16 Knauft (1996), p. 239.

17 Jantzen (1998), p. 94.

18 Raschke (1996), pp. 40ff; Irigaray [1974] (1993), pp. 32–3, quoted in Jantzen (1998), p. 272. Jantzen develops Irigaray's work to develop a new feminist philosophy of religion based on imagination and desire.

19 Foucault (1976a), p. 94.

20 Castelli (1992), p. 205. See also Castelli (1991).

21 Jantzen (1995), p. 327.

22 R. King (1999), p. 211.

23 Ibid., p. 1.

24 Pasewark (1993), p. 336.

25 R. King (1999), p. 208. See Parrish (1996), pp. x–xi.

26 Foucault (1980c).

27 Giddens (1992), p. 18. See also Foucault (1975a), pp. 138, 193.

28 Foucault (1982i), p. 40.

29 Foucault (1980c), p. 203.

30 Asad (1993), pp. 43–54.

31 Foucault's work on the Christian technology of the self was explored early on by scholars at the 1982 University of Vermont seminar. See Martin (1988); Paden (1988); Rothwell (1988). Jantzen (1995) also picks up the idea of a technology of self in her discussion of Christian mysticism. The wider analysis of the government of self has, however, been limited. The literature on Foucault's ethics of the self is continually expanding. See, for example, Davidson (1986, 1994); MacIntyre (1990); Connelly (1993); Bernauer and Mahon (1994).

32 See my collection of pieces that would have formed the background to the fourth volume of Foucault's *History of Sexuality* and my discussion of this work in Carrette (1999a).

33 Hadot (1995), p. 211. Cf. Cameron (1986); Goldhill (1995).

34 Hadot (1995), p. 208.

35 Nilson (1998), p. 112, quoting Foucault (1984i), p. 732. Nilson usefully combines a Nietzschean thematic into a reading of Foucault's final works and in places highlights the Nietzsche–Foucault critique of Christianity. As Nilson states:

> It can hardly be denied ... that with his final studies, Foucault was following Nietzsche's call for the *Umwertung* (revaluation) of an anachronistic tradition bequeathed by Christianity, but still having effect in all areas of modern society, in order to free our view for a culture of the self yet to be created.
>
> (Nilson, 1998, p. 60; cf. pp. 113–14)

36 Cupitt (1995), p. 12. Cf. Cupitt (1988), pp. 38ff. Cupitt's work takes little account of the critical perspectives of race, gender and sexuality, but it has been taken up with some enthusiasm in the UK by those developing 'non-essentialist' forms of religious practice.

37 The 'specific intellectual' engages in 'local, specific struggles' and stands in opposition to the 'universal intellectual' of the nineteenth and early twentieth century. See Foucault (1976g), pp. 127–31. Cf. Foucault (1972c); (1977f), p. 124; (1984c), p. 265.
38 Foucault (1966a), p. 387.

Bibliography

Works by Michel Foucault

In order to appreciate the chronology of Foucault's works, which is often lost by using the translation dates, the works are ordered by the year of the original versions in French or, occasionally, English. In certain cases I also follow David Macey's extensive bibliography by following the date on which the original lecture or interview occurred. (See Macey, 1993, pp. 543ff.) I have used where possible the English translation followed by the original French or Italian source. The bibliography includes material from the Foucault archive, originally held at the Bibliothèque du Saulchoir, Paris, which is 'not reproducible' and can be consulted only in the library. This material is indicated by the library code reference followed by an asterisk. The Foucault archive is now held at l'Institut Mémoires de l'Édition Contemporain (IMEC), Paris.

Abbreviations

DE   *Dits et écrits 1948–1988* (4 vols), ed. Daniel Defert and François Ewald. Paris: Gallimard, 1994.

FE   *The Foucault Effect: Studies in Governmentality*, ed. Graham Burchell, Colin Gordon and Peter Miller. Hemel Hempstead: Harvester Wheatsheaf, 1991.

FL   *Foucault Live: Interviews 1961–1984*, ed. Sylvère Lotringer. 2nd edition. New York: Semiotext(e), 1996.

FR   *The Foucault Reader: An Introduction to Foucault's Thought*, ed. Paul Rabinow. London: Penguin, 1991.

LCP   *Language, Counter-Memory, Practice: Selected Essays and Interviews*, ed. Donald Bouchard. Ithaca: Cornell University Press, 1977. Trans. Donald Bouchard and Sherry Simon.

PK   *Power/Knowledge: Selected Interviews and Other Writings 1972–1977*, ed. Colin Gordon. Hemel Hempstead: Harvester Wheatsheaf, 1980.

PPC   *Politics, Philosophy, Culture: Interviews and Other Writings 1977–1984*, ed. Lawrence D. Kritzman. London: Routledge, 1988.

RC   *Religion and Culture by Michel Foucault*, ed. Jeremy R. Carrette. Manchester: Manchester University Press/New York: Routledge, 1999.

(1954a) 'Dream, Imagination and Existence' in *Dream and Existence: Michel Foucault and Ludwig Binswanger*, ed. Keith Hoeller. Atlantic Highlands, NJ: Humanities Press, 1993, pp. 31–105. Trans. Forest Williams. Originally 'Introduction' to Ludwig Binswanger, *Le Rêve et l'existence*, trans. Jacqueline Verdeaux, intro. and notes by Michel Foucault. Paris: Desclée de Brouwer, 1954.

(1954b) (Revised 1962, 1966) *Mental Illness and Psychology*. Berkeley: University of California Press, 1987. Trans. Alan Sheridan. Originally published as *Maladie mentale et psychologie*. Paris: Presses Universitaires de France, 1962/6; revised version of *Maladie Mentale et Personalité*. Paris: Presses Universitaires de France, 1954.

(1961a) *Historie de la folie à l'âge classique*. Paris: Gallimard, 1972. Originally published Paris: Plon, 1961.

(1961b) *Madness and Civilization: A History of Insanity in the Age of Reason*, abridged version of *Historie de la folie*. [London: Tavistock 1967]. London: Routledge, 1991. Trans. Richard Howard.

(1961c) 'Madness Only Exists in Society' in FL, pp. 7–9. Originally published in *Le Monde*, 12 July 1961.

(1962a) 'The Father's "No" ' in LCP, pp. 68–86. Trans. Donald Bouchard and Sherry Simon. Originally published in *Critique*, no. 178, Mar. 1962.

(1962b) 'Introduction' in *Rousseau (J.-J.), Rousseau juge de Jean-Jacques. Dialogues* in DE I, pp. 172–88.

(1962c) 'Dire et voir chez Raymond Roussel' in DE I, pp. 205–15. Originally published in *Lettre ouverte*, no. 4, 1962.

(1962/1968) 'Religious Deviations and Medical Knowledge' in RC, pp. 50–6. Trans. Richard Townsend. Originally published as 'Les deviations religieuses et le savoir medical' in *Hérésies et sociétés dans l'Europe préindustrielle XIe–XVIIIe siècle*, ed. Jacques Le Goff. Paris: Mouton et H.S.S., 1968. Paper originally delivered at Royaumont, 27–30 May, 1962. (Also published in DE I, pp. 624–35.)

(1963a) (Revised 1972) *The Birth of the Clinic: An Archaeology of Medical Perception*. London: Routledge, 1991. Trans. Alan Sheridan Smith. Originally published *Naissance de la clinique: Une Archéologie du regard médical*. Paris: Pressses Universitaires de France, 1963 (revised 1972).

(1963b) *Death and the Labyrinth: The World of Raymond Roussel*. London: Athlone, 1987. Trans. Charles Ruas. Originally published *Raymond Roussel*, Paris: Gallimard, 1963.

(1963c) 'A Preface to Trangression' in LCP, pp. 29–52. Trans. Donald Bouchard and Sherry Simon. Originally published in *Critique*, no. 195–6, Aug.–Sept. 1963. (Also published in RC, pp. 57–71.)

(1963d) 'Language to Infinity' in LCP, pp. 53–67. Trans. Donald Bouchard and Sherry Simon. Originally published in *Tel Quel*, no. 15, Autumn 1963.

(1963e) 'Distance, aspects, origine' in DE I, pp. 272–85. Originally published in *Critique*, no. 198, Nov. 1963.

(1963f) 'Un "nouveau roman" de terreur' in DE I pp. 285–7. Originally published in *France-Observateur*, no. 710, Dec. 1963.

(1964a) 'The Prose of Actaeon' in Pierre Klossowski, *The Baphomet*. New York: Eridanos, 1988, pp. xxi–xxxviii. Trans. Sophie Hawkes and Stephen Sartarelli. Originally published in *La Nouvelle Revue Française*, no. 135, 1964. (Also published in RC, pp. 75–84.)

(1964b) 'Debat sur le roman' (conference discussion, Sept. 1963) in DE I, pp. 338–90. Originally published in *Tel Quel*, no. 17, Spring, 1964. Part translation 'The Debate on the Novel' in RC, pp. 72–4. Trans. Elizabeth Ezra.

(1964c) (Revised 1967) 'Fantasia of the Library' in LCP, pp. 87–109. Originally published in *Cahiers Renaud-Barrault*, no. 59, 1967 and in the German translation of *The Temptation* by Anneliese Botond. Frankfurt: Insel, 1964.

(1964d) (Revised 1967) 'Nietzsche, Freud, Marx' in *Transforming the Hermeneutic Context: From Nietzsche to Nancy*, ed. G.L. Ormiston and A.D. Schrift. New York: SUNY, 1990, pp. 59–67. Trans. A.D. Schrift. Conference paper at Royaumont. July 1964. Originally published in *Nietzsche: Cahiérs du Royaumont*. Paris: Les Éditions du Minuit, 1964.

(1964e) 'Le Mallarmé de J.-P. Richard' in DE I, pp. 427–37. Originally published in *Annales: Économies, sociétés, civilisations*, no. 5, Sept.–Oct. 1964.

(1966a) *The Order of Things: An Archaeology of the Human Sciences*. London: Routledge, 1991. Trans. Alan Sheridan. Originally published as *Les Mots et les choses: Une Archéologie des sciences humaines*. Paris: Gallimard, 1966.

(1966b) 'The Order of Things' (interview with Raymond Bellour) in FL, pp. 13–18. Trans. John Johnston. Originally published in *Les Lettres Françaises*, 31 Mar. 1966.

(1966c) 'Maurice Blanchot: The Thought from the Outside' in *Foucault/Blanchot*. New York: Zone Books, 1987, pp. 7–60. Trans. Jeffrey Mehlman and Brian Massumi. Originally published in *Critique*, no. 229, June 1966.

(1966d) 'Qu'est-ce qu'un philosophe?' (interview with M.-G.Foy) in DE I, pp. 552–3. Originally published in *Connaissance des hommes*, no. 22, Autumn 1966. English translation 'Philosophy and the Death of God' in RC, pp. 85–6. Trans. Elizabeth Ezra.

(1966e) 'André Breton: A Literature of Knowledge' in FL, pp. 10–12. Trans. John Johnston. Originally published in *Arts-Loisirs*, no. 54, Oct. 1966.

(1967a) 'Of Other Spaces', *Diacritics*, vol. 16, no. 1, Spring 1986, pp. 22–7. Trans. Jay Miskowiec. Originally published *Architecture – Mouvement – Continuité*, no. 5, Oct. 1986.

(1967b) 'The Discourse of History' (interview with Raymond Bellour) in FL, pp. 19–32. Trans. John Johnston. Originally published in *Les Lettres Françaises*, 15 June 1967.

(1967c) 'Qui êtes-vous, professeur Foucault?' in DE I, pp. 601–20. Originally published in Italian in *La Fiera letteraria*, no. 39, Sept. 1967. English translation 'Who Are You, Professor Foucault?' in RC, pp. 87–103. Trans. Lucille Cairns.

(1968a) *This is Not A Pipe*. Berkeley: University of California Press, 1982. Trans. James Harkness. Originally published as 'Ceci n'est pas une pipe' in *Cahiers du chemin*, Jan. 1968. Revised and expanded as *Ceci n'est pas une pipe*. Montpellier: Fata Morgana, 1973.

(1968b) 'Foucault Responds to Sartre' in FL, pp. 51–6. Trans. John Johnston. Originally published in *La Quinzaine Littéraire*, no. 46, 1–15 Mar. 1969.

(1968c) 'Politics and the Study of Discourse' in FE, pp. 53–72. Trans. Anthony Nazzaro, revised by Colin Gordon and subsequently by Graham Burchell, Colin Gordon and Peter Miller. Originally published in *Esprit*, no. 371, May 1968.

(1969a) *The Archaeology of Knowledge.* London: Routledge, 1991. Trans. Alan Sheridan Smith. Originally published as *L'Archéologie du savoir*. Paris: Gallimard, 1969.

(1969b) 'What is an Author?' in FR, pp. 101–20 (also in LCP, pp. 113–38). Trans. Donald Bouchard and Sherry Simon. Originally published in *Bulletin de la Société Française de Philosophie*, no. 63, July–Sept. 1969.

(1969c) 'The Birth of a World' in FL, pp. 65–7. Trans. John Johnston. Originally published in *Le Monde des Livres*, no. 3, May 1969.

(1969d) 'The Archaeology of Knowledge' in FL, pp. 57–64. Trans. John Johnston. Originally published in *La Quinzaine Littéraire*, Apr.–May 1969.

(1970a) 'The Discourse on Language' (inaugural lecture at the Collège de France), appendix in *The Archaeology of Knowledge*. New York: Pantheon, 1972, pp. 215–37. Trans. Rupert Swyer.

(1970b) 'Presentation', Georges Bataille, *Oeuvres complètes*, Vol. 1: *Premiers Écrits 1922–1940*. Paris: Gallimard, 1970, pp. 5–6. (Also published in DE II, pp. 25–7.)

(1970c) 'Theatrum philosophicum' in LCP, pp. 165–96. Trans. Donald Bouchard and Sherry Simon. Originally published in *Critique*, no. 282, Nov. 1970.

(1970d) 'Foreword' to the English Language edition of *The Order of Things*. London: Routledge, 1991, pp. ix–xiv.

(1971a) 'Nietzsche, Genealogy, History' in LCP, pp. 139–64. Trans. Donald Bouchard and Sherry Simon. Originally published in *Homage à Jean Hyppolite*. Presses Universitaires de France, 1971.

(1971b) 'A Conversation with Michel Foucault' (interview with John K. Simon), *Partisan Review*, vol. 38, no. 2, 1971, pp. 192–201. Republished as 'Rituals of Exclusion' in FL, pp. 68–73.

(1971c) 'My Body, This Paper, This Fire', *Oxford Literary Review*, vol. IV, no. 1, Autumn 1979, pp. 5–28. Trans. Geoff Bennington. Originally published in *Paideia*, Sept. 1971.

(1971d) 'Human Nature: Justice versus Power', dialogue with Noam Chomsky, televised in Nov. 1971 by Dutch Broadcasting Company, in *Reflexive Water. The Basic Concerns of Mankind*, ed. Fons Elder. London: Souvenir Press, 1974, pp. 134–97.

(1971e) 'Revolutionary Action: "Until Now"' in LCP, pp. 218–33. Trans. Donald Bouchard and Sherry Simon. Originally published in *Actuel*, no. 14, Nov. 1971.

(1971f) 'History of Systems of Thought' in LCP, pp. 199–204. Trans. Donald Bouchard and Sherry Simon. Summary of 1971 lectures at the Collège de France.

(1972a) 'Michel Foucault on Attica: An Interview', with John K. Simon, Apr. 1972, in *Telos*, no. 19, Spring 1974, pp. 154–61. Republished as 'On Attica' in FL, pp. 113–21.

(1972b) 'On Popular Justice: A Discussion with Maoists' in PK, pp. 1–36. Trans. John Mepham. Originally published in *Les Temps Modernes 310 bis (hors sie)*, May 1972.

(1972c) 'Intellectuals and Power' (discussion with Gilles Deleuze) in LCP, pp. 205–17. Trans. Donald Bouchard and Sherry Simon. Originally published in *L'Arc*, no. 49, 1972.

(1972d) 'An Historian of Culture' in FL, pp. 95–104. Trans. Jared Becker and James Cascaito. Originally published in Italian in *Il Bimestre*, no. 22–3, Sept.–Dec. 1972.

(1972e) 'Confining Societies' (discussion panel) in FL, pp. 83–94. Trans. Jeanine Herman. Originally published *Esprit*, no. 413, Apr.–May 1972.

(1973a) Foreword and Appendix to *I, Pierre Rivière, Having Slaughtered My Mother, My Sister and My Brother....* New York: Pantheon, 1975, pp. vii–xiv, 199–212. Trans. Frank Jellinek.

(1973b) 'Power and Norm: Notes' (notes from lecture at the Collège de France, 28 Mar. 1973) in Morris and Patton (1979), pp. 59–66. Trans. W. Suchting.

(1973c) 'The Equipment of Power' (discussion with Gilles Deleuze and Félix Guattari) in FL, pp. 105–12. Trans. Lysa Hochroth. Originally published in *Recherches*, no. 13, Dec. 1973.

(1974) 'Film and Popular Memory' in FL, pp. 122–32. Trans. Martin Jordin. Originally published in *Cahiers du Cinéma*, no. 251–2, July–Aug. 1974.

(1975a) *Discipline and Punish: The Birth of the Prison*. London: Penguin, 1991. Trans. Alan Sheridan. Originally published as *Surveiller et punir: Naissance de la prison*. Paris: Gallimard, 1975.

(1975b) 'An Interview with Michel Foucault', *History of the Present*, no. 1, Feb. 1985, pp. 2–3, 14. Interview with Jean-Louis Ezine. Trans. Renée Morel. Originally published as 'Sur la sellette' in *Les Nouvelles Littéraires*, 17 Mar. 1975.

(1975c) 'Prison Talk' in PK, pp. 37–54. Trans. Colin Gordon. Originally published in *Magazine Littéraire*, no. 101, June 1975.

(1975d) 'Body/Power' in PK, pp. 55–62. Trans. Colin Gordon. Originally published in *Quel Corps?*, no. 2, 1975.

(1975e) 'On Literature' (interview with Roger-Pol Droit conducted 20 June 1975) in FL, pp. 150–3. Trans. John Johnston. First published in *Le Monde Sans Visa*, 6 Sept. 1986.

(1975f) 'Talk Show' (radio interview with Jacques Chancel) in FL, pp. 133–45. Trans. Phillis Aronov and Dan McGrawth.

(1975g) 'From Torture to Cellblock' in FL, pp. 146–9. Trans. John Johnston. Originally published in *Le Monde*, 21 Feb. 1975.

(1975h) 'Schizo-Culture: Infantile Sexuality' (lecture at Columbia University at the 'Schizo-Culture' Conference, 1975) in FL, pp. 154–67.

(1975i) 'Schizo-Culture: On Prisons and Psychiatry' (panel discussion at the 'Schizo-Culture' Conference, 1975) in FL, pp. 168–80.

(1975j) 'Sade: Sargent of Sex' in FL, pp. 186–9. Trans. John Johnston. Originally published in *Cinématographe*, no. 16, Dec. 1975–Jan. 1976.

(1975k) 'White Magic and Black Gown' in FL, pp. 287–91. Trans. Lysa Hochroth. Originally published in *Actes, Cahiers d'action juridique*, no. 5–6, Dec. 1974–Jan. 1975.

(1976a) *The History of Sexuality, Volume 1: An Introduction*. London: Penguin, 1990. Trans. Robert Hurley. Originally published as *Histoire de la sexualité I: La Volonté de savoir*. Paris: Gallimard, 1976.

(1976b) 'Two Lectures' (lectures from Collège de France, 7 and 14 Jan. 1976) in PK, pp. 78–108. Trans. Kate Soper. Originally published in Italian collection *Microfisica del potere*, ed. A. Fontana and P. Pasquino. Turin: Einaudi, 1977.

(1976c) 'The Politics of Health in the Eighteenth Century' in PK, pp. 166–82. Trans. Colin Gordon. Originally published as Introduction to *Généalogie des équipements de normalisation: les équipements sanitaires*. Fontenay-sur-Bois: CERFI, 1976.

(1976d) 'Questions of Geography' in PK, pp. 63–77. Trans. Colin Gordon. Originally published in *Hérodote*, no. 1, Jan.–Mar. 1976.

(1976e) 'The Politics of Soviet Crime' in FL, pp. 190–5. Trans. Mollie Horwitz. Originally published in *Le Nouvel Observateur*, no. 585, 26 January–1 February 1976.

(1976f) 'Sorcery and Madness' in FL, pp. 200–6. Trans. John Johnston. Originally published in *Le Monde*, 23 Apr. 1976.

(1976g) 'Truth and Power' in PK, pp. 109–33. Trans. Colin Gordon. Originally published in extracts in *Politique hebdo*, no. 247, 29 Nov. 1976 and as an introduction to the Italian collection of Foucault's work *Microfisica del potere*, ed. A. Fontana and P. Pasquino. Turin: Einaudi, 1977.

(1976h) 'Paul's Story' in FL, pp. 181–5. Trans. Lysa Hochroth. Originally published in *Cahiers du cinéma*, no. 262–3, Jan. 1976.

(1976i) 'I, Pierre Rivière …' in FL, pp. 203–206. Trans. John Johnston. Originally published in *Pariscope*, 10–16 Nov. 1976.

(1976j) 'War in the Filigree of Peace. Course Summary', *Oxford Literary Review*, vol. 4, no. 2, 1980, pp. 15–19. Trans. Ian McLeod. Originally published in *Annuaire du Collège de France*, 1976 and republished in *Résumé des cours*, 1970–82. Paris: Julliard.

(1976k) 'The Social Extension of the Norm' in FL, pp. 196–9. Trans. Lysa Hochroth. Originally published in *Politique hebdo*, no. 212, 4–10 Mar. 1976.

(1977a) 'Preface' to English translation of Gilles Deleuze and Félix Guattari, *Anti-Oedipus: Capitalism and Schizophrenia*. New York: Viking, 1977, pp. 7–8. Trans. Robert Hurley, Mark Sheen and Helen Lane.

(1977b) 'The Eye of Power' in PK, pp. 146–65. Trans. Colin Gordon. Originally published as foreword to Jeremy Bentham, *Le Panoptique*. Paris: Belford, 1977.

(1977c) 'The History of Sexuality' in PK, pp. 183–93. Trans. Leo Marshall. Originally published in *La Quinzaine Littéraire*, no. 247, 1–15 Jan. 1976.

(1977d) 'The Life of Infamous Men' in Morris and Patton (1979), pp. 76–91. Trans. Paul Foss and Meaghan Morris. Originally published in *Cahiers du chemin*, no. 29, 15 Jan. 1977.

(1977e) 'Power and Strategies' in PK, pp. 134–45. Trans. Colin Gordon. Originally published in *Les Révoltes logiques*, no. 4, Winter 1977.

(1977f) 'Power and Sex: An Interview with Michel Foucault' in PPC, pp. 110–24. Trans. David Parent. Originally published in *Le Nouvel Observateur*, no. 644, 12 Mar. 1977.

(1977g) 'The Anxiety of Judging' in FL, pp. 241–54. Trans. John Johnston. Originally published in *Le Nouvel Observateur*, no. 655, 30 May 1977.

(1977h) 'The Confession of the Flesh' (discussion) in PK, pp. 194–228. Trans. Colin Gordon. Originally published in *Ornicar?*, 10 July 1977.

(1977i) 'Confinement, Psychiatry, Prison' in PPC, pp. 178–210. Trans. Alan Sheridan. Originally published in *Change: La Folie encerclée*, no. 32–3, Oct. 1977.

(1977j) 'The Dangerous Individual', address to the Law and Psychiatry Symposium at York University, Toronto, in PPC, pp. 125–51. Trans. Alain Baudot and Jane Couchman.

(1977k) 'Le pouvoir, une bête magnifique' (interview with M.Osorio) in DE III, pp. 368–82. Originally published in *Quadernos para el dialogo*, no. 238, Nov. 1977.

(1977l) 'Pouvoir et savoir' (interview with S. Hasumi) in DE III, pp. 399–414. Originally published in *Umi*, Dec. 1977.

(1978a) 'Introduction' to Georges Canguilhem, *On the Normal and the Pathological*. Boston: Reidel, 1978, pp. ix–xx. Trans. Carolyn Fawcett.

(1978b) 'Govermentality' in FE, pp. 87–105. Trans. Rosi Braidotti. Originally published in *Aut-Aut*, no. 167–8, Sept.–Dec. 1978. Italian transcript of a Collège de France lecture in Feb. 1978.

(1978c) 'Sexual Morality and the Law' (radio discussion with Guy Hocquenhem and Jean Danet) in PPC, pp. 271–85. Trans. Alan Sheridan. Originally published in *Recherches*, no. 37, Apr. 1979.

(1978d) 'Questions of Method' (round table discussion held on 20 May 1978) in FE, pp. 73–86. Trans. Colin Gordon. Originally published in *L'Impossible Prison: Recherches sur les système pénitentaire au XIXe siècle*. Paris: Seuil, 1980.

(1978e) 'On Power' in PPC, pp. 96–109. Trans. Alan Sheridan. Originally published in *L'Express*, 13 July 1984.

(1978f) 'Interview with Michel Foucault', *New German Critique*, no. 16, Winter 1979, pp. 155–6. Trans. J.D. Leakey. Originally published in *Der Spiegel*, no. 32, Oct. 1978.

(1978g) *Remarks on Marx: Interviews with Duccio Trombadori*. New York: Semiotext(e), 1991. Trans. R. James Goldstein and James Cascaito. Originally published in Italian as *Colloqui con Foucault*. Salerno: 10/17 Cooperative editrice, 1978.

(1978h) 'Foucault at the Collège de france I: A Course Summary', *Philosophy and Social Criticism*, vol. 8, no. 2, Summer 1981, pp. 1–44. Trans. James Bernauer. Originally published in *Annuaire du Collège de France*, 1978.

(1978i) 'Michel Foucault and Zen: A Stay in a Zen Temple' in RC, pp. 110–14. Trans. Richard Townsend. Originally published in *Umi*, no. 197, Aug.–Sept. 1978.

(1978j) 'Sexualité et politique' (interview with C. Nemoto and M. Watanabe) in DE III, pp. 522–31. Originally published in *Asahi Jaanaru*, no. 19, May 1978.

(1978k) 'La philosophie analytique de la politque' in DE III, pp. 534–51. Conference in Tokyo. Originally published in *Asahi Jaanaru*, June 1978.

(1978l) 'Sexuality and Power' in RC, pp. 115–30. Trans. Richard Lynch. Originally published in *Gendai-shisô*, July 1978.

(1978m) 'Clarifications on the Question of Power' in FL, pp. 255–63. Trans. James Cascaito. Originally published in *Aut-Aut*, no. 167–8, Sept.–Dec. 1978.

(1978n) *Vingt Ans et après*. Paris: Seuil, 1978. Dialogues with Thierry Voeltzel from 1976 onwards. Translated extract 'On Religion' in RC, pp. 106–9. Trans. Richard Townsend.

(1978o) 'À quoi rêvent les Iraniens?' in DE III, pp. 688–94. Originally published in *Le Nouvel Observateur*, Oct. 1978.

(1978p) 'Le chef mythique de la révolte de l'Iran' in DE III, pp. 713–16. Originally published in *Corriere della sera*, Nov. 1978.

(1979a) 'The Spirit of the World Without Spirit' (discussion with Claire Brière and Pierre Blanchet) in PPC, pp. 211–26. Trans. Alan Sheridan. Originally published as an afterword to *Iran: La Révolution au nom de Dieu*. Paris: Seuil, 1979.

(1979b) 'Is It Useless to Revolt?', *Philosophy and Social Criticism*, vol. 8, no.1, Spring 1981, pp. 1–9. Trans. James Bernauer. Originally published in *Le Monde*, 11 May 1979. (Also published in RC, pp. 131–4.)

(1979c) 'Omes et Singulatim: Towards a Criticism of "Political Reason"'. The Tanner Lectures on Human Values, delivered at Stanford University, 10 and 16 Oct. 1979. (Originally published in *The Tanner Lectures On Human Values*,

Volume 2, ed. Sterling M. McMurrin. Salt Lake City: University of Utah Press, 1981, pp. 223–54.) Reprinted as 'Politics and Reason' in PPC pp. 57–85. (Also published as 'Pastoral Power and Political Reason' in RC, pp. 135–52.)

(1979d) 'Foucault at the Collège de France II: A Course Summary', *Philosophy and Social Criticism*, vol. 8, no. 3, Fall 1981, pp. 349–59. Trans. James Bernauer. Originally published in *Annuaire du Collège de France*, 1978.

(1979e) 'Introduction' to *Herculine Barbin; Being the Recently Discovered Memoirs of a Nineteenth-Century French Hermaphrodite*. Brighton: Harvester Press, 1980, pp. vii–xvii. Dated 1980. Trans. Richard McDougall, Originally read to *Arcadie*, Congress, May 1979.

(1979f) 'The Simplest of Pleasures' in FL, pp. 295–7. Trans. Mike Riegle and Gilles Barbedette. Originally published in *Le Gai Pied*, no. 1, Apr. 1979.

(1979g) Discussion at Stanford, 11 Oct. 1979. Bibliothèque du Saulchoir. Cassette. C9*.

(1980a) 'The Masked Philosopher' in PPC, pp. 323–30. Trans. Alan Sheridan. Originally published in *Le Monde*, 6 Apr. 1980. Foucault's identity was concealed.

(1980b) 'Sexuality and Solitude', James Lecture delivered on 20 Nov. 1980 at the New York Institute for the Humanities. Originally published in *London Review of Books*, 21 May–3 June 1981, pp. 3, 5–6. (Also published with comparative notes between two versions of the lecture in RC, pp. 182–7.)

(1980c) 'Subjectivity and Truth' and 'Christianity and Confession', Dartmouth Lectures, 17/24 Nov. 1980 (including Howison lectures, Berkeley, 20–1 Oct.). Originally published as 'About the Beginning of the Hermeneutics of Self: Two Lectures at Dartmouth' in *Political Theory*, vol. 21, no. 2, May 1993, pp. 198–227. Trans. Mark Blasius. (Also published in RC, pp. 158–81.)

(1980d) 'On the Government of Living' in RC, pp. 154–7. Trans. Richard Townsend. Originally published in *Annuaire du Collège de France*, 1980. (Also published in DE IV, pp. 125–9.)

(1980e) 'Du gouvernement des vivants', Cours du Collège de France. Bibliothèque du Saulchoir. Typescript of lectures, 9 Jan.–5 Mar. 1980. D251*.

(1980f) Discussion with philosophers, 23 Oct. 1980. Berkeley. Bibliothèque du Saulchoir. Cassette. C16*.

(1980g) 'Power, Moral Values and the Intellectual', interview with Micheal D. Bess, San Francisco, 1980. Bibliothèque du Saulchoir. Typescript D384(b)* and cassette. C20*.

(1980h) 'Truth is the Future' in FL, pp. 298–301. Originally published in *The Three Penny Review*, vol. 1, no. 1, Winter–Spring 1980.

(1981a) 'Friendship as a Way of Life' in FL, pp. 203–11. Trans. John Johnston. Originally published in *Le Gai Pied*, no. 25, Apr. 1981.

(1981b) 'Is It Really Important to Think?' (interview with Didier Eribon), *Philosophy and Social Criticism*, vol. 9, no. 1, Spring 1982, pp. 29–40. Trans. Thomas Keenan. Originally published in *Libération*, no. 30–1, May 1981.

(1981c) 'Passion According to Werner Schroeter' (recorded 1981) in FL, pp. 313–21. Trans. John Johnston. Originally published in *Werner Schroeter*. Paris: Cinémathèque Française et Goethe Institute, 1982.

(1981d) 'Foucault, Michel, 1926–' in Gutting (1994), pp. 314–19. Originally published in *Dictionnaire des philosophes*, ed. D. Huisman. Presses Universitaires de France, 1981.

(1982a) 'The Social Triumph of the Sexual Will' (conversation with Gilles Berbe-dette), *Christopher Street*, no. 64, May 1982, pp. 36–41. Trans. Brendan Lemon.

(1982b) 'Michel Foucault, An Interview: Sex, Power and the Politics of Identity' (conducted by Bob Gallagher and Alexander Wilson in June 1982), *The Advocate*, no. 400, 7 Aug. 1984, pp. 26–30, 58.

(1982c) 'The Subject and Power', Afterword to Hubert L. Dreyfus and Paul Rabinow, *Michel Foucault: Beyond Structuralism and Hermeneutics*. Hemel Hempstead: Harvester Press, 1982, pp. 208–26.

(1982d) 'Space, Knowledge and Power' (inteview conducted by Paul Rabinow) in FR, pp. 239–56. Trans. Christian Hubert. Originally published in *Skyline*, Mar. 1982.

(1982e) 'Sexual Choice, Sexual Act: Foucault and Homosexuality' (interview with James O'Higgins) in PPC, pp. 286–303.

(1982f) 'The Battle for Chastity' in PPC, pp. 227–241. Trans. Anthony Foster. Origi-nally published in *Communications*, no. 35, May 1982. (Also published in RC, pp. 188–97.)

(1982g) 'The Minimalist Self' (interview with Stephen Riggins, 22 June 1982) in PPC, pp. 3–16. Originally published in English in the Canadian journal *Ethos*, vol. 1, no. 2, Autumn 1983.

(1982h) 'Truth, Power Self: An Interview with Michel Foucault' (conducted by Rux Martin, 25 Oct. 1982) in Martin *et al.* (1988), pp. 9–15.

(1982i) 'Technologies of the Self' (University of Vermont Seminar) in Martin *et al.* (1988), pp. 16–49.

(1982j) 'The Political Technology of Individuals' (University of Vermont Lecture) in Martin *et al.* (1988), pp. 145–62.

(1982k) 'L'Hermeneutique du sujet' in DE IV, pp. 353–65. Originally published in *Annuaire du Collège de France*, 1982.

(1982l) 'Response to Speech by Susan Sontag', *Soho News*, 2 Mar. 1982, p. 13.

(1982m) 'History and Homosexuality' (discussion) in FL, pp. 363–70. Trans. John Johnston. Originally published in *Masques*, no. 13, Spring 1982.

(1983a) 'Social Security' (interview with Robert Bono) in PPC, pp. 159–77. Trans. Alan Sheridan. Originally published in *Sécurité sociale: l'enjeu*. Paris: Syros, 1983.

(1983b) 'Kant on Enlightenment and Revolution', lecture at the Collège de France, 5 Jan. 1983, published as 'The Art of Telling the Truth' in PPC, pp. 86–95. Trans. Alan Sheridan. Originally published in *Magazine littéraire*, no. 207, May 1984.

(1983c) 'What is Enlightenment?' (lecture at Berkeley, autumn 1983) in FR, pp. 32–50. Trans. Catherine Porter.

(1983d) 'An Exchange with Michel Foucault' (exchange of letters between Foucault and Lawrence Stone) in P. Burke (1992), pp. 59–70. Originally published in *New York Review of Books*, 13 Mar. 1983.

(1983e) 'Structuralism and Post-Structuralism: An Interview with Michel Foucault' (interview with Gérard Raulet), *Telos*, no. 55, Spring 1983, reprinted in PPC, pp. 17–53. Trans. Jeremy Harding. Originally published in *Spuren*, nos. 1–2, 1983.

(1983f) 'Politics and Ethics: An Overview' (edited interviews, conducted in Apr. 1983 with Paul Rabinow, Charles Taylor, Martin Jay, Richard Rorty and Leo Lowen-thal) in FR, pp. 373–80. Trans. Catherine Porter.

(1983g) 'On the Genealogy of Ethics: An Overview of Work in Progress' (interview with Hubert L. Dreyfus and Paul Rabinow) in FR, pp. 340–72.

(1983h) 'Contemporary Music and the Public' in PPC, pp. 314–30. Trans. John Rahn. Originally published in *CNAC Magazine*, no. 15, May–June 1983.

(1983i) 'An Interview with Michel Foucault' (interview with Charles Ruas), published as Postscript to *Death in the Labyrinth*, pp. 169–86. Trans. Charles Ruas.

(1983j) 'L'écriture de soi' in DE IV, pp. 415–30. Originally published in *Le Corps écrit*, no. 5, 1983.

(1983k) Discussion with Hubert L. Dreyfus and Paul Rabinow, Berkeley, 15 Apr. 1983. Bibliothèque du Saulchoir. Typescript. D250(4)*.

(1983l) Discussion with Hubert L. Dreyfus and Paul Rabinow, Berkeley, 19 Apr. 1983. Bibliothèque du Saulchoir. Typescript. D250(5)*.

(1983m) Discussion with Hubert L. Dreyfus and Paul Rabinow, Berkeley, 21 Apr. 1983. Bibliothèque du Saulchoir. Typescript. D250(6)*.

(1983n) 'Discourse and Truth: The Problematization of Parrhesia'. Notes to the seminar given by Foucault at the University of California at Berkeley. 10 Oct.– 30 Nov. 1983. Edited by Joseph Pearson, 1985. Bibliothèque du Saulchoir. D213*.

(1983o) 'What Our Present Is' (interview with André Berten conducted in 1983) in FL, pp. 407–15. Trans. Lysa Hochroth. Originally published in *Cahiers du GRIFFE*, nos. 37–8, 1988.

(1983p) 'Problematics' (interview with Thomas Zummer in Nov. 1983) in FL, pp. 416–22. Originally published in *Crash: Nostalgia for the Absence of Cyberspace*, ed. R. Reynolds and T. Zummer. New York: Thread Waxing Space, 1994.

(1983q) 'The Culture of Self'. Discussion in the History Department, University of California, Berkeley. Bibliothèque du Saulchoir. Cassette. C84*.

(1983r) Discussion with Michel Foucault, 21 Apr. 1983. (With Paul Rabinow, Hubert L. Dreyfus, Charles Taylor Robert Bellah, Martin Jay and Leo Lowenthal.) Bibliothèque du Saulchoir. Typescript. D250(7)*.

(1983/4a) 'What Calls for Punishment?' (interview with Foulek Ringelheim, Dec. 1983, revised and corrected by Foucault on 16 Feb. 1984) in FL, pp. 423–31.

(1983/4b) 'Preface to *The History of Sexuality, Volume 2*' in FR, pp. 33–9. (Original undated typescript.)

(1984a) *The Use of Pleasure: The History of Sexuality, Volume 2*. London: Penguin, 1992. Trans. Robert Hurley. Originally published as *Histoire de la sexualité 2: L'Usage des plaisirs*. Paris: Gallimard, 1984.

(1984b) *The Care of the Self: The History of Sexuality, Volume 3*. London: Penguin, 1990. Trans. Robert Hurley. Originally published as *Histoire de la sexualité 3: Le Souci de soi*. Paris: Gallimard, 1984.

(1984c) 'The Ethic of the Care for the Self as a Practice of Freedom' in Bernauer and Rasmussen (1991), pp. 1–20. Trans. Joseph Gauthier. Originally published in *Concordia*, no. 6, 1984.

(1984d) 'The Concern for Truth' (interview with François Ewald) in PPC, pp. 255–67. Trans. Alan Sheridan. Originally published in *Magazine littéraire*, no. 207, May 1984.

(1984e) 'An Aesthetics of Existence' in PPC, pp. 47–53. Trans. Alan Sheridan. Originally published in *Panorama*, no. 945, 28 May 1984.

(1984f) 'Polemics, Politics and Problematizations' (based on discussions with Paul Rabinow and Thomas Zummer, May 1984) in FR, pp. 381–90. Trans. Lydia Davies.

(1984g) 'The Return of Morality' (interview with Gilles Barbedette and André Scala, conducted on 29 May 1984; final interview) in PPC, pp. 242–54. Trans. Thomas Levin and Isabelle Lorenz. Originally published in *Les Nouvelles*, 28 June–5 July 1984.

(1984h) 'A Last Interview with French Philosopher Michel Foucault' (conducted by Jamin Raskin, Mar. 1984), *City Paper*, vol. 8, no. 3, 27 July–2 Aug. 1984, p. 18.

(1984i) 'Une esthétique de l'existence' in DE IV, pp. 730–5. Originally published in *Le Monde*, July 1984.

(1989) *Résumé des cours*, 1970–82. Paris: Julliard.

General bibliography

Alcoff, L. and Potter, E., eds (1993) *Feminist Epistemologies*. London: Routledge.

Allen, B. (1993) *Truth in Philosophy*. Cambridge, MA: Harvard University Press.

Allison, D.B., ed. (1985) *The New Nietzsche: Contemporary Style of Interpretation*. Cambridge, MA: MIT Press.

Almansi, G. (1982) 'Foucault and Magritte' in *History of European Ideas*, vol. 3, no. 3, pp. 303–9.

Anderson, K. (1989) 'Towards a New Reason: Guilt, Language and Nature in the Work of Roland Barthes and Francis Ponge' in *Ideology and Religion in French Literature*, ed. H. Cockerham and E. Ehrman. Camberley: Porphyrogenitus, pp. 23–48.

Ansell-Pearson, K. (1994) *An Introduction to Nietzsche as Political Thinker*. Cambridge: Cambridge University Press.

Antonopoulos, A. (1991) 'Writing the Mystic Body: Sexuality and Textuality in the *écriture-féminine* of Saint Catherine of Genoa', *Hypatia*, vol. 6, no. 3, pp. 185–207.

Appignanesi, L., ed. (1989) *Ideas From France: The Legacy of French Theory: ICA Documents*. London: Free Association Books.

Arac, J., ed. (1991) *After Foucault: Humanistic Knowledge, Postmodern Challenges*. New Brunswick, NJ: Rutgers.

Armstrong, T.J., trans. (1992) *Michel Foucault: Philosopher*. Hemel Hempstead: Harvester Wheatsheaf.

Artaud, A. [1932] (1988) 'The Theater of Cruelty: First Manifesto' in Artaud (1988), pp. 242–51.

—— (1965) *Artaud Anthology*, ed. J. Hirschmann. San Francisco: City Lights.

—— (1968) *Collected Works, Volume 1*. London: Calder and Boyars.

—— (1974) *The Death of Satan and Other Mystical Writings*. London: Calder and Boyars.

—— (1988) *Antonin Artaud: Selected Writings*, ed. S. Sontag. Berkeley: University of California Press.

—— (1993) *The Theatre and Its Double*. London: Calder.

Asad, T. (1993) *Genealogies of Religion: Discipline and Reasons of Power in Christianity and Islam*. Baltimore: Johns Hopkins University Press.

Balakian, A. (1947) *Literary Origins of Surrealism: A New Mysticism in French Poetry*. New York: King's Crown Press.

—— [1959] (1986) *Surrealism: The Road to the Absolute*. Chicago: University of Chicago Press.

Ball, S.J., ed. (1990) *Foucault and Education: Disciplines and Knowledge*. London: Routledge.

Barber, S. (1993) *Antonin Artaud: Blows and Bombs*. London: Faber and Faber.

Barthes, R. [1971] (1989) *Sade/Fourier/Loyola*. Berkeley: University of California Press.

Bartkowski, F. (1988) 'Epistemic Drift in Foucault' in Diamond and Quinby (1988), pp. 43–58.

Bataille, G. [1928] (1982) *Story of the Eye*. London: Penguin.

—— [1939] (1985) 'The Sacred' in Bataille (1985), pp. 240–5.

—— [1945] (1992) *On Nietzsche*. New York: Paragon House.

—— (1950) 'Letter to René Char on the Incompatibilities of the Writer' in Stoekl (1990), pp. 29–43.

—— [1954] (1988) *Inner Experience*. New York: SUNY.

—— (1955) 'Hegel, Death and Sacrifice' in Stoekl (1990), pp. 9–28.

—— [1957] (1987) *Eroticism*. London: Marion Boyars.

—— [1957] (1990) *Literature and Evil*. London: Marion Boyars.

—— [1961] (1988) *Guilty*. Venice, CA: Lapis Press.

—— [1962] (1991) *The Impossible*. San Francisco: City Lights.

—— [1973] (1989) *Theory of Religion*. New York: Zone Books.

—— (1985) *Visions of Excess: Selected Writings 1927–1939*, ed. A. Stoekl. Minneapolis: University of Minneapolis Press.

—— (1994) *The Absence of Myth: Writings on Surrealism* (introduction and ed. M. Richardson). London: Verso.

Baudrillard, J. [1977] (1987) *Forget Foucault*. New York: Semiotext(e).

Baynes, K, Bohman, J. and McCarthy, T. (1987) *After Philosophy: End or Transformation?* Cambridge, MA: MIT Press.

Beaujour, M. (1972) 'Eros and Nonsense: Georges Bataille' in Simon (1972), pp. 149–73.

Beauvoir, S. de (1951) 'Must We Burn Sade?' in Sade [1785] (1990), pp. 3–64.

Behr, J. (1993) 'Shifting Sands: Foucault, Brown and the Framework of Christian Asceticism', *The Heythrop Journal*, vol. 34, no.1, Jan., pp. 1–21.

Bell, V. (1993) *Interrogating Incest: Feminism, Foucault and the Law*. London: Routledge.

Benhabib, S. and Cornell, D. (1987) *Feminism As Critique: On the Politics of Gender*. Minneapolis: University of Minnesota Press.

Bernauer, J.W. (1982) 'Foucault's Political Analysis', *International Philsophical Quarterly*, vol. 22, no.1, issue 85, pp. 51–64.

—— (1983) 'America's Foucault', *Man and World*, 16, pp. 389–405.

—— (1986) 'The Sounds of Silence', *Commonweal*, vol. CXIII, no. 1, pp. 17–20.

—— (1987a) 'The Prisons of Man: An Introduction to Foucault's Negative Theology', *International Philosophical Quarterly*, vol. 27, no. 4, issue 108, pp. 365–80.

—— (1987b) 'Oedipus, Freud, Foucault: Fragments of an Archaeology of Psychoanalysis' in *Pathologies of the Modern Self: Postmodern Studies on Narcissism, Schizophrenia and Depression*, ed. D.M. Levin. New York: New York University Press, pp. 349–61.

—— (1987c) 'Michel Foucault's Ecstatic Thinking' in Bernauer and Rasmussen (1991), pp. 45–82.

—— (1989) 'Beyond Life and Death: On Foucault's Post-Auschwitz Ethic' in Armstrong (1992), pp. 260–79.

—— (1990) *Michel Foucault's Force of Flight: Towards an Ethics for Thought.* London: Humanities.

Bernauer, J.W. and Mahon, M. (1994) 'The Ethics of Michel Foucault' in Gutting (1994), pp. 141–58.

Bernauer, J.W. and Rasmussen, D., eds (1991) *The Final Foucault.* Cambridge, MA: MIT Press.

Bevis, P., Cohen, M. and Kendall, G. (1989) 'Archaeologizing Genealogy: Michel Foucault and the Economy of Austerity' in Gane and Johnson (1993), pp. 193–215.

Blanchot, M. (1949) 'Sade' in Sade (1991), pp. 37–72.

—— [1950] (1973) *Thomas the Obscure (New Version).* New York: Davis Lewis.

—— [1955] (1982) *The Space of Literature.* Lincoln: University of Nebraska Press.

—— [1969] (1993) *The Infinite Conversation.* Minneapolis: University of Minnesota Press.

—— (1986) 'Michel Foucault as I Imagine Him' in *Foucault/Blanchot.* New York: Zone Books, 1987, pp. 63–109.

Boon, J.A. (1972) *From Symbolism to Structuralism: Lévi-Strauss in a Literary Tradition.* Oxford: Blackwell.

Bouchard, D.F., ed. [1977] (1992) *Language, Counter-Memory, Practice: Selected Essays and Interviews by Michel Foucault.* Ithaca: Cornell University Press.

Boundas, C. and Olkowski, D., eds (1994) *Gilles Deleuze and the Theater of Philosophy.* London: Routledge.

Bouyer, L. (1981) 'Mysticism: An Essay on the History of the Word' in *Understanding Mysticism,* ed. R. Woods. London: Athlone, pp. 42–55.

Bove, P.A. (1986) *Intellectuals in Power: A Genealogy of Critical Humanism.* New York: Columbia University Press.

—— (1988) 'The Foucault Phenomenon: the Problematics of Style', Foreword in Deleuze [1986] (1988), pp. vii–xl.

Boyne, R. (1990) *Foucault and Derrida: The Other Side of Reason.* London: Unwin Hyman.

Braidotti, R. (1991) *Patterns of Dissonance: A Study of Women in Contemporary Philosophy.* Cambridge: Polity Press.

Breton, A. (1933) 'Raymond Roussel' in Brotchie (1987), pp. 57–9.

—— (1936) *What is Surrealism?* London: Faber and Faber.

—— (1960) *Nadja.* New York: Grove Weidenfeld.

—— (1972) *Manifestoes of Surrealism.* Michigan: Michigan University Press.

—— (1978) *What is Surrealism? Selected Writings,* ed. F. Rosemont. London: Pluto Press.

Breton, A. and Soupault, P. [1920] (1985) *Magnetic Fields.* London: Atlas Press.

Brodribb, S. (1993) *Nothing Mat(t)ers: A Feminist Critique of Postmodernism.* North Melbourne: Spinifex.

Brotchie, A., ed. (1987) *Raymond Roussel: Life, Death and Works.* London: Atlas Press.

Brown, P. (1988) *The Body and Society: Men, Women and Sexual Renunciation in Early Christianity.* New York: Columbia University Press.

Brummett, B. (1980) 'Towards a Theory of Silence as a Political Strategy', *The Quarterly Journal of Speech*, vol. 66, pp. 289–303.

Bruns, G.L. (1997) *Maurice Blanchot: The Refusal of Philosophy*. Baltimore: John Hopkins University Press.

Burchell, G., Gordon, C. and Millar, P. (1991) *The Foucault Effect*. Hemel Hempstead: Harvester Wheatsheaf.

Burke, P., ed. (1992) *Critical Essays on Michel Foucault*. Aldershot: Scolar Press.

Burke, S. (1992) *The Death and Return of the Author*. Edinburgh: Edinburgh University Press.

Butler, J. (1989) 'Foucault and the Paradox of Bodily Inscriptions', *Journal of Philosophy*, vol. 8, no.11, pp. 601–7.

—— (1990) *Gender Trouble: Feminism and the Subversion of Identity*. London: Routledge.

—— (1994) 'Bodies that Matter' in *Engaging with Irigaray: Feminist Philosophy and Modern European Thought*, ed. C. Burke, M. Schor and M. Whitford. New York: Columbia University Press, pp. 141–73.

Cameron, A. (1986) 'Redrawing the Map: Early Christian Territory After Foucault' (review article of *Historie de la Sexualité*, Vols 2 and 3), *Journal of Roman Studies*, vol. 76, pp. 266–71.

Canguilhem, G. (1978) *The Normal and the Pathological*. Boston: Reidel.

Caplan, P., ed. (1987) *The Cultural Construction of Sexuality*. London: Routledge.

Caputo, J.D. (1989) 'Mysticism and Transgression: Derrida and Meister Eckhart' in *Derrida and Deconstruction*, ed. H.J. Silverman. London: Routledge, pp. 24–39.

—— (1993a) 'Heidegger and Theology' in *Heidegger*, ed. C. Guignon. Cambridge: Cambridge University Press. pp. 270–88.

—— (1993b) 'On Not Knowing Who We Are: Madness, Hermeneutics, and the Night of Truth in Foucault' in *Foucault and the Critique of Institutions*, ed. J.D. Caputo and M. Yount. Pennsylvania: Pennsylvania State University Press, pp. 233–62.

Cardinal, R. (1986) *Breton: Nadja*. London: Grant and Cutler.

Carrette, J.R., ed. (1999a) *Religion and Culture by Michel Foucault*. Manchester: Manchester University Press/New York: Routledge.

Carrette, J.R. (1999b) 'Prologue to a Confession of the Flesh' in Carrette (1999a), pp. 1–47.

Carrette, J.R. and Keller, M. (1999) 'Religions, Orientation and Critical Theory: Race, Gender and Sexuality at the 1998 Lambeth Conference', *Theology and Sexuality*, vol. 11, Sept., pp. 19–41.

Carrette, J.R. and King, R. (1998) 'Giving Birth to Theory: Critical Perspectives on Religion and the Body' (review article), *Scottish Journal of Religious Studies* (Special Edition), vol. 19, no. 1, pp. 123–43.

Carter, A. (1979) *The Sadeian Woman: An Exercise in Cultural History*. London: Virago.

Cassian, J. (1985) *Conferences*. New York: Paulist Press.

Castel, R. (1994) ' "Problematization" as a Mode of Reading History' in Goldstein (1994), pp. 237–52.

Castelli, E. (1991) *Imitating Paul: A Discourse of Power*. Louisville, KY: Westminster/John Knox.

—— (1992) 'Interpretations of Power in 1 Corinthians', *Semeia*, 54, pp. 199–222.

Caws, M.A. (1966) *Surrealism and the Literary Imagination*. The Hague: Mouton and Co.

Certeau, M. de. (1986) *Heterologies: Discourse on the Other*. Manchester: Manchester University Press.

Chasseguet-Smirgel, J. (1983) 'Perversion and the Universal Law' in *International Review of Psycho-Analysis*, vol. 10, pp. 293–301.

Chidester, D. (1986) 'Michel Foucault and the Study of Religion', *Religious Studies Review*, vol. 12, no. 1, pp. 1–9.

Choucha, N. (1991) *Surrealism and the Occult*. Oxford: Mandrake.

Cixous, H. (1976) 'The Laugh of Medusa' in Marks and Courtivron (1981), pp. 245–64.

Clark, E.A. (1988) 'Foucault, The Fathers and Sex', *Journal of the American Academy of Religion*, vol. 56, no. 4, pp. 619–41.

Clark, T. (1992) *Derrida, Heidegger, Blanchot: Sources of Derrida's Notion and Practice of Literature*. Cambridge: Cambridge University Press.

Clatterbaugh, K. (1997) *Contemporary Perspectives on Masculinity*. 2nd edition. Boulder, CO: Westview.

Coakley, S., ed. (1997) *Religion and the Body*. Cambridge: Cambridge University Press.

Cocteau, J. (1958) *Opium: The Diary of a Cure*. New York: Grove Press.

Cohen, A. and Dascal, M., eds (1989) *The Institution of Philosophy: A Discipline in Crisis?* La Salle, IL: Open Court.

Connolly, W.E. (1993) 'Beyond Good and Evil: The Ethical Sensibility of Michel Foucault', *Political Theory*, vol. 21, no. 3, pp. 365–89.

Cooey, P.M. (1994) *Religious Imagination and the Body: A Feminist Analysis*. Oxford: Oxford University Press.

Cooper, B. (1981) *Michel Foucault: An Introduction to the Study of His Thought*. New York: Edwin Mellon Press.

Corbin, H. (1977) *Spiritual Body and Celestial Earth: From Mazdean Iran to Shi'ite Iran*. Princeton, NJ: Princeton University Press.

Cousins, M. and Hussain, A. [1984] (1990) *Michel Foucault*. London: Macmillan Educational.

Cupitt, D. (1987) *The Long-Legged Fly*. London: SCM.

—— (1988) *New Christian Ethics*. London: SCM.

—— (1995) *Solar Ethics*. London: SCM.

Dallen, J. [1986] (1991) *The Reconciling Community: The Rite of Penance*. Collegeville, MN: Pueblo Book/ Liturgical Press.

Daly, M. (1973) *Beyond God the Father: Toward a Philosophy of Women's Liberation*. Boston: Beacon Press.

Davidson, A.I. (1986) 'Archaeology, Genealogy, Ethics' in Hoy (1986), pp. 221–33.

—— (1994) 'Ethics as Ascetics: Foucault, the History of Ethics and Ancient Thought' in Gutting (1994), pp. 115–40.

——, ed. (1997) *Foucault and His Interlocutors*. Chicago: University of Chicago Press.

Davis, C. (1990) 'Our Modern Identity: The Formation of the Self', *Modern Theology*, vol. 6, no. 2, Jan., pp. 159–71.

—— (1994) *Religion and the Making of Society: Essays in Social Theology*. Cambridge: Cambridge University Press.

Dean, C.J. (1992) *The Self and Its Pleasures: Bataille, Lacan, and the History of the Decentered Subject*. Ithaca: Cornell University Press.

Dean, M. (1994) *Critical and Effective Histories: Foucault's Methods and Historical Sociology*. London: Routledge.

Deleuze, G. [1962] (1983) *Nietzsche and Philosophy*. London: Athlone.

—— [1967] (1991) *Masochism*. New York: Zone Books.

—— [1969] (1990) *The Logic of Sense*. London: Athlone.

—— (1973) 'Nomad Thought' in Allison (1985), pp. 142–9.

—— [1986] (1988) *Foucault*. Minneapolis: University of Minnesota Press.

Deleuze, G. and Guattari, F. [1972] (1984) *Anti-oedipus: Capitalism and Schizophrenia*. London: Athlone.

Derrida, J. [1967] (1978) *Writing and Difference*. London: Routledge.

—— [1972] (1982) *Margins of Philosophy*. Chicago: University of Chicago Press.

Descombes, V. (1980) *Modern French Philosophy*. Cambridge: Cambridge University Press.

Dews, P. (1989) 'The Return of the Subject in Late Foucault', *Radical Philosophy*, no. 51, pp. 37–41.

Diamond, I. and Quinby, L., eds (1988) *Feminism and Foucault: Reflections On Resistance*. Boston: Northeastern University Press.

Donnelly, M. (1982) 'Foucault's Genealogy of the Human Sciences' in Gane (1986), pp. 15–32.

Dreyfus, H.L. (1987) 'Foreword' to the US edn of Foucault (1954b), pp. vii–xliii.

—— (1992) 'On the Ordering of Things: Being and Power in Heidegger and Foucault' in Armstrong (1992), pp. 80–95.

Dreyfus, H.L. and Rabinow, P. (1982) *Michel Foucault: Beyond Structuralism and Hermeneutics*. Hemel Hempstead: Harvester Wheatsheaf.

Dumm, T.L. (1996) *Michel Foucault and the Politics of Freedom*. London: Sage.

Durgnat, R. (1977) *Luis Buñuel*. Berkeley: University of California Press.

During, S. (1992) *Foucault and Literature*. London: Routledge.

Dworkin, A. (1984) *Pornography*. London: Women's Press.

—— (1988) *Intercourse*. London: Arrow Books.

Eilberg-Schwartz, N. (1994) *God's Phallus and Other Problems for Men and Monotheism*. Boston: Beacon Press.

Elders, F. (1974) *Reflexive Water: The Basic Concerns of Mankind*. London: Souvenir Press.

Ellenberger, H. (1970) *The Discovery of the Unconscious*. New York: Basic Books.

Eribon, D. (1992) *Michel Foucault*. London: Faber and Faber.

Erickson, V.L. (1993) *Where Silence Speaks: Feminism, Social Theory and Religion*. Minneapolis: Fortress Press.

Featherstone, M., Hepworth, M. and Turner, B.S. (1991) *The Body and Social Process*. London: Sage.

ffrench, P. (1995) *The Time of Theory: A History of 'Tel Quel' 1960–1983*. Oxford: Clarendon Press.

ffrench, P. and Lack, R.-F., eds (1998) *The Tel Quel Reader*. London: Routledge.

Fiorenza, E.S. (1983) *In Memory of Her: A Feminist Theological Reconstruction of Christian Origins*. London: SCM.

Flaubert, G. [1874] (1983) *The Temptation of St Antony*. London: Penguin.

Flax, J. (1983) 'Political Philosophy and the Patriarchal Unconscious: A Psychoanalytic Perspective on Epistemology and Metaphysics' in *Discovering Reality: Feminist Perspectives on Epistemology, Metaphysics, Methodology, and Philosophy of Science*, ed. S. Harding and M.B. Hintikka. Dordrecht, Holland: D. Reidel, pp. 245–79.

—— (1990) *Thinking Fragments: Psychoanalysis, Feminism and Postmodernism in the Contemporary West*. Berkeley: University of California Press.

Flowers, J.E. (1983) *Literature and the Left in France*. London: Methuen.

Flynn, T.R. (1985) 'Truth and Subjectivity in the Later Foucault' *Journal of Philosophy*, vol. 82, no. 10, Oct., pp. 531–40.

—— (1991) 'Foucault as Parrhesiast: His Last Course at the Collège de France (1984)' in Bernauer and Rasmussen (1991), pp. 102–18.

—— (1993) 'Foucault and the Eclipse of Vision' in *Modernity and the Hegemony of Vision*, ed. D.M. Levin. Berkeley: University of California Press, pp. 273–86.

Fowlie, W. (1953) *Age of Surrealism*. London: Denis Dobson.

Fraser, N. (1989) *Unruly Practices: Power, Discourse and Gender in Contemporary Social Theory*. Cambridge: Polity Press.

Freeman, J. and Welchman, J.C. (1989) *The Dada and Surrealist Word-Image*. Cambridge, MA: MIT Press.

Freud, S. [1908] (1959) 'Character and Anal Eroticism', *Standard Edition*, vol. 9. London: Hogarth Press/Institute of Psycho-Analysis, pp. 169–75.

Gablik, S. (1985) *Magritte*. London: Thames and Hudson.

Gallop, J. (1981) *Intersections: A Reading of Sade with Bataille, Blanchot, and Klossowski*. Lincoln: University of Nebraska Press.

—— (1988) *Thinking Through the Body*. New York: Columbia University Press.

—— (1989) 'French Feminism' in Hollier (1989), pp. 1045–9.

Gandel, K. and Kotkin, S. (1985) 'Foucault in Berkeley', *History of the Present*, no. 1, Feb., pp. 6, 15.

Gane, M., ed. (1986) *Towards A Critique of Foucault*. London: Routledge and Kegan Paul.

Gane, M. and Johnson, T., eds (1993) *Foucault's New Domains*. London: Routledge.

Geertz, G. (1978) 'Stir Crazy' (review of *Discipline and Punish*), *New York Review of Books*, 26 Jan. 1978, pp. 3–6. In P. Burke (1992), pp. 139–46.

Giddens, A. (1992) *The Transformation of Intimacy: Sexuality, Love and Eroticism in Modern Societies*. Cambridge: Polity Press.

Gilchrist, R. (1994) *Gender and Material Culture: The Archaeology of Religious Women*. London: Routledge.

Goldenberg, N.R. (1979) *Changing of the Gods: Feminism and the End of Traditional Religion*. Boston: Beacon Press.

Goldhill, S. (1995) *Foucault's Virginity: Ancient Erotic Fiction and The History of Sexuality*. Cambridge: Cambridge University Press.

Goldstein, J. (1984) 'Foucault Among the Sociologists: The "Disciplines" and the History of the Professions', *History and Theory*, vol. 23, pp. 170–92.

——, ed. (1994) *Foucault and the Writing of History*. Oxford: Blackwell.

Goodall, J. (1994) *Artaud and the Gnostic Drama*. Oxford: Clarendon Press.

Greene, N. (1967) 'Antonin Artaud: Metaphysical Revolutionary', *Yale French Studies*, no. 39, pp. 188–97.

—— (1975) 'Thomas, Come Back', *Novel*, vol. 8, no. 2, Winter, pp. 175–7.

Gregg, J. (1994) *Maurice Blanchot and the Literature of Transgression*. Princeton, NJ: Princeton University Press.

Grimshaw, J. (1986) *Feminist Philosophers: Women's Perspectives On Philosophical Traditions*. Hemel Hempstead: Harvester Wheatsheaf.

Grosz, E. (1989) *Sexual Subversions: Three French Feminists*. St Leonards, NSW: Allen and Unwin.

—— (1991) 'Introduction: Feminism and the Body', *Hypatia*, vol. 6, no. 3, pp. 1–5.

—— (1993a) 'Nietzsche and the Stomach for Knowledge' in *Nietzsche, Feminism and Political Theory*, ed. P. Patton. London: Routledge, pp. 49–70.

—— (1993b) 'Bodies and Knowledge: Feminism and the Crisis of Reason' in Alcoff and Potter (1993), pp. 187–215.

—— (1994) *Volatile Bodies: Toward a Corporeal Feminism*. Bloomington and Indianapolis: Indiana University Press.

—— (1995) *Space, Time and Perversion*. London: Routledge.

Gutting, G. (1989) *Michel Foucault's Archaeology of Scientific Reason*. Cambridge: Cambridge University Press.

——, ed. (1994) *Foucault. The Cambridge Companion*. Cambridge: Cambridge University Press.

Habermas, J. (1987a) 'The Critique of Reason as an Unmasking of the Human Sciences: Michel Foucault' in Kelly (1995), pp. 47–77.

—— (1987b) 'Some Questions Concerning the Theory of Power: Foucault Again' in Kelly (1995), pp. 79–107.

—— (1989) 'Taking Aim at the Heart of the Present: On Foucault's Lecture on Kant's "What is Enlightenment?"' in Kelly (1995), pp. 149–54.

Hacking, I. (1981) 'The Archaeology of Foucault', *The New York Review of Books*, vol. 28, no. 8, pp. 32–7.

Hadot, P. (1995) *Philosophy as a Way of Life*. Oxford: Blackwell.

Halperin, D.M. (1995) *Saint Foucault: Towards a Gay Hagiography*. Oxford: Oxford University Press.

Harootunian, H.D. (1991) 'Foucault, Genealogy, History: The Pursuit of Otherness' in Arac (1991), pp. 110–37.

Harstock, N. (1987) 'Foucault on Power: A Theory for Women?' in *Feminism/Postmodernism*, ed. L.J. Nicholson. London: Routledge, 1990, pp. 157–75.

Hart, K. (1991) *The Trespass of the Sign: Deconstruction, Theology and Philosophy*. Cambridge: Cambridge University Press.

Hatab, L.J. (1990) *Myth and Philosophy: A Contest of Truths*. La Salle, IL: Open Court.

Hayman, R. (1977) *Artaud and After*. Oxford: Oxford University Press.

Hearn, J. and Morgan, D., eds (1990) *Men, Masculinities and Social Theory*. London: Unwin Hyman.

Hedges, E. and Fishkin, S., eds (1994) *Listening to 'Silences': New Essays in Feminist Criticism*. Oxford: Oxford University Press.

Heidegger, M. [1927] (1993) *Being and Time*. Oxford: Blackwell.

Hollier, D., ed. (1988) *The College of Sociology 1937–39*. Minneapolis: University of Minnesota Press.

——, ed. (1989) *A New History of French Literature*. Cambridge, MA: Harvard University Press.

Hooke, A.E. (1987) 'Is Foucault's Antihumanism Against Human Action?', *Political Theory*, vol. 15, no. 1, pp. 38–60.

Horowitz, G. (1987) 'No Sex, No Self, No Revolution', *Poltical Theory*, vol. 15, no. 1, pp. 61–80.

Hoy, D.C., ed. (1986) *Foucault: A Critical Reader*. Oxford: Blackwell.

Huppert, G. (1974) 'Divinatio et Eruditio: Thoughts on Foucault' in Smart (1994), Vol. II, pp. 55–68.

Irigaray, L. [1974] (1993) *An Ethics of Sexual Difference*. London: Athlone.

—— (1977) '"Frenchwomen," Stop Trying' in *This Sex Which is Not One*. Ithaca: Cornell University Press, 1985, pp. 198–204.

—— (1993) *Sexes and Genealogies*. New York: Columbia University Press.

Jacobs, M. (1992) *Sigmund Freud*. London: Sage.

Jambet, C. (1989) 'The Constitution of the Subject and Spiritual Practice' in Armstrong (1992), pp. 233–47.

James, W. [1901–2] (1960) *The Varieties of Religious Experience*. Glasgow: Collins.

Jameson, F. (1991) *Postmodernism, or the Cultural Logic of Late Capitalism*. London: Verso.

Janet, P. (1926) 'The Psychological Characteristics of Ecstasy' in Brotchie (1987), pp. 38–42.

Jantzen, G.M. (1989) 'Mysticism and Experience', *Religious Studies*, vol. 25, pp. 295–315.

—— (1995) *Power, Gender and Christian Mysticism*. Cambridge: Cambridge University Press.

—— (1998) *Becoming Divine: Towards a Feminist Philosophy of Religion*. Manchester: Manchester University Press.

Jarry, A. [1895] (1992) *Caesar Antichrist*. London: Atlas Press.

Jaworski, A. (1993) *The Power Of Silence: Social and Pragmatic Perspectives*. London: Sage.

Jay, M. (1986) 'In the Empire of the Gaze: Foucault and the Denigration of Vision in Twentieth-Century Thought' in Hoy (1986), pp. 175–204.

Jordan, M. (1997) *The Invention of Sodomy in Christian Theology*. Chicago: University of Chicago Press.

Kant, I. [1793] (1960) *Religion Within the Limits of Reason Alone*. New York: Harper Torchbooks.

Kantorowicz, E.H. (1957) *The King's Two Bodies: A Study in Mediaeval Political Theology*. Princeton, NJ: Princeton University Press.

Katz, J.N. (1995) *The Invention of Heterosexuality*. New York: Plume/Penguin.

Katz, S.T., ed. (1978) *Mysticism and Philosophical Analysis*. London: Sheldon.

Kauppi, N. (1994) *The Making of an Avant-Garde: Tel Quel*. Berlin and New York: Mouton de Gruyter.

Kearney, R. (1986) *Modern Movements In European Philosophy*. Manchester: Manchester University Press.

Kelley, D. (1990) 'Antonin Artaud: "Madness" and Self-Expression' in *Modernism and the European Unconscious*, ed. P. Collier and J. Davies. Cambridge: Polity Press, pp. 230–45.

Kelly, M., ed. (1995) *Critique and Power: Recasting the Foucault/Habermas Debate*. Cambridge, MA: MIT Press.

King, A.S. (1996) 'Spirituality: Transformation and Metamorphosis', *Religion*, vol. 26, pp. 343–51.

King, R. (1999) *Orientalism and Religion: Postcolonial Theory, India and 'the Mystic East'*. London: Routledge.

Klossowski, P. [1953 and 1959] (1989) *Roberte Ce Soir and The Revocation of the Edict of Nantes: Two Novels*. London: Marion Boyars.

—— [1965] (1988) *The Baphomet*. Hygiene, CO: Eridanos.

—— [1967] (1992) *Sade My Neighbour*. London: Quartet Books.

—— (1969) 'Nietzsche's Experience of the Eternal Return' in Allison (1985) pp. 107–120.

Knauft, B.M. (1996) *Genealogies of the Present in Cultural Anthropology*. London: Routledge.

Kroker, A. and Cook, D. (1988) *The Postmodern Scene*. London: Macmillan.

Krondofer, B., ed. (1996) *Men's Bodies, Men's Gods: Male Identities in a (Post-) Christian Culture*. New York: New York University Press.

Kusch, M. (1991) *Foucault's Strata and Fields: An Investigation into Archaeological and Genealogical Science Studies*. Dordrecht: Kluwer Acadmic Publishers.

Lala, M.-C. (1990) 'The Conversions of Writing in George Bataille's "L'Impossible"' in Stoekl (1990), pp. 237–45.

Lalonde, M.P. (1993) 'Power/Knowledge and Liberation: Foucault as a Parabolic Thinker', *Journal of the American Academy of Religion*, vol. 61, no. 1, pp. 81–100.

Lampe, G.W.H., ed. (1961) *A Patristic Greek Lexicon*. London: Oxford University Press.

Landry, D. and Maclean, G., eds (1996) *The Spivak Reader*. London: Routledge.

Lash, S. (1984) 'Genealogy and the Body: Foucault/ Deleuze/ Nietzsche' in Smart (1994), Vol. III, pp. 14–32.

Le Brun, A. (1990) *Sade: A Sudden Abyss*. San Francisco: City Lights.

Lecercle, J.-J. (1985) *Philosophy Through the Looking Glass*. London: Hutchinson.

Lemert, C. and Gillan, G. (1982) *Michel Foucault: Social Theory and Transgression*. New York: Columbia University Press.

Levinson, H.S. (1981) *The Religious Investigations of William James*. Chapel Hill: University of North Carolina Press.

Lewis, H. (1990) *Dada Turns Red: The Politics of Surrealism*. Edinburgh: Edinburgh University Press.

Liebmann Schaub, U. (1989) 'Foucault's Oriental Subtext', *PMLA*, vol. 104, pp. 306–16.

Lloyd, G.E.R. (1986) 'The Mind on Sex', *The New York Review of Books*, 13 Mar., pp. 24–8.

Louth, A. (1981) *The Origins of the Christian Mystical Tradition*. Oxford: Clarendon Press.

—— (1989) *Denys the Areopagite*. London/Wilton: Geoffrey Chapman/Morehouse-Barlow.

McCarthy, T. (1991) *Ideals and Illusion: On Reconstruction and Deconstruction in Contemporary Theory*. Cambridge, MA: MIT Press.

Macey, D. (1993) *The Lives of Michel Foucault*. London: Hutchinson.

MacIntyre, A. (1990) *Three Rival Versions of Moral Enquiry*. London: Duckworth.

—— (1993) 'Miller's Foucault, Foucault's Foucault', *Salmagundi*, no. 97, Winter, pp. 29–99.

McNay, L. (1992) *Foucault and Feminism*. Boston: Northeastern University Press.
—— (1994) *Foucault: A Critical Introduction*. Cambridge: Polity Press.
McNeil, M. (1993) 'Dancing with Foucault: Feminism and Power-Knowledge' in Ramazanoglu (1993), pp. 147–75.
McWhorter, L. (1989) 'Culture or Nature? The Function of the Term "Body" in the Work of Michel Foucault', *Journal of Philosophy*, vol. 56, no. 11, pp. 608–14.
Mahon, M. (1992) *Foucault's Nietzschean Genealogy: Truth, Power and the Subject*. Albany: SUNY.
Major-Poetzl, P. (1983) *Michel Foucault's Archaeology of Western Culture: Towards a New Science of History*. Brighton: Harvester Press.
Malraux, A. [1926] (1974) *The Temptation of the West*. New York: Jubilee Books.
—— [1928] (1956) *The Conquerors*. Boston: Beacon.
Marks, E. and Courtivron, I. de, eds (1981) *New French Feminisms: An Anthology*. Hemel Hempstead: Harvester Wheatsheaf.
Martin, L.H. (1988) 'Technologies of the Self and Self-knowledge in the Syrian Thomas Tradition' in Martin *et al.* (1988), pp. 50–63.
Martin, L.H., Gutman, H. and Hutton, P.H., eds (1988) *Technologies of the Self: A Seminar with Michel Foucault*. London: Tavistock.
Megill, A. (1979) 'Foucault, Structuralism, and the Ends of History', *Journal of Modern History*, vol. 51, Sept., pp. 451–503.
—— (1985) *Prophets of Extremity: Nietzsche, Heidegger, Foucault and Derrida*. Berkeley: University of California Press.
—— (1987) 'The Reception of Foucault by Historians', *Journal of the History of Ideas*, vol. 48, no. 1, pp. 117–41.
Mellor, P. and Shilling, C. (1997) *Re-forming the Body: Religion, Community and Modernity*. London: Sage.
Mendez, C.W. (1980) 'Virginia Woolf and the Voices of Silence', *Language and Style*, vol. 13, no. 4, pp. 94–112.
Merquior, J. (1985) *Foucault*. London: Fontana.
Messner, M.A. (1997) *Politics of Masculinities: Man in Movements*. Thousand Oaks, CA: Sage.
Midelfort, H.C.E. [1980] (1988) 'Madness and Civilisation in Early Modern Europe: A Reappraisal of Michel Foucault' in *After the Reformation: Essays in Honor of J.H. Hexter*, ed. B.C. Malament. Manchester: Manchester University Press, pp. 247–65.
Milbank, J. (1990) *Theology and Social Theory: Beyond Secular Reason*. Oxford: Blackwell.
Miller, J. (1993a) *The Passion of Michel Foucault*. London: HarperCollins.
—— (1993b) 'Foucault's Politics in Biographical Perspective', *Salmagundi*, no. 97, Winter, pp. 30–44.
—— (1993c) 'Policing Discourse: A Response to David Halperin', *Salmagundi*, no. 97, Winter, pp. 94–9.
Minson, J. (1985) *Genealogies of Morals: Nietzsche, Foucault, Donzelot and the Eccentricity of Ethics*. London: Macmillan.
Mir, G.C. (1968) *Aux Sources de la Pédagogie des Jésuites: le 'Modus parisiensis'*. Roma: Institutum Historicum S.I.
Moore, S.D. (1992) *Mark and Luke in Post-Structuralist Perspective: Jesus Begins to Write*. New Haven: Yale University Press.

Morris, M. (1979) 'The Pirate's Fiancée: Feminists and Philosophers, or Maybe Tonight It'll Happen' in Diamond and Quinby (1988), pp. 21–42.

Morris, M. and Patton, P., eds (1979) *Michel Foucault: Power, Truth, Strategy.* Sydney: Feral.

Mrosovsky, K. (1980) 'Introduction' in Flaubert [1874] (1983), pp. 3–56.

Mulvey, L. (1989) *Visual and Other Pleasures.* London: Macmillan.

Nadeau, M. (1973) *The History of Surrealism.* London: Penguin.

Nelson, J. (1992a) *The Intimate Connection: Male Sexuality, Masculine Spirtuality.* London: SPCK.

—— (1992b) *Body Theology.* Louisville, KY: Westminster/John Knox.

Nietzsche, F. [1883–5] (1969) *Thus Spoke Zarathustra.* London: Penguin.

—— [1886] (1973) *Beyond Good and Evil.* London: Penguin.

—— [1887] (1967) *On The Genealogy of Morals.* New York: Vintage.

—— [1887] (1974) *The Gay Science.* New York: Vintage.

—— [1883–8] (1968) *The Will To Power.* New York: Vintage.

—— [1888] (1968) *The Anti-Christ.* London: Penguin.

Nilson, H. (1998) *Michel Foucault and the Game of Truth.* London: Macmillan.

Norris, C. (1993) *The Truth About Postmodernism.* Oxford: Blackwell.

O'Brien, P. (1989) 'Michel Foucault's History of Culture' in *The New Cultural History*, ed. L. Hunt. Berkeley: University of California Press, pp. 25–46.

O'Farrell, C. (1989) *Foucault: Historian or Philosopher?* London: Macmillan.

O'Hara, D. (1991) 'What was Foucault?' in Arac (1991), pp. 71–96.

Osborne, K.B. (1990) *Reconciliation and Justification: The Sacrament and Its Theology.* New York: Paulist Press.

Owen, D. (1994) *Maturity and Modernity: Nietzsche, Weber, Foucault and the Ambivalence of Reason.* London: Routledge.

Paden, W.E. (1988) 'Theaters of Humility and Suspicion: Desert Saints and New England Puritans' in Martin *et al.* (1988), pp. 64–79.

Parrish, S.M. (1996) *Hierarchy and Its Discontents: Culture and the Politics of Consciousness in Caste Society.* Philadelphia: University of Pennsylvania Press.

Pasewark, K.A. (1993) *A Theology of Power: Being Beyond Domination.* Minneapolis: Fortress Press.

Pefanis, J. (1991) *Heterology and the Postmodern: Bataille, Baudrillard and Lyotard.* Durham, NC: Duke University Press.

Peterson, D., ed. (1982) *A Mad People's History of Madness.* Pittsburgh: University of Pittsburgh Press.

Poggioli, R. (1968) *The Theory of the Avant-Garde.* Cambridge, MA: Belknap Press.

Porter, R. (1987) *Mind-Forg'd Manacles: A History of Madness in England from the Restoration to the Regency.* London: Penguin.

—— (1988) 'Sex in the Head' (review of Foucault's *History of Sexuality*, Vol. 3), *The London Review of Books*, vol. 10, no. 13, pp. 13–14.

Prado, C.G. (1995) *Starting With Foucault: An Introduction to Genealogy.* Boulder, CO: Westview Press.

Prince, G. (1989) 'The *Nouveau Roman*' in Hollier (1989), pp. 988–93.

Prosser MacDonald, D. (1995) *Transgressive Corporeality: The Body, Poststructuralism, and the Theological Imagination.* New York: SUNY.

Pseudo-Dionysius (1987) *Pseudo-Dionysius, The Complete Works.* Classics of Western Spirituality. London: SPCK/Mahwah. NJ: Paulist Press.

Pyper, H. (1993) 'Surviving Writing: The Anxiety of Historiography in the Former Prophets' in *The Hebrew Bible and the New Literary Criticism*, ed. J.C. Exum and D.J. Clines. Sheffield: JSOT.

Racevskis, K. (1983) *Michel Foucault and the Subversion of the Intellect*. Ithaca: Cornell University Press.

Rajchman, J. (1985) *Michel Foucault: The Freedom of Philosophy*. New York: Columbia University Press.

—— (1991) *Truth and Eros: Foucault, Lacan and the Question of Ethics*. London: Routledge.

Ramazanoglu, C., ed. (1993) *Up Against Foucault: Explorations of Some Tensions between Foucault and Feminism*. London: Routledge.

Raschke, C.A. (1996) *Fire and Roses: Postmodernity and the Thought of the Body*. Albany, NY: SUNY.

Ray, S.A. (1987) *The Modern Soul: Michel Foucault and the Theological Discourse of Gordon Kaufman and David Tracy*. Philadelphia: Fortress Press.

Richardson, M. (1994a) *Georges Bataille*. London: Routledge.

——, ed. (1994b) *The Absence of Myth: Writings on Surrealism by George Bataille*. London: Verso.

Richman, M.E. (1982) *Reading Georges Bataille: Beyond the Gift*. Baltimore: Johns Hopkins University Press.

Romano, C. (1981) 'Michel Foucault's New Clothes', *The Village Voice*, vol. 26, 29 Apr.–5 May, pp. 40–3.

Rorem, P. (1984) *Biblical and Liturgical Symbols Within the Pseudo-Dionysius Synthesis*. Toronto: Pontifical Institute of Mediaeval Studies.

—— (1993) *Pseudo-Dionysius: A Commentary on the Texts and an Introduction to Their Influence*. Oxford: Oxford University Press.

Roth, M.S. (1981) 'Foucault's "History of the Present"', *History and Theory*, vol. 20, pp. 32–46.

Rothwell, K.S. (1988) 'Hamlet's "Glass of Fashion": Power, Self, and the Reformation' in Martin *et al.* (1988), pp. 80–8.

Roussel, R. (1966) *Locus Solus*. London: Calder and Boyars.

—— (1970) *Impressions of Africa*. London: Calder and Boyars.

Ruether, R.R. (1983) *Sexism and God-Talk: Towards a Feminist Theology*. London: SCM.

Rycroft, C. (1977) *A Critical Dictionary of Psychoanalysis*. London: Penguin.

Sade, Marquis de [1785] (1990) *The One Hundred and Twenty Days of Sodom*. London: Arrow Books.

—— (1791) *Justine, or Good Conduct Well Chastised* in Sade (1991), pp. 447–743.

—— (1795) *Philosophy in the Bedroom* in Sade (1991), pp. 177–367.

—— [1797] (1991) *Juliette*. London: Arrow Books.

—— (1991) *Three Complete Novels: Justine, Philosophy in the Bedroom, Eugénie De Franval and Other Writings*. London: Arrow Books.

Said, E.W. (1972) 'Michel Foucault as an Intellectual Imagination' in Smart (1994), Vol. I, pp. 37–63.

—— (1978) *Orientalism*. London: Routledge and Kegan Paul.

Sarup, M. (1993) *Post-Structuralism and Postmodernism*. Hemel Hempstead: Harvester Wheatsheaf.

Sawhney, D.N., ed. (1994) *The Divine Sade*. Warwick: PLI–Warwick Journal of Philosophy. Warwick University.

Sawicki, J. (1991) *Disciplining Foucault*. London: Routledge.

Scarry, E. (1985) *The Body in Pain: The Making and Unmaking of the World*. New York: Oxford University Press.

Schrift, A.D. (1988) 'Foucault and Derrida on Nietzsche and the End(s) of Man' in Smart (1994), Vol. 2, pp. 278–92.

Sedgwick, P. (1982/7) *Psycho Politics*. London: Pluto Press.

Segal, J. (1992) *Melanie Klein*. London: Sage.

Seidler, V.J., ed. (1992) *Men, Sex and Relationships: Writings from Achilles' Heel*. London: Routledge.

Seigel, J. (1990) 'Avoiding the Subject: A Foucaultian Itinerary', *Journal of the History of Ideas*, vol. 51, pt 2, pp. 273–99.

Sells, M.A. (1994) *Mystical Languages of Unsaying*. Chicago: University of Chicago Press.

Shamdasani, S. (1993) 'Automatic Writing and the Discovery of the Unconscious', *Spring*, vol. 54, pp. 100–31.

Shattuck, R. (1958) *The Banquet Years: Origins of the Avant-Garde in France 1885 to World War I*. New York: Anchor Books.

Sheridan, A. (1980) *Michel Foucault: The Will to Truth*. London: Tavistock.

—— (1984) 'Diary', *London Review of Books*, vol. 6, no. 13, 19 July – 1 Aug., p. 21.

Shilling, C. (1993) *The Body and Social Theory*. London: Sage.

Shiner, L. (1982) 'Reading Foucault: Anti-Method and the Genealogy of Power-Knowledge', *History and Theory*, vol. 21, pp. 382–98.

Shortland, M. (1986) 'Bodies of History: Some Problems and Perspectives', *History of Science*, vol. 24, pp. 303–26.

Shumway, D.R. (1989) *Michel Foucault*. Charlottesville: University of Virginia Press.

Silverman, H.J. (1988) *Philosophy and Non-Philosophy Since Merleau-Ponty*. London: Routledge.

Simon, J.K. (1963) Review of Michel Foucault, *Histoire de la folie*, *Modern Language Notes*, vol. 78, no. 1, pp. 85–8.

——, ed. (1972) *Modern French Criticism: From Proust and Valéry to Structuralism*. Chicago: University of Chicago Press.

Simons, J. (1995) *Foucault and the Political*. London: Routledge.

Smart, B. (1985) *Michel Foucault*. London: Routledge.

——, ed. (1994) *Michel Foucault: Critical Assessments*, Vols I–III. London: Routledge.

Smith, H. (1989) *Beyond the Postmodern Mind*. Wheaton: Quest.

Soper, K. (1994) 'Ruling Passion Strong in Death', *Radical Philosophy*, vol. 66, Spring, pp. 44–6.

Soskice, J.M. (1985) *Metaphor and Religious Language*. Oxford: Clarendon Press.

Stauth, G. (1991) 'Revolution in Spiritless Times: An Essay on Michel Foucault's Enquires into the Iranian Revolution' in Smart (1994), Vol. III, pp. 379–401. Originally published by Dept of Sociology National University of Singapore and *International Sociology*, 1991.

Stein, E. (1992) 'Introduction' in *Forms of Desire: Sexual Orientation and the Social Constructionist Controversy*, ed. E. Stein. London: Routledge, pp. 3–9.

Steiner, G. (1992) *Heidegger*. 2nd edition. London: Fontana.

Stiernotte, A.P., ed. (1959) *Mysticism and the Modern Mind*. New York: Liberal Arts Press.

Still, A. and Velody, I., eds (1992) *Rewriting the History of Madness: Studies in Foucault's 'Histoire de la Folie'*. London: Routledge.

Stoekl, A. (1989) 'The Avant-Garde Embrace Science' in Hollier (1989), pp. 929–35.

——, ed. (1990) *Yale French Studies No.78: On Bataille*. New Haven: Yale University Press.

Stoler, A.L. (1995) *Race and the Education of Desire: Foucault's 'History of Sexuality' and the Colonial Order of Things*. Durham, NC: Duke University Press.

Sturrock, J., ed. (1979) *Structuralism and Since*. Oxford: Oxford University Press.

—— (1993) *Structuralism*. 2nd edition. London: Fontana.

Suleiman, S.R. (1989) 'As Is' in Hollier (1989), pp. 1011–18.

Szasz, T.S. (1971) *The Manufacture of Madness: A Comparative Study of the Inquisition and the Mental Health Movement*. London: Routledge and Kegan Paul.

Tambling, J. (1990) *Confession: Sexuality, Sin, the Subject*. Manchester: Manchester University Press.

Tannery, C. (1991) *Malraux: The Absolute Agnostic*. Chicago: University of Chicago Press.

Taylor, M. (1984) *Erring: A Postmodern A/theology*. Chicago: University of Chicago Press.

Thomson, A. (1987) 'Mots relatifs aux Actes de Raymond Roussel – Selections from the Critical Writings About Roussel's Theatre' in Brotchie (1987), pp. 13–24.

Turner, B.S. (1991) *Religion and Social Theory*. London: Sage.

—— (1992) *Regulating Bodies: Essays in Medical Sociology*. London: Routledge.

—— (1996) *The Body and Society: Explorations in Social Theory*. 2nd edition. London: Sage.

Tyler, S.A. (1978) *The Said and Unsaid: Mind, Meaning and Culture*. New York: Academic Press.

Tzara, T. (1992) *Seven Dada Manifestos and Lampisteries*. London: Calder/Riverrun Press.

Vernon, M. (1996) 'Following Foucault: The Strategies of Sexuality and the Struggle to be Different', *Theology and Sexuality*, no. 5, Sept., pp. 76–96.

Veyne, P. (1993) 'The Final Foucault and his Ethics', *Critical Inquiry*, no. 20, Autumn, pp. 1–9.

Visker, R. (1995) *Michel Foucault: Genealogy as Critique*. London: Verso.

Voltaire [1733] (1994) *Letters Concerning the English Nation*. Oxford: Oxford University Press.

Wakefield, N. (1990) *Postmodernism: The Twilight of the Real*. London: Pluto Press.

Welch, S. (1985) 'The Truth of Liberation Theology: "Particulars of a Relative Sublime"' in Diamond and Quinby (1988), pp. 207–28.

White, H.V. (1973) 'Foucault Decoded: Notes from the Underground', *History and Theory*, vol. 12, pp. 23–54.

—— (1987) *The Content of the Form: Narrative Discourse and Historical Representation*. Baltimore: Johns Hopkins University Press.

Wills, D. (1985) *Self De(con)struct: Writing and the Surrealist Text*. Occasional monograph of the Department of Modern Languages, James Cook University of North Queensland.

Wolin, R. (1992) *The Terms of Cultural Criticism: The Frankfurt School, Existentialism, Poststructuralism*. New York: Columbia University Press.
Wood, D. (1990) *Philosophy at the Limit*. London: Unwin Hyman.

Index

Adorno,T. 67
aesthetics 150–1, 176
Allen, B. 138, 161, 174, 179
Allison, D.B. 175
Almansi, G. 59, 163
anal 153
Anderson, K. 97,171
Annales school 9, 87
Antony, St. 35
anxiety 58, 76, 81, 83, 167
Apollinaire, G. 57, 69
archaeology 10, 11–12, 18, 20, 21, 22, 28, 31, 42, 151, 157; definition of 94–5, 144; mysticism and negative theology 86–108
architecture 119–20, 127
Aristotle 125, 177
Artaud, A. 13, 34, 50, 53–5, 61,163
Asad, T. x, 153, 174, 181
asceticism 119
atheism xi, 2
Augustine, St. 121
automatic writing 50, 59
Avant-garde (French) xi, 4, 6, 36, 44, 47, 48, 50, 60, 61, 85, 142, 143; definition of 62; and Foucault's theological model 63–85

Bachelard, G. 9, 87, 96, 155, 170
Balakian, A. 49, 162
Barber, S. 54, 163
Barthes, R. 7, 97, 166
Bartkowski, F. 74, 166
Bataille, G. xi, xii, 14, 35, 46, 47, 51, 52, 56, 60, 65, 66, 67, 69, 75, 79, 139, 143, 163, 165, 166, 167; and Sade 70–4; sexuality and theology 81–2
Beauvoir, S. de 68, 165
Behr, J. 153

belief and practice 43, 109–14, 132, 146, 150
Bentham, J. 20
Bernauer, J.W. 27, 80, 86, 90, 91, 96, 101, 138, 153, 155, 157, 158, 168, 169, 170, 171, 172, 178, 179, 181
Bevis, P. 37, 133–5, 178
binary/non-binary thought xi, 6, 27, 30, 35, 36, 37, 41, 43, 48, 63, 103–6, 110, 114, 124, 129, 138, 147
Binswanger, L. 9, 10
Blanchot, M. xi, 14, 35, 46, 47, 52, 67, 69, 73, 76, 81, 85, 88, 89, 90, 139, 165, 167, 170; and Foucault's theological model 77–8; negative theology 90–1
Blavier, A. 163
body 4, 5, 6, 13, 19, 22, 36, 42, 44, 48, 49, 60, 61, 62, 64, 71, 78, 82, 83, 86, 130, 131, 139, 141, 142, 143, 146–7; Artaud on 54–5; and belief 109–14, 126; docility 19, 71, 118, 168; and soul 19, 109, 113, 116, 117, 122–8, 164, 165, 166, 168, 176, 177, 180
body theology xi, 6, 67, 70, 81–4, 109–28, 132, 139, 143, 146–7, 167, 177
Bouchard, D.F. 167
Bouyer, L. 99, 172
Bove, P.A. 8, 155
Boyne, R. 29, 159
Braidotti, R. 162, 164
Breton, A. 46, 47, 50, 51, 52, 53, 162
Brodribb, S. 74, 80, 164, 166
Brown, P. 3, 154
Brown, S. 165
Brummett, B. 32, 159
Bruns, G.L. xi, 153
Buddhism 144, 148; *see also* Zen
Buñuel, L. 61

Butler, J. 125, 164, 177

Cameron, A. 154, 181
Canguilhem, G. 9, 87, 96, 155, 170
Caplan, P. 164
Caputo, J.D. 169
Cardinal, R. 50, 162
Carrette, J.R. 157, 162, 164, 165, 169,
    180, 181
Carter, A. 68, 165
Caruso, P. 47
Cassian, J. 40, 121, 135, 143
Castel, R. 131, 153, 178
Castelli, E. 148, 153, 181
Catholicism 21, 25, 121, 151, 167
Caws, M.A. 97
Certeau, M. de. 8, 61, 104, 155, 164, 173
Cervantes, M. de (*Don Quixote*) 15, 16
Chasseguet-Smirgel, J. 165
Chidester, D. 153
Choucha, N. 162, 164
Christianity 1–6, 19, 47, 55, 61, 74, 148,
    173, 178, 181; and the body 83–6,
    109–28; and confession 25–43;
    Foucault's critique of 142–5; and the
    History of Sexuality 20–4; and
    mysticism 92–108; and political
    spirituality 129–37, 141; and silence
    31–2
Christology 123, 158
Cixous, H. 74, 166
Clark, E.A. 131, 153, 154, 178
Clark, T. 78, 167
Clatterbaugh, K. 164
Coakley, S. 181
Cocteau, J. 162
Cohen, A. 37, 133–5, 165, 178
confession 4, 19, 21, 22, 25–43, 112, 128,
    132, 134, 136, 160, 176; concept of
    37–9, 160
Connolly, W.E. 138, 178, 180, 181
Cooey, P.M. 111, 174, 180
Cooper, D. 12
Corbin, H. 139, 180
Courtivron, I. de 159, 174
Cousins, M. 39, 153, 155, 157, 161
critical theory 7, 51, 53
cultural studies x, 1, 144–5
Cupitt, D. 105–6, 151, 174, 181

Dada 50
Dali, S. 61
Dallen, J. 160

Daly, M. 180
Darwin, C. 77
Dascal, M. 165
Davidson, A.I. x, 153, 178, 181
Davis, C. 153
Dean, C.J. 68–9, 73–4, 164, 165, 166
Dean, M. 133, 178, 179
death 13, 72, 73, 75, 77, 80, 166
death of God 3, 5, 9, 14, 17, 55, 61, 63,
    64, 65, 71, 78, 79–84, 85, 109, 111,
    132, 167
death of man 17–18, 75, 79–81, 107–8,
    169
Deleuze, G. 19, 86, 90, 115, 124, 127,
    155, 165, 177; the fold and reading
    Foucault 3, 153–4; and metaphysics
    116, 122, 124, 126, 165;
    phantasy/phantasm 115–16, 127, 165;
    philosophical work of 175
Derrida, J. 7, 35, 51, 85, 104, 158, 166,
    173; Foucault and silence 28–9
Descartes, R. 49, 77, 162
Descombes, V. 79, 167, 171, 174
desire 65, 72, 77, 82, 83, 101, 115, 177,
    181
Desnos, R. 51
Diamond, I. 164
discipline 113, 118–20
discourse 7, 10–11, 18, 21, 25, 32, 35, 36,
    37, 38, 39, 91, 93–108, 146, 158, 173;
    and God 97, 99; sexed 127
Donnelly, M. 118, 157, 175, 176
Dreyfus, H.L. x, 10, 86, 95, 135, 153,
    155, 157, 169, 170, 171
dualism *see* binary/non-binary thought
Dumézil, G. 44, 47
Dumm, T.L. 177
During, S. 161
Durkheim, E. 71
Dworkin, A. 68, 69, 72–4, 165, 166

Eilberg-Schwartz, N. 181
Ellenberger, H. 165
Epicurus 24
episteme x, 15
Eribon, D. 86, 154, 157, 159, 161, 169,
    174, 175, 179
Erickson, V.L. 159
Esslin, M.
ethics 22, 24, 26, 132, 150, 178, 179, 180;
    and politics 133, 136, 138
Ewald, F. 98
exagoreusis 38, 40, 42
existentialism 8

exomologesis 38

feminism 64, 68, 74, 111, 127, 147, 148, 181
Feuerbach, L. 79
ffrench, P. 45–7, 161, 162, 163, 167
Fiorenza, E.S. 180
Fishkin, S. 159
Flaubert, G. 35, 77
Flax, J. 164, 166, 168
Flynn, T.R. 61, 104, 164, 173, 179
Foucault, M.: and Artaud 53–5; and Derrida 28–9; and history 38–9, 130–2, 178; main works (*Archaeology of Knowledge* 5, 11, 25, 35, 50, 86–108, 169, 170, 173, 176; *Birth of the Clinic* 12, 13–14; *Discipline and Punish* 5, 19–20, 22, 109–26; *Historie de la folie* 10, 11, 22, 28–9, 44, 65, 130; *History of Sexuality: Volume 1* 4, 9, 21, 25, 26, 29, 36, 37, 65, 130, 132–6, 178, 181; *History of Sexuality: Volume 2* 21, 24, 132–6; *History of Sexuality: Volume 3* 21, 24, 132–6; *Madness and Civilization* 11–12, 14, 28–9, 73, 114; *The Order of Things* 12, 13, 14, 15–18, 57, 65, 76–80, 82); reading of ix–xii, 2; religious question 2, 3, 5, 6, 20, 28, 40, 42, 43, 44, 47, 60, 74, 85, 108, 114, 122, 129; religious sub-text 1, 3, 4, 6, 8, 9, 14, 18, 25, 108, 109, 129, 142, 143, 151; and Sade 62–7; theological model 75–84, 112 (*see also* political spirituality; spiritual corporality)
Fowlie, W. 162
Fox, G. 121
Fraser, N. 110, 164, 174
Freeman, J. 162, 163
Freud, S. 46, 96, 153, 172

Gablik, S. 162
Galileo, G. 77
Gallop, J. 76, 68, 69, 70, 71, 74, 78, 83, 165, 166, 167, 168
Gane, M. 157
gay identity 7, 66, 150, 155; *see also* homosexuality; male identity
gaze 13, 20, 57, 104, 119, 173
Geertz, G. 176
gender identity 5, 30, 64, 65, 70, 74, 126–8, 147, 148, 168, 173, 181
genealogy 9, 18, 20, 21, 39, 40, 87, 88,

111, 121, 124, 131, 144, 151, 157; defining features of 114–17, 174–5
Giddens, A. 149, 181
Gilchrist, R. 127, 177
Gillan, G. 87, 155, 169
gnosticism 53, 70
God 14, 14–16, 17, 18, 27, 40, 46, 53, 70, 71, 72, 75–84, 86, 91, 93, 97–108, 119–20, 122, 127, 158, 165, 173; and sexuality 81–2; *see also* death of God
Goethe, J.W. von 52
Goldhill, S. 134, 154, 178, 181
Goldstein, J. 156, 178
Goodall, J. 53, 163
governmentality 6, 22, 43, 131, 133, 138, 142, 177, 179
Greene, N. 54, 163, 167
Gregg, J. 167
Grimshaw, J. 166, 168
Grosz, E. 115, 127, 163, 174, 175, 177
Guattari, F. 19, 175
Gutting, G. x, 86, 153, 155, 170

Habermas, J. 160
Hadot, P. 150, 178, 181
Halperin, D.M. 154, 155, 164
Harkness, J. 163, 174
Harstock, N. 164
Hart, K. 169
Hatab, L.J. 177
Hayman, R. 53, 163
Hearn, J. 164
Hedges, E. 159
Hegel, G.W.F. 69, 79, 166
Heidegger, M. 9, 85, 95, 96, 103, 169, 171
heterology *see* otherness
heterosexuality xii, 70
heterotopias 58, 107
Hinduism 148
history *see* Foucault
history of science x, 9, 86–8, 94, 169
Hölderlin, F. 13, 14, 34, 53, 77
Hollier, D. 166
homosexuality xii, 34, 70, 106, 154–5; *see also* gay identity
Horkheimer, M. 67
Hoy, D.C. 9, 155
human sciences 1, 11, 17
humanism 88
Hume, D. 175
Huppert, G. 164
Hussain, A. 39, 153, 155, 157, 161

Illich, I. 27
imagination *see* theology as imaginative
    process
immanence 5, 86, 136, 139, 143, 145–6,
    169; rule of 145; *see also*
    transcendence; binary/non-binary
    thought
Iran 137, 139–40, 141, 163, 179, 180
Irigaray, L. 7, 68, 74, 80, 125, 165, 168,
    181
Islam 137, 139–40, 144, 179

Jambet, C. 137, 138, 139, 179, 180
James, W. 2, 99, 168
Jameson, F. 154
Janet, P. 53, 69
Jantzen, G.M. 93, 99, 147, 148, 153, 156,
    166, 168, 171, 172, 180, 181
Jarry, A. 50, 61, 164
Jaworski, A. 28–33, 36, 158, 159
Jay, M. 61, 104, 163, 164, 173
Jesuits 107, 118
Jordan, M. 181

Kafka, F. 52
Kant, I. 10, 17, 67, 80, 95, 170, 171, 174,
    175
Kantorowicz, E.H. 123–4, 176
Katz, J.N. 164
Kauppi, N. 161, 167
Kearney, R. 76, 167
Keller, M. 180
Kendell, G. 37, 133–5, 178
King, A.S. 154
King, R. x, 144, 148, 149, 153, 180, 181
Klein, M. 175
Klossowski, P. 14, 47, 61, 69, 70–1, 73,
    139, 140, 165, 167, 168
Knauft, B.M. 147, 181
Kojève, A. 79
Krafft-Ebing, R. von 69
Krondofer, B. 181
Kusch, M. 86–9, 157, 161, 169, 170, 174

Lacan, J. 7, 33, 166
Lack, F. 161, 167
Laing, R.D. 12
Lalonde, M.P. 153
Lampe, G.W.H. 160
Landry, D. 153
language 14–15, 49–50, 53, 55, 56, 58,
    65, 76–8, 82, 85, 88, 90, 112, 115, 139,
    165, 167; and anxiety 58, 78;

labyrinths of 52, 89, 108; limits of 49,
    78, 98, 99, 102, 104; and negation 94,
    97, 100, 107; and sexuality 75, 82;
    and theology 14–15, 17, 75–8, 81–2,
    85
Lash, S. 114, 115, 168, 174, 175
Le Brun, A. 73, 166
Lemert, C. 87, 155, 169
Levinson, H.S. 2, 153
Lévi-Strauss, C. 47
Lewis, II. 162
Liebmann Schaub, U. 141, 180
limit/liminality 51, 72, 81–2, 85, 94, 95
literary studies/theory x, 1, 8, 14, 34–5,
    44, 48, 51, 52, 63, 68
Lloyd, G.E.R. 134, 178
Louth, A. 96, 171
Luibheid, C. 99

Mably, G. de 123
McCarthy, T. 179
Macey, D. 70, 86, 89, 153, 157, 159, 161,
    163, 164, 165, 167, 169, 170, 174, 175,
    179, 180
MacIntyre, A. 181
Maclean, G. 153
McNay, L. 64, 153, 154, 164, 168
McNeil, M. 164
madness 3, 6, 9, 10, 12, 13, 26, 28, 29,
    32, 44, 45, 47, 54, 65, 156, 158, 173;
    history of 12–13
Magritte, R. 53, 56–9, 99, 163, 172
Mahon, M. 138, 167, 178, 179, 181
Major-Poetzl, P. 86, 174
male identity 5, 64, 65, 74, 75, 76, 78,
    80–4, 126, 168
Mallarmé, S. 52, 77
Malraux, A. 167,174
Marcus Aurelius 24
Marks, E. 159, 174
Marx, K. 71, 163
Marxism 8, 9, 10, 60, 71, 140
masochism 69
Massignon, L. 139
Mauss, M. 71
medicine 9, 13, 21
Megill, A. 86–7, 88, 101, 104–5, 169,
    170, 173, 178
Mellor, P. 181
Mendez, C.W. 159
Messner, M.A. 164
metaphor 95, 103–5, 173
metaphysics 44, 49, 54, 74, 80, 116–17,
    122, 124, 126, 165, 166

Midelfort, H.C.E. 156, 176, 178
Milbank, J. 153
Miller, J. 47, 65, 66, 86, 88, 91, 159, 162, 165, 168, 169, 170, 172, 179
Miller, J.-A. 38
Mir, G.C. 118
monasticism 19, 32, 112, 113, 118–20, 121, 176
Moore, S.D. 153
Morgan, D. 164
Morris, M. 164
Mrosovsky, K. 35, 77
mysticism 85–6, 118, 139, 168, 169, 170, 173, 181; and archaeology 90–108

Nadeau, M. 162
negative theology xi, 35, 85, 90–108, 169, 170
Nelson, J. 78, 167
Neo-Platonism 94, 96–7, 104, 106, 108
Nerval, G. de 13, 53
New Testament 148
Nietzsche, F. 2, 17, 46, 47, 52, 53, 54, 55, 61, 75, 77, 79–80, 81, 109, 135, 150, 167, 172, 175, 177, 181; on body and soul 114–17, 124–5, 126, 127, 177
Nilson, H. 150, 181

occult 53, 169
O'Farrell, C. 48, 51, 137, 155, 157, 162, 163, 170, 179
Old Testament 15, 76, 81
orientalism 141
Osborne, K.B. 160
otherness (heterology) 10, 17, 49, 51, 55, 56, 57, 58, 60, 106–7, 129, 140, 170
Owen, D. 114, 174

panopticon 20, 121
parrhēsia 179
Parrish, S.M. 149, 181
Pasewark, K.A. 149
Paul, St. 123, 148
Pefanis, J. 51, 163
Peterson, D. 29, 158
phantasm/phantasy *see* Deleuze
phenomenology 8, 9, 10, 11, 101
philosophy x, xii, 1, 2, 7, 8, 10, 48, 49, 51, 52, 54, 55, 60, 61, 63, 78, 83, 93, 160, 173; exit from 83, 167; and liminality 51, and literature 48; refusal of xi; theology 110–13, 128; thinking differently 52

Pinel, P. 12
Plato 26, 96, 104, 177; *see also* Neo-Platonism
Plotinus 96, 171
Poggioli, R. 162
political spirituality xi, 4, 5, 20, 27, 32, 43, 108, 109, 112, 128, 129, 133, 136–41, 142, 147, 151, 152, 163, 177
politics of knowledge 8–9, 19, 37, 47, 48, 131, 132
Ponge, F. 97
Porter, R. 44, 156, 161, 178
postmodern 7, 91, 154, 167
post-structuralist xi, 50, 92, 99, 102, 104, 105
power x, 6, 30–3, 34, 38, 39, 66, 109, 110, 119, 129, 130, 136, 138, 139, 140, 144, 146, 148, 149, 157, 161, 173, 176, 177; bio- 22, 141; pastoral 130, 132, 133, 136; power–knowledge x, xii, 6, 8, 9, 19, 20, 101, 114, 115, 124, 126, 146, 148, 150, 167; and silence 30–2, 33–4; techniques of 19, 32, 109
Prado, C.G. 161, 174, 179
problematisation (problematics) 9, 10, 130–2, 138, 139, 141, 142, 177, 178
Proculus 96
prison (penal) 9, 19, 20, 32, 120, 122, 126
Prosser MacDonald, D. 167, 177, 181
Pseudo-Dionysius 56, 77, 85, 86, 90–108
psychoanalysis 13, 17, 22, 38, 50, 104, 107, 116, 134
psychology 8, 9, 10, 46, 53, 55, 107
Puritan spirituality *see* Quakers
Pyper, H. 81, 167, 168

Quakers (Society of Friends) 44, 112, 120–1, 123, 176
queer theory x; *see also* male identity
Quinby, L. 164

Rabinow, P. x, 86, 95, 135, 153, 155, 157, 169, 170, 171
race and ethnicity 106, 141, 181
Radbertus, P. 123
Rajchman, J. 179
Ramazanoglu, C. 164
Raschke, C.A. 167, 177, 181
Ratramnus of Corbie 123
Ray, S.A. 88, 153, 170
Reformation 38, 137
religion: concept of x, xi, 1, 5, 6; and

culture 143, 144–5; disappearance of 151–2; and politics 129–41
religious studies x, 1, 144, 150, 151
Richardson, M. 71, 72, 81, 166
Richman, M.E. 71, 166
Riggins, S. 34
Robbe-Grillet, A. 45
Rorem, P. 92, 99, 100, 104, 170, 171, 172, 173, 174
Rose, M. 87
Roth, M.S. 178
Roussel, R. 14, 34, 45, 53, 56, 58–9, 99
Ruether, R.R. 180
Rycroft, C. 167, 175

Sade, M. de, xi, xii, 5, 16, 34, 45, 47, 61, 62, 63, 64, 65–75, 77–8, 81–3, 109, 143, 164, 165, 166, 167, 168
Sadism 69
sado-masochism 65, 69
Said, E.W. 67, 144, 165
Same/Other 17, 51, 106–7, 179; *see also* otherness (heterology)
Sanguinetti, E. 60
Sartre, J.-P. 79, 80
Sarup, M. 174
Sawicki, J. 164
Schrift, A.D. 80, 167, 168
Segal, J. 175
Seidler, V.J. 164
Seigel, J. 31, 154, 170
self 22, 23, 24, 27, 36, 40, 42, 43, 47, 91, 118, 121, 138, 140, 141, 143, 149–51, 161, 169, 177, 178, 179, 180, 181; technologies of 23, 36, 43, 66, 110, 111, 121, 128, 131, 133, 135, 136, 140, 143, 144, 149–51, 160, 176, 178, 181
Sells, M.A. 103–4, 173
Seneca 24
sexuality xi, xii, 5, 7, 9, 20, 21, 22, 23, 27, 37, 39, 40, 41, 64, 70, 75, 77, 111, 116, 126–8, 130–6, 143, 145, 146–7, 160, 181; and God 81–4
Shamdasani, S. 50, 162
Shattuck, R. 162
Sheridan, A. 86, 87, 157, 169
Shilling, C. 153, 174, 181
Shumway, D.R. 16, 156
silence 4, 5, 10, 12, 13, 25, 43, 47, 48, 58, 62, 98–103, 109, 111, 130, 134, 142, 147, 158, 159, 172; and archaeology 93, 98–103; and the body 114–15; and confession 25–43; and power 30–2, 33
Simon, J.K. 31

Simons, J. 177
Smart, B. 157
sociology 1, 71, 110, 111
sodomy 70
Sollers, P. 45, 46
Sontag, S. 54, 163
Soskice, J.M. 173
soul 19, 55, 96, 109–10, 113, 116, 124–5, 165, 177; and body 122–8, 165–6, 176; sexed 117, 127
Soupault, P. 162
space 103–6, 111, 119–20, 122, 173
Spinoza, B. 175
spiritual 45, 46, 47, 49–50, 52, 57, 59–61; definition of 6, 154, 179–80
spiritual corporality xi, 4, 5, 20, 27, 42, 43, 44, 48, 50, 55, 61, 63, 64, 65, 73, 74, 76, 79–84, 86, 108, 109, 112, 122, 126, 129, 142, 143, 147, 151, 152, 167, 169; definition of 4–5, 63, 132–5, 139 140
Spivak, G.C. x
Stauth, G. 137, 139, 140, 179, 180
Stein, E. 164
Steiner, G. 169
Stoicism 26
Stoler, A.L. 141, 145, 180
structuralism 14, 88; *see also* post-structuralist
Sturrock, J. 170
subject 6, 9, 22, 24, 26, 38, 39, 40, 65, 107–8, 143, 160, 161
Suleiman, S.R. 167
surrealism 4, 6, 44–62, 85–6, 143, 169; definition of 162; and spiritual experience 45–7

Tambling, J. 39, 161
Tannery, C. 174
Taylor, M. 169
Tel Quel 45–6, 53, 59, 60, 68, 154, 161, 167
Tertullian 38, 160
theology x, xi, xii, 6, 14, 60, 63, 67, 70, 75, 78, 81, 90–108, 110, 121, 123, 138, 142, 146, 150, 151, 161, 169, 179; and the body 109–128; illusion of 122–6, 177; as imaginative process 127–8, 147, 177, 181; philosophical 110, 112, 113, 128; sexed 127–8; and sexuality 75–84; 146–7; space and time 119–20; *see also* body theology
transcendence 5, 86, 97, 99, 100, 103–6,

107, 108, 117, 139, 143, 145–6, 169, 180; *see also* immanence
transgression 48, 72, 81, 156
Trombadori, D. 158
truth 6, 7, 23, 27, 32, 38, 39, 40, 107, 117, 137, 138, 140, 149, 150, 159, 161, 174,179
Tuke, S. 12
Turner, B.S. 110, 153, 174, 181
Tyler, S.A. 36, 159
Tzara, T. 162

unconscious 10

Velàzquez: *Las Meninas* 15
Valery, P. 155
Van Gogh, V. 13, 53

Vernon, M. 155
Visker, R. 59–60, 163
Voltaire 176

Wakefield, N. 154
Weber, M. 135
Welch, S. 153, 163
Welchman, J.C. 162, 163
White, H.V. 178
Wills, D. 51–2, 162, 163
Wolin, R. 162
women 33, 74, 83–4, 106, 159 168; and silence 33
Woolf, V. 33

Zen 141; *see also* Buddhism